MW00606213

A DIFFERENT STORY

The Rise of
Narrative in Psychotherapy

A DIFFERENT STORY

The Rise of
Narrative in Psychotherapy

by

C. Christian Beels, M.D., M.S.

Zeig, Tucker & Theisen, Inc.
Phoenix, Arizona

Library of Congress Cataloging-in-Publication data

Beels, C. Christian.
    A different story : the rise of narrative in psychotherapy / by C. Christian Beels.
        p. cm.
    Includes bibliographical references and index.
    ISBN: 1-891944-34-7
    1. Psychotherapy—Philosophy.   2. Family psychotherapy—Philosophy.
3. Storytelling—Therapeutic use.   4. Personal construct theory.   5. Beels, C.
Christian. I. Title.

RC437.5.B42 2000
616.89´14—dc21   00–043716

Copyright © 2001 by Zeig, Tucker & Theisen, Inc.
All rights reserved. No part of this book may be reproduced by any process
whatsoever without the written permission of the copyright owner.

Published by
Zieg, Tucker & Theisen, Inc.
3614 North 24th Street
Phoenix, AZ 85016

Manufactured in the United States of America

10 9 8 7 6 5 4 3 2 1

For Margaret, with love

CONTENTS

ACKNOWLEDGMENTS

THIS BOOK HAS COME ABOUT through "the love and labor of many," as I learned to say at school, and I especially want to mention two indispensable readers and editors. It was Marie Winn who first thought the project could be done, and then patiently taught me how to do it — an incalculable gift. Phyllis Vine read the final draft and gave it much of whatever discipline and direction it now has. I have learned so much from these two wonderful writers and good friends. After their tutelage, what remains of vanity and other faults is my own

I owe a particular debt to those who have read and criticized all or parts of previous drafts: Joan Bamberger, Lou Breger, Charles Burg, Francis and Katharine Cunningham, Stephen Chinlund, Elizabeth Dalton, Christine Dinsmore, David Epston, Richard Evans, Gladys Foxe, Judith Friedman, Gene Goodheart, Henry Grunebaum, Brigid Marcuse, Katharine McQuarrie, David Moltz, Valerie Moylan, Peggy Papp, Steve Rosenheck, Bennett Simon, Shan Sullivan, and Michael White. Other invaluable help came from Susan Heath, Gilbert Levin, Jim Levine, Marilyn Mendelsohn, and Paul Mishler.

Suzi Tucker has provided encouragement and graceful correction throughout — without her recognition that there was something here to say, it would not have happened.

My wife, Margaret, and children, Jessica and Alexander, read, criticized, suggested, and endured. My life with them in the years of this book's gestation has been marvelously full of grace and patience that no thanks can requite, but I offer it here anyway.

Where it was possible to contact them, I reviewed with the patients the way their stories are told. They are the real heroes here.

INTRODUCTION

Fɪꜰᴛᴇᴇɴ-ʏᴇᴀʀ-ᴏʟᴅ Mᴇʀᴄᴇᴅᴇs Vᴀʀɢᴀs had just been discharged from her second stay at a local psychiatric hospital. The behavior that had originally alarmed her family — scratching her arms and cutting her wrists, drinking alcohol, taking dangerous drugs, and staying out of school — had not entirely disappeared, and now, as she and her parents sat in my office, they had yet another problem. Although the antidepressant medication prescribed at the hospital was mitigating her suicidal mood to some extent, Mercedes had made it clear that she was finished with the hospital, and that she didn't like any of the psychiatrists to whom she had been introduced for possible outpatient treatment. Her parents, Fausto and Maria, obviously were trying to remain calm.

As they settled down on the sofa and easy chairs in my office, I invited them into my usual opening ceremony. I asked them to help me make a map of the family: their ages, work, where they live, what they do. Maria was a social worker, and a family therapist as well — she had heard me speak at a conference. So this was one source of their calm — she and I both knew that a meeting such as this could well start with no agreement about the nature of the problem, and no solution in sight. Simply collecting all the stories together, even without resolving the differences of opinion, could produce the beginning of collaboration. They had already accomplished something just by getting here.

Mercedes was keeping a watchful distance, so I asked the parents to help me complete my map. Fausto and Maria had originally come to the United States from Argentina, where Fausto's large merchant family controlled a mining business that had diversified into the export and import of many other products. As the head of the New York branch of the family, Fausto had long been recognized for his business skill and ruthlessness, but also for his generosity to the family and his philanthropy in the world and the church. He had very high moral standards, and prided himself on his consistency in maintaining these. In the family, this meant that he expected both Mercedes and her older brother, Raul, to be consistent in excelling at school. He reviewed their report cards as he reviewed the performance of his companies and their employees, reducing Mercedes to tears when she was young and provoking more rebellious responses now that she was in high school. Maria had done her best to mediate between Fausto and Mercedes. Raul, either owing to his self-discipline, or because he was older, or a boy, had been able to distance himself from Fausto's angry lectures, but Mercedes took her father's criticism much harder. At this point in the discussion, Mercedes joined in to say that Raul's leaving for college the year before had focused her parents' attention on her and her troubles at school. She missed her brother, both on that account and because she liked having him around to talk to.

I was a little apprehensive about having everything so neatly explained in the first 10 minutes. Was there something we weren't talking about that might explode? Maria was trying to be understanding and positive in her description of Fausto's good intentions. Maria, as well as the social workers at the hospital, had identified Fausto's demanding behavior as the root of Mercedes' problem, and by the time the family came in to see me he had recognized what was happening and was asking for guidance. I felt there was something solid about their agreement in this regard, and I decided to accept it as a good thing. And Mercedes, I thought, sounded adult and reasonable in the way she talked about not being able to learn anything more from the hospital, and not wanting to become more identified with the "crazy" behavior there.

I could see that the three had a lot going for them, and told them so. I noted especially their ability to talk sympathetically with one another, at least in the office. I told them that I would be willing to help them organize their household so that it would be a more effective place than the hospital for Mercedes to take her next steps. The formal "working" atmosphere of a family meeting in my office encouraged Mercedes to think and talk constructively. Another good sign. At home, the sudden flare-ups of emotion, her tantrums in reaction to her father, seemed to occur at times when everyone's guard was down. Could they predict when this was going to happen? Sometimes. Good — I asked them to keep notes.

Fausto then asked how we were going to find Mercedes a psychiatrist when she kept rejecting them. I told Mercedes that she was right to be careful in her choice of an individual therapist, since it would be good to be able to stay with the same person long enough to really get to know him or her. So first impressions were important, I explained, and after asking her what sort of therapist she preferred based on her experience so far, I said I would keep sending her to candidates until she found someone with whom she thought she could work. As her own therapist became part of the team, we would be able to work out a plan for talking among us so that her relationship with her therapist would be as confidential as possible, but at the same time we would not be ambushed by the emergence of something dangerous or harmful. She agreed.

Over the next weeks, she worked down to the fifth person on my list, a very patient and imaginative analytically trained woman psychiatrist who shared her sense of humor, and Mercedes committed herself to that individual therapy. Why did she reject the other four? I have no idea, and in my view her reasons really were not important. Selecting a person with whom she could start her own story — that was important. So was my confidence that eventually she would do so.

My first meeting with the Vargas family was in 1987. I had been doing family therapy for 25 years, and teaching it for almost as long in the city and state hospitals of New York. I was leaving state service that year to work full time seeing patients in private practice in my office in the same Manhattan apartment house in which I lived. So this was a turning point in my life as well as in theirs, and as I met with them off and on for the next 10 years, we all learned from the experience. In that first meeting, I learned again to pick out the positives in the account of defeat and frustration that the family brings with them. By inviting Mercedes to interview possible therapists, I was uncovering a positive side of what her parents thought was a problem. I was also encouraging her to step into a position of responsibility.

This way of proceeding would not have occurred to a psychiatrist in 1955 when I went to medical school to learn psychiatry and become a psychoanalyst. At that time, a suicidal 15-year-old girl would have been too young to be admitted to most long-term psychiatric hospitals. We would have had to find one with an adolescent ward. Or she might have stayed at home between suicidal episodes. But whether at home or in the hospital, the therapist would have been chosen for her, the treatment recommended would have been classical psychoanalytic sessions three or four times a week, and any objections on her part would have been analyzed as "resistance," a manifestation of her psychopathology. There would have been an absolute split between what happened in the office, where all was calm, neutral, and secret, and the tumultuous world of the patient and her family. That split would have protected the analyst's office as a clean examining table for looking at that part of the tumult that the patient harbored within herself. Psychiatry had become the sole proprietor and master of this apparently scientific procedure over the previous 50 years. That was why in 1955 I had to become a medical psychiatrist in order to learn it.

§

It is possible now to look back and see that psychoanalysis in its beginnings was actually the first narrative therapy.[1] At the start of his career, Freud discovered a special form of storytelling and attentive listening and found that, for those hysterical victims of trauma who made up his early cases, that kind of telling and listening was a remarkable cure. Later, Freud and his disciples, responding to the scientific mystique of their time, burdened his great discovery with a medical and scientific superstructure, entailing a psychology of instincts, perception, consciousness, and memory, and an account of the mental development of the child. Thus weighted down, psychoanalysis lost its distinction as a narrative approach to the relief of trauma and became instead the biological theory of mental life that went on to dominate psychiatry and psychotherapy, especially in the United States.

Although my career began with an apprenticeship in psychoanalytic psychiatry, I had the good fortune to find an alternative path leading back to an interest in narrative — in the telling of the story and the respectful inquiry of the audience — as a central phenomenon in many different kinds of psychotherapeutic practice. That path began in the social and community psychiatry of the 1960s, and the family therapy practice that was at the heart of the social psychiatrist's work. Social psychiatry looked outward at the mind's environment rather than inward into its interior. Family therapy introduced my generation of therapists to the idea that when problems are seen in their family context, they involve many

---

[1] For a discussion of this idea from the point of view of modern psychoanalysis, see Spence (1982) and Malcolm (1983).

stories, which have as many meanings as there are family members. In working with the family, the truth that makes us free could be an upward construction of a common purpose rather than a downward analysis of hidden motives and secret hurts. The careful and considerate witnessing of the story could be done by family members, who would be responsible for carrying the story forward, as well as by the analyst who, in her[2] silence and privacy, would be more a stand-in than a primary player.

But the narrative focus of family therapy is not only on the story — it is also on the *audience* of family members who gather around to give it meaning. Who should or could be in that audience, and how might they behave? How might they receive the story so that it can go forward? The idea of choosing an audience for the story brings forward the idea of *membership* as an essential ingredient in therapy. Of what group should the teller be a member in order to get the most fruitful hearing: The family? A group of families? A group of others with similar afflictions? A group that is an audience to the therapy conversation itself? The social view of therapy is that the search for the right audience may be as important as the search for the right story. Mercedes Vargas had, in addition to her own therapist, many audiences: family meetings, long walks with her mother, special meetings with her father and me, Alcoholics Anonymous and other twelve-step meetings, school discussion groups, in all of which she was encouraged to try out new versions of her story.

Family therapy, like other new developments that appeared in the 1960s, was built on psychoanalysis in many ways, and it certainly would not have emerged at all except in the "culture of therapy" that analysis had established. But more interesting than their common roots are the ways in which they differ — ways in which the new therapies are the philosophical opposites of the approaches of Freud and his successors. Whereas analysis was an inward exploration of the individual's psychology, the new therapy is an outward exploration of social possibilities — rather than private truth, consequences. Analysis mined the past; the new therapy looks to the future. Analysis considered motives; the new therapy is about intentions. The inward search for insight, that was the hallmark of analysis, has been replaced by an outward search for resources.

---

[2] For the sake of rhythm and imagery, I prefer not to use the "his or her" locution, but instead to change the gender of the general pronoun in each chapter. Here, and in even-numbered chapters, such persons will be female.

Analysis reduced complexity by trying to track down underlying truths, decoding childhood memories to find out what "really happened" in the ur-world of the child's emotional experience. The new therapy seeks multiple versions of different, often relative, truths, and it welcomes additional lines of inquiry. And whereas analysts fought long battles over the orthodoxy of their beliefs, the new therapy generates and welcomes heterodoxy. It seeks to reflect the cultural diversity of modern society.

From here, it was a short step to the more recent uses of the narrative approach. Once it was clear that stories other than the narratives of childhood trauma in Freud's great cases had healing value — that indeed, what was needed was another story besides the one the patient brought to consultation — then the possibilities for those different stories proliferated. There could be stories of contemporary adult life, of political affliction, of learning new skills, of working with a partner to make a marriage or raise a child, of oppression and defiance, of liberation, and of discovery and invention, depending on the direction in which the teller and the audience took the story. Helping people to tell a good story gives the power of the storyteller back to its true owner. The Vargas family in that first meeting decided to begin the story of remaking their home into a better place in which Mercedes could take her next steps toward her new life. That was what we all agreed on, and we could begin work on it in spite of our differences.

§

My interest, in this book, is not in "narrative therapy," which seems, at least in America, to be in danger of becoming another school with its own special methods and language. What I am interested in, rather, is the way a narrative approach to therapy diffuses school loyalties. Family therapists, breaking out of their school practice of seeing the family together, are rediscovering individual therapy as the construction of a personal story of recovered membership, creating a solidarity of the client's own choosing. Psychoanalysts who take narrative as their model have begun to see their work as a conversation — as an exchange of interpretations, a comparison of one story with another — rather than as the one-way offering of the analyst's interpretation to the patient. These recent changes in psychoanalysis may come to provide a bridge between it and other narrative practices.

That synergy would help us to appreciate that this most recent wave of therapies does not constitute a new revolution, a new discovery, after all. Seen more accurately, it represents a rediscovery of practices known to folk healers of all societies throughout human history: hypnotic trance, shamanic healing ceremonies, meditation, and other arts linking the mind with the group and the body. What the modern healers have added is a systematic, sometimes even scientific, curiosity about the local conditions that make these practices work, and about the way the new stories are put together.

What criterion of truth guides the construction of a new story, an alternative to the one brought in by the patient or the family? It is not science but ethics. The new social therapies, of which family therapy is the prototype, emphasize the moral and political organization of the group, the ethical relationship between the therapist and the family or individual, the *pragmatic* consequences of adopting one story or another.[3] I chose to see the positive aspect of Merecedes' rejecting one therapist after another because getting tough with her about it or interpreting her ambivalence obviously wouldn't *work,* whereas joining her in her caution had a better chance. That determined my belief.

§

If there has been a scientific contribution to the development of the narrative point of view, it came from anthropology. Family therapists, finding themselves dealing with people who were, for the most part, in a different social class and had different social experiences from those of the professionals, had to overcome barriers to understanding between cultures. They had to embrace the different languages and values of an alienated or immigrant clientele. Learning to think like anthropological consultants rather than analytic experts, family therapists approached the local conditions of their clients' lives with respect. This anthropological view helped them to see that there is no "average" or ideal family form, no universal prescription for a healthy family, no correct treatment for everyone.

---

[3] A connection between these ideas and the new pragmatism in philosophy is Richard Rorty's (1991) view of science as a community for the open discussion of experience rather than as a method of demonstrating objective truth.

The influence of anthropology, and the recognition of the function of the audience, has inspired a rediscovery of the role of ritual in psychotherapy. Ritual can be used deliberately as a means of changing or redefining our sense of membership; for instance, by choosing or inventing special practices or alliances that are not obvious in the dailiness of our lives. Rather than explaining religion out of modern life by calling it "the future of an illusion," we have looked into our clients' experience of it and embraced the comparative study of ritual and the altered states achievable through hypnosis and meditation. The need for ritual associations and memberships can be seen all around us — at worst, in the alarming growth and spread of fanatical cults among the young and alienated. Cults provide a good example of the crucial role of the ethics of the therapeutic group in determining the effect of membership. One of the responsibilities of our new profession is the design and promotion of ethical associations and memberships that are not cults: that are open, not secret, that are easy to leave or change, that do not rely on the claims of a cult leader. Consultation with families, schools, and the like to help them to become open in this sense, to choose their stories from an open book, has been an important part of the work.

In order to accomplish this kind of open practice, it has been necessary at last to give up our most treasured possession, the very idea of the hero-therapist, the cult leader. In setting aside heroes such as Freud, we have moved the authority of the master therapists and their theories away from center stage. This has allowed us to discover in their place another kind of hero, the client traveling on his or her pilgrimage, in the good company of many others, exchanging, like Chaucer's pilgrims, the stories of their travels. The discovery of that hero's journey is one of the subjects of this book.

The other players involved are the professionals who, like me, were in the right place at the right time, through choice or fortune. I entered this story as a teacher choosing to become a psychoanalyst. My good fortune since then has been to be in a series of places — of audiences and memberships — where I have had the opportunity to learn and then to change my mind, to become part of the community psychiatry and family therapy movements that founded what we thought at the time was a second revolution.

Only now, perhaps with the perspective of age, do we realize that in thinking of ourselves as the vanguard of that revolution, we were assuming a heroic posture little different from that of the analysts we were trying to replace. A narrative perspective requires that, along with giving up heroes, we would have to give up the vanity of revolution itself. This is the real message of the new therapeutic scene: everything works some of the time (even classical psychoanalysis), and the problem is to find out what, when, and for whom — a proper subject for research.

Since their practitioners labored in the pragmatic vineyards outside the academy, the new therapies were little noticed as a cultural force by the literary and philosophical establishment that earlier had taken up psychoanalysis with such enthusiasm. Having little to contribute to the illumination of high culture, they have had no academic celebrity. This book may do something to remedy that, but I have another purpose here in exploring the relations between psychotherapy and the devotions of the professional class. Psychoanalysis, to the degree that it provided that class with a personal religion, became a sacred text, and the classical analysts, the priests of the religion, were unable to change it in response to the experience of practice. The newer therapies have been free to change, not only because we are less burdened by sacred tradition, but also because we have had different forms of ordination. Rather than lie down on our teachers' couches, we gather in groups to watch their work on videotape and argue with each other and with them about what they are doing.

Like anthropologists, we have been concerned with the language and practices of daily life, with a search for what in those practices works (or fails) to alleviate suffering. And as that search has brought us closer into the company of patients, families, and fellow workers, it has also brought to us an experience of membership that is stronger than the consolation of belief. The constant correction of theories by practice is not possible — is demoralizing — without that kind of encouragement. How that company has carried us all forward is, for me, the personal part of the story.

CHAPTER ONE
An Education for Confidence

I TOOK THE FIRST STEPS on my journey in 1955, when I decided to leave teaching at an Episcopal boys' boarding school and enter medical school to become a psychoanalyst. Looking back, I can see that like all initiations in the healing arts, this was partly an effort to cure myself of something.[1] And like all initiates, I had to use the rituals that the culture provided. This story, then, is not only about me; it is also about that culture and its rituals, the United States just after its victory in World War II, when classical Freudian analysis flourished as never before or since. It was a time of unrivaled confidence and the innocence — or ignorance — that goes with it. We Americans were invincibly proud of the little we knew and were cheerfully going straight ahead with it. Psychoanalysis was an essential part of our victorious march, and those who were not keeping up the pace and felt the strain turned to it for relief from their symptoms of fatigue, or from the terror of being left behind.

What was the ailment of which I was trying to heal myself by going from teaching to analysis? The first unmistakable symptom, I think, came the day six years earlier when I graduated from another such boys' boarding school, St. Paul's, in Concord, New Hampshire. St. Paul's was an institution at the center of that American straight-on well-bred confidence: white, Protestant, male, rich, and Eastern Establishment. I was there on scholarship because I represented what passed for diversity in such a place: I was from west of the Mississippi.

On the morning of graduation day, I entered the chapel of St. Paul's for the last communion service of my class, my "form" as it was called in the English tradition. The chapel had seemed to me an enormous church

---

[1] Ellenberger (1981) was the master historian of the efforts of therapists, from Mesmer to Sullivan, to heal themselves, and I have relied on his model.

when I first entered it in the ninth grade, a "New Boy" from the remote province of Oklahoma. On this day four years later, it still seemed large — large enough to hold the whole school family of 500, boys, masters, and even guests. All the girls the top two forms could invite to a dance would fit into the balcony above the entrance doors. The school had marched in and out of chapel, not only twice on Sunday, but every morning (with a hymn, a psalm and a prayer), every year since it was founded in 1860 by the Reverend Henry Augustus Coit. The 85 boys in my form were about to file out of that long parade by graduating that afternoon, piling our trunks, books, posters, and record players into our parents' cars for the drive home.

I could hardly wait. My family had moved from Oklahoma to New York, and I wanted to escape this New Hampshire "rustication" (as the Reverend Coit had called it) for that Great City, civilization, and above all, women. Four years of monastic privation in that all-male world were ending. I took a deep breath and gazed down from the choir stall that enclosed me, to one side of the altar where, beyond the shafts of light that poured from the stained glass overhead, my form-mates were gathering at the altar rail, kneeling to take their last Communion as members of the school. I was not a communicant, and so, with a handful of others, I waited, as I had done every Sunday, for the members of the Episcopal Church to eat the Body and drink the Blood of Our Lord and Savior Jesus Christ. I shuddered a little every time I heard the liturgy, since it seemed to me as gruesome and primitive as football, another ritual from which I had excused myself as soon as I was allowed. But then, I thought, I would be delivered from all this in only a few hours.

I took another deep breath, and suddenly left my body sitting there in the choir stall while I rose up into the dark vault of the bell tower and looked down at the service far below. I couldn't tell if I were awake or dreaming, or how long I was up there. Then the darkness around me cleared, and I found myself reunited with my body, which had joined the others marching out of the chapel into the sunshine, a little blinded by the tears in my eyes. The tears were a surprise too, the only clues to any emotion I might have connected with all this. And like most other signs of intense emotion in my life, I did my best to ignore this one, moving through the rest of the day with the calm and confidence implied by the description written on all our diplomas: *Puer optimae spei*, "Boy of best hope."

How could I have acknowledged any anxiety when everything was working out perfectly? Like others in my form, my acceptance at college had been agreed upon in a conversation between our vice-rector and the Harvard admissions man; I don't think I was interviewed beyond a hand-shake and a few words. I had told my father — we talked about it per-haps twice — that I would study medicine. This was almost a decision by default since I was not interested in law or business, and I had some curiosity about biology. Sex, really, was what I was interested in, and I had spent much of my earlier years reading medical books about it. So medicine seemed a fine idea to me. I was sure it would all work out.

§

The confidence of privileged youth at Harvard matched the mood of the country, with an expanding economy and opportunities every-where for that small cohort of us born during and after the Great De-pression. The glittering pavements of Manhattan, to which I returned as often as I could get there, were crowded with people who walked as if they knew it was the capital of the world. In such a mood, acquiring what Harvard called a General Education at the hands of the faculty of arts and sciences was such an exhilarating assignment that most of us at-tributed any discomfort we were feeling to not having the right girl-friend. That was something to worry about. From the promptings of our hormones and the expectations of our friends, we fashioned a ritual of healing: true love and sincere sex, whatever sex meant in 1950, were the greatest solace our predicament had to offer.

Accordingly, as soon as I arrived in Harvard Yard, I moved quickly to find a reassuring romance, and once I found her, I held fast to her until the middle of my senior year. At that critical point, just after pro-posing marriage, I realized how badly matched we were and broke it off. But the passion and turbulence she and I had been able to generate for the better part of three years anesthetized me to other experiences. She was the daughter of an alcoholic retired English professor of great gen-tility and breeding who lived in a dark Victorian house on a shady side street in Cambridge, and I was able to feel, somehow, that I belonged there. I didn't notice until almost too late that the fact was that I didn't belong there or, more important, that I didn't like being there at all. My blindness baffled me. Why marriage? Why not just meet lots of women and get to know them? That seemed too much of an exploration for me to take on, too much of an adventure in the open field.

Another kind of exploration and adventure that I turned away from that senior year at Harvard was a Fulbright scholarship in biology to

study the asymmetry of snails at the University of Utrecht. I decided I
was not going to be a biologist, and certainly not a medical doctor. I was
going to *teach* biology at St. George's School, a New England Episcopal
boarding school for boys just like St. Paul's.

§

What ailed me? I had no idea. In fact, I would not have seen myself
as harboring an ailment. My decision to be a schoolteacher rather than
a doctor did not seems so retrograde, so defensive. Defensive against
what? Plenty of other people were changing their minds about marriage
and career. My friends were either going to Marine Corps officer training
or enlisting in the army to get their service over with. The Pax Ameri-
cana still required the occupation of Germany, and the Korean War was
under way. While at St. George's, I avoided the draft by serving as a
pharmacist's mate in the weekend Naval Reserve. The world was not the
safe and confident place it was when I left Oklahoma in 1945, and only
America had the atomic bomb.

Many years later, as a family therapist, I would have turned to look
at the shape and disposition of my family for some understanding of my
behavior. When I was born in 1930 in Tulsa, Oklahoma, I was an only
child of a family hit by the Depression. Before I was born, my mother
taught business writing at a secretarial school, the only time she ever
worked. My father had a degree in chemistry from the University of
Missouri and had done graduate study at the Colorado School of Mines.
But like many young men in those years, he gave up his professional
dream of being a chemist for the first job he could find. He started work
as a land-lease agent for the Oklahoma company of the recently dismem-
bered Rockefeller oil trust, a job that sent him traveling most of the time
and for which my family moved out of the state and back three times
(six moves) before I was 10. I didn't then think of my life as oppressed
by the exigencies of oil exploration, I just thought we had to move a lot.

The years from age 10 to age 15 in Tulsa were my first opportunity
to learn how to make friends in a neighborhood. We even built a house,
but this settling did not last long. My parents decided that the prospect
of a Tulsa high school education should be improved upon, and so I was
sent east to St. Paul's.

I see now that this was an effort at class promotion on my parents'
part, a move that may have had something to do with family history. My

father's father, who was Dutch, after receiving an engineering degree from Heidelberg, left his banking family in the Netherlands, first to become a prospector in California, and then a surveyor on the new branch of the Union Pacific Railroad from Chicago to Port Arthur, Texas. After laying out the streets of Port Arthur, he married my English grandmother and they moved to Kansas City, where my grandfather worked for the Gallup Map Company.

My mother's father, who was from Winsted, Connecticut, had been the president of a bank that failed in a crash in 1888. He moved to Kansas City to speculate in land in Kansas and Oklahoma and eventually repaid the bank's creditors. The family stayed in Kansas City, but went back to the Winsted farm in the summers. My mother remembered those girlhood Connecticut summers. So even though they both grew up in Kansas City, my parents had allegiances to banking-class origins in New England and in Europe, where my father had visited his Dutch family as a young man.

But if recapturing a place in the banking class and the larger world was behind my parents' sending me from Oklahoma to St. Paul's, I never thought about it in that way at the time. One did not talk about social class in the Tulsa oil business. Everyone knew who was rich, but it was all new money, sometimes as new as last year. Tulsa liked to think of itself as a frontier town in Indian Territory, a bunch of ordinary hardworking people who had gotten to wherever they were on their own.

And for quite other reasons, no one talked about class at St. Paul's, any more than we would have belched at the dinner table. We knew that not everyone went to a school that provided a passport to the Ivy League, but it was bad form to talk about it other than lightly, just as it was bad form to wear a school team sweater with the letter outside. Thus earnestly casual, I would not have connected my family's constant mobility during my school and college years with any anxious or alienated feelings of mine. My father was posted from New York to The Hague, back to New York, then to London. I had to view these less as dislocations than as chances to see the world.

If I were to follow one method of narrative analysis and examine this story for what is not explicitly told, for the knowledge pushed to the margins and played down, I would find a search for "home." St. Paul's had been my home, more than any of the places my parents had paused in their journeys. I can see that losing that home was the experience I was trying not to have — not to be aware of — as I left my body in the choir stall. Home, not the girl, was what I was looking for in the professor's house in Cambridge, and in the return to teach at boarding school. But in that education, "home", with its sense of clinging to the limitations of where you started out, was an unthinkable, unworthy thought. Success was something both my father and I had achieved at the sacrifice of a home (he turned to gardening passionately wherever he could). And as for class, the other unthinkable thought, I was so far from knowing what class destinations my unused passport was valid for, that I did not even think about setting out. I short-circuited all these imponderable thoughts and, with only a moment's hesitation, went straight "home" to boarding school at St. George's.

§

At Harvard, besides romance, we had heard much about one other cure for fear and doubt, and that was psychoanalysis. Although most of us only read about it, its account of negative emotions and their remedies held a fascination for our undergraduate minds that was far out of proportion to what we actually knew about it from either reading or experience. The idea of psychoanalysis both consoled and inspired us, but since we were too sophisticated for emotions like consolation and inspiration, we became interested in Freud and analysis "intellectually."

The consolation was in its approach to personal experiences of fear, depression, mental blindness, and sexual frustration, all of which we were living through at some moments of our outwardly confident lives. The inspiration came from Freud's stance as one of the intellectual heroes of the nineteenth century. There was a popular course called "Darwin, Marx, and Freud," the three scientific revolutionaries who had created the modern world by displacing Victorian man from his proud estate. Darwin had demoted him from his place as a special creature of God, Marx from his place as a rightful steward of capitalist prosperity, and Freud from his image of himself as a man whose passions, even in his family, were governed by reason and duty. (Woman's passions were something else.)

Freud was good for everything, from ideas for an English paper to getting a laugh at a cocktail party. Some of us actually read him: all of us discussed him, to the annoyance of our more classically minded professors. To them, the theory was too easy: it served for everything. To us, it was the heady stuff of revolution, and that was not easy to come by in the American middle class of the 1950s.

§

But there was another, larger reason that we were turning to systems such as Freud's and Marx's. Our professors were telling us, in various ways, that we were engaged with them in the completion of a project that dated from the Enlightenment and that had reached a peak in Europe in the nineteenth century: the discovery, classification, and description of Great Ideas.

That was what General Education at Harvard was all about. We were to take enough general courses in the arts, the social sciences (which included both history and psychology), and the natural sciences, so that we could write and converse in all three disciplines. Then we were allowed to specialize as a way of preparing to make a living or of digging more deeply into an area of scholarship. One of my favorite social scientists, Max Weber, would have noted the similarity between this system of education and that of the Chinese, who, even at the beginning of this century, required civil servants to pass examinations in the Confucian classics. And my history teacher at St. Paul's would have pointed out that the British Empire was established by men who modeled themselves on Julius Caesar by studying his memoirs of the Gallic Wars in the original Latin — which was why I had to do the same. Latin and Caesar were matters of class and cultural solidarity, a system of recruitment and recognition (and exclusion). But that use of a classical education as a device for power and exclusion was another unpleasant thought. I found it much easier to think of General Education as the study of religious texts in a secular society. Sacred studies, the reading of the Gospels, the chanting of psalms and singing of hymns at St. Paul's had prepared me to recognize such religious activity.

At Harvard, I joined eagerly in the worship of Great Ideas. They shone in the firmament of General Education, embodied in the figures of its patron saints: Plato, Augustine, Dante, Aeschylus, Milton, John Stuart Mill, Max Weber, and so on. I tried to hold my place in the choir, answering the professors' lectures with term papers on themes announced by the section men: "Contrast and compare Aquinas' and Mill's views of natural religion" or "Describe the Hobbesean man's criticism of the Lockean state." We were allowed to choose an occasional solo aria; mine was "The Oedipus Complex in King Lear." Writing that term paper, I put two burnished icons of the religion side by side and earned an A from my section man.

As a biology major, I felt more than a little inferiority in the hierarchy of this church. The humanities and the social sciences were the natural haunt of Great Ideas, and I had to hunt for the ones also lurking in the sciences. The origin of life was certainly a Great Idea in biology. And the mechanism of Darwinian evolution was being challenged. On the left, the Russian geneticist Lysenko claimed to show that animals could inherit their parents' learned, as opposed to genetically selected, characteristics — so there was a way for social experiences such as communism to affect the descent of man. From the right, the Jesuit PierreTeilhard de Chardin argued that the origin of life could not have been an accident. I read Laurence Henderson's *The Fitness of the Environment*, which showed that, accident or not, the earth's atmosphere is the only place we know in the universe where life could have arisen. These and many other scientific wonders seemed to me objects of contemplation as profound as *The Divine Comedy, Paradise Lost,* and the Book of Genesis, and certainly on the same cosmic plane as those poetic accounts of beginnings and ends. Then, one morning in my sophomore year, I picked up the newspaper to find that a group of physicists at Columbia had duplicated the conditions for the origin of life (Miller, 1969). They had produced amino acids in a large tank of hot seawater by passing lightning bolts through a nitrogen-and-carbon-dioxide-rich atmosphere above its surface. This experiment produced the elements of organic beginnings in a very short time, without God, and apparently answered Teilhard de Chardin's claim that if life were due to chance, there was not even time to throw the dice.

In news like this, and in the pages of *Scientific American,* I saw the ideas that interested me: the social organization of apes as the prototype of human society; embryology — the egg's development into a tiny vertebrate as a recapitulation of evolution I could watch under my microscope; D'Arcy Thompson's *Growth and Form,* describing formulas for the curve at the edge of a leaf; and the Pythagorean spiral of the chambered nautilus shell. I was looking for evidence to support Thompson's quotation from Plato: "God is a Geometer." I had a vision of teaching these things in a high school biology course. It was what I had wanted to know about six years earlier.

The ideas of Freud were some of the best meeting points for biology and philosophy — I emphasize his *ideas.* What held my interest in psychoanalysis was Freud the philosopher and critic of culture, the author of *Civilization and Its Discontents,* not the model of psychoanalytic practice. *Becoming* a psychoanalyst had not entered my mind. I didn't want to be a doctor, and analysis as a profession was an even more remote and unimagined terminus at the far end of post-postgraduate training. I dutifully spent some time with psychology and sociology. It seemed to me that those "social sciences" were masquerading as part of the heroic laboratory tradition of chemistry and physics. It was a strain: they were both obviously natural histories. The pretension to "theory" only filled them with the gas of pseudoscientific notions, mostly incapable of laboratory proof, ultimately tedious, and, as I realized after taking anthropology, culture-bound. When they did succeed in the laboratory, they produced oddities, like the behaviorism of Skinner, who showed he could teach pigeons to play Ping-Pong and wrote a book called *Beyond Freedom and Dignity*. It was not an appealing perspective to me.

What did appeal was the aspect of Freudian psychoanalysis that was part of the same project as General Education: the European nineteenth-century quest for discovering great truths and expressing them in literature and philosophy at a high level of generalization. Analysis was part of the medical-scientific arm of that endeavor: its goal, to hold the known world together in a scientific synthesis that would fill the void left by the collapse of theology (Sulloway, 1992). Certainly the synthesis had to be scientific. The nineteenth century marveled at such scientific discoveries as the periodic table of the chemical elements, which explained all the substances in creation; the cell biology of Pasteur, which seemed to encompass countless aspects of life and health; and the march of the physicists into the heart of the atom to find the secrets of light, radio, and X rays. Many writers of that century saw that scientists had discovered profound connections between apparently incongruous domains. Psychoanalysis united science and art with the same confident style of exegesis. Freud himself was the master of this kind of broad, erudite theorizing, and he presented his thoughts as a secret key to such disciplines as art criticism, the paleohistory of human society, and the origins of warfare and religion. Term papers, indeed.

§

In college, I mainly saw the heroic side of Freud. He was a contemporary of another scientific hero, Pasteur,[2] who had saved children from

---

[2] I encountered Pasteur, Koch, Semmelweis, and others in I. B. Cohen's history of science course, which I took by happy accident because it solved a

rabies, saved the wine crop of France, made milk safe to drink, and done decisive battle in his laboratory with the myth of the spontaneous generation of life. It seemed to me that Freud marched in the train of nineteenth-century medical heroes, along with Robert Koch, the discoverer of a treatment for syphilis, and Ignaz Semmelweis, the doctor who unmasked the infectious nature of childbed fever with his famous warning to obstetricians: "Even a gentleman with clean hands may carry the disease." Freud was just such a myth-exposer, a shiner of light into dark corners of the mind, a demonstrator of reality where false and comforting (but unhealthy and disease-producing) fantasies and delusions had been before. In this sense, Freud's method seemed to be truly a psycho-analysis, a taking apart, a clearing away of appearances and getting down to the basic physiological facts.

Of course, Freud, in some crucial respects, was *not* a scientist like Pasteur. Not only did he limit his exploration of his field; he was subject to another criticism, as L. L. Whyte (1948) had pointed out. Both Marx and Freud unscientifically assigned motives to their opponents: class bias for Marx and unconscious resistance for Freud. This polemic device was a bid to be removed from the usual scientific requirement of submitting to counterdemonstrations, to falsification. I knew this, but since I, too, was mainly interested in the ideas, I kept on reading and thinking about where all this would go in my high school biology course — under "sex" or under "the brain"?

§

A steady diet of Great Ideas in the humanities was making me feel a little queasy and lightheaded, especially when I compared it with the gritty, humbler fare of physics and chemistry, where the contrarian attitude of experimental science prevailed. I wanted to borrow from my science courses the habit of interrogating ideas, of asking, "Where would this *not* be true?" I needed a way of being critical, of raising questions about those ideas without going through the seemingly endless process of becoming an expert in every field. The antidote that I found for intoxication with the Great Ideas of General Education was anthropology.

---

schedule and distribution problem. The history of science and the history of religion were both trails that came together later in an unpredictable way.

If an idea is a candidate for elevation in our culture, how does it fare in other cultures? In the spring of my freshman year, I took Clyde Kluckhohn's introductory course and felt at once that I had connected with something of profound importance. Indeed, it almost provided an antidote to the cultural trap — a way out from the victory march. Could I become an anthropologist?

Cultural anthropology brought the exploratory spirit of natural history to human affairs. It said, "Do you want to understand religion? Well, look at this religion, and this one, and this. How can we understand this vast collection of religions? What are their similarities and differences? Why do shamans occur in the world across a great arc from Russia to Polynesia and again in the native Alaskan and North American peoples? Why do those cultures think of trance as a natural journey of the soul, while we think of it as something abnormal?" Or "What are all the different stories that describe the killing of a god so that the world can be saved, and how is the story of Jesus a special one?" The natural history approach to human thought, even to human irrationality, could lead to understanding by finding a pattern of meaning in example after example and then sharpening that pattern with exceptions that made you stop and think. There were ancient African kingdoms that had bureaucratic governments, tax collectors, secret police, and even universities, all without a written language (Herskovitz, 1940). What did that say about the importance of writing in the technical elaboration of other civilizations?

Anthropology could do without the lust for scientific respectability that so contorted sociology and psychology. It just went on collecting fascinating stories. Content to be a natural history rather than an experimental science, it was nevertheless able to be systematic. One of its projects was putting the stories systematically into the Yale Cross-Cultural Index.[3] This compendium of all known cultures and their institutions provided a body of data in which, through computerized statistical inquiry, you could ask such questions as "Does the Evil Eye appear more often in pastoral than in farming societies?"

The ethnographic descriptions of cultural anthropology were my first taste of the possibilities of narrative method, the search for pattern by constantly rereading or rehearing stories as they are told by the people who originate them. And although I was fascinated by this kind of inves-

---

[3] Now called the Human Relations Area Files.

tigation, as I was by the analysis of poetry or fiction, I could see that becoming an anthropologist would have taken me too far from home. Instead of that or any other exploration, I spent two years as a teacher, and it had a decisive effect.

§

As a convert to the religion of Great Ideas, I was rather like one of those younger sons in Jane Austen's novels who, having failed to inherit, went to the university and was considering taking clerical orders. I was looking around for an available parish, which in Austen's day was appropriately called a "living." Graduating from Harvard in 1953, I went to teach at St. George's School in Newport, Rhode Island, because I was not quite sobered up from my intoxication with Great Ideas, and I was looking for an occupation where I could keep playing with them. The fact was, I was more interested in teaching than in science.

And that was my affinity with Freud, who was clearly also interested in Great Ideas and in the mysterious organic origins of things. And Freud, too, was more interested in teaching than in science. That was what made him such a spectacular lecturer at Clark University, where he launched psychoanalysis in America. It also led him, at certain critical points in his career, to press for theory and generalization when he should have looked for more examples.

At St. George's, in the experience of teaching classes and being a dormitory master and drama coach, I began to put some of the Great Ideas in perspective. They did not, as it turned out, belong in a high school biology course. I tried to introduce other innovations at the school: a singing group, an honor society dinner, a new way of organizing the curriculum. The administration tolerated some of these intrusions well enough, but some of the senior masters wanted me just to be quiet and do my job. The alienation and depression I had experienced occasionally before returned with such intensity that I began to think I did have an ailment. Or was it my surroundings? I was clearly in the wrong place doing the wrong thing, but where should I go?

If, during my last year at St. George's, I had taken my depression to an analyst, what would he (probably he, not she) have said? I would have heard very little from him, but from subsequent practice, I can take a guess at his summary of my problem in 1954. "This only child of a remote, depressed father and an infantile dependent mother is suffering neurotic symptoms of depression and anxiety because of conflict over

Oedipal strivings with his father. Having been sent to an Eastern establishment boarding school in order to fulfill his father's ambitions, he has adopted the position of teacher in such a school both as a reproach to the father — 'you sent me into this game and now I'm going to stay in it by not getting out and competing in the world' — and as an expression of impotence. It expresses his inability to leave the training phase and get on with the next challenge in his life, which was intended to be medical school. He is involved in a passive protest, a self-castration. His aggressive, competitive energies are neutralized in futile criticism of the school's administration, whereas his criticism of his father's dominance of the family is unexpressed. By becoming a teacher, he seeks his mother's dominated role, that of nurturing servant and nursemaid, a tutor in the household of the larger society, rather than finding a position of mastery in it. His passive longings and wish to unite with his mother are expressed in his attraction to cooking, the theater and other interests of hers, and his avoidance of contact sports, such as football, shows his avoidance of assertion. The Oedipal attachment to his mother is hidden behind an apparent contempt for her intellectual limitations, which also reflects, on another level, his envious competition with, or identification with, his father's intellectual abilities."

It is fairly easy to make up these psychoanalytic formulations. This one fits many of the facts, and it is a fair sample of the paragraphs I later learned to produce at case conferences in residency training. It rests on several assumptions: (1) the normality of competition, (2) the gender stereotypes of assertiveness for men and passivity for women, and (3) the notion that anyone, having once intended to be a doctor and having signed up for premedical courses in college, should then "normally" carry out that program. The assumptions about the gender roles of mother, father, and son are necessary to the theory of the Oedipus complex on which the analysis is based. Without these assumptions, the grid loses its form, and the story falls apart. But above all, the analysis takes the school experience and my return to it as a teacher to be a *symbol* or a *symptom* of a conflict whose emotional reality lies in childhood sexuality, and whose contrasting "real" reality lies in the world of structure and function.

§

From a narrative standpoint, looking back on that time, I would take a different view of my ailment. I was depressed because I was in too

much of a hurry to establish myself as a finished person with a function
in that world. My education for confidence had enticed me into imper-
sonating the expertise of a teacher, a kind of work that I had, after all,
observed firsthand for almost a decade. I wanted the training part of my
life to be over, and was unwilling to face the idea that it had only begun.
Going to medical school in order to begin a further training in psychiatry, and after that in analysis, was an acceptance of having to spend the
rest of my life learning — an idea I could not have borne in college
where all the bright people seemed to have come to the end of their ignorance. At least, that was how I imagined them. The rewriting of that
story uses material at hand to link the past to the future, defining how
that future could be different. Where did the new material come from?

First, there was a change of audience: a change from the confident
and finished inhabitants of the common rooms at Harvard. My most important new audience for my newly embraced uncertainty was Margaret,
the woman I later married, who visited me at St. George's. Her response
to my little world of classrooms and drama coaching and soccer was,
"What is a nice boy like you doing in a place like this?" At that point,
we were both making important changes in our lives. She was changing
her major at Radcliffe from seventeenth-century history and literature to
social relations — the General Education equivalent of psychology. She
joined a group of students who visited mental patients at Boston State
Hospital. Her family and some friends looked askance at what they
thought was an intellectual step down, but she and I, in similar ways,
knew we were trying to find a certain kind of life work, rather than immediate academic prestige. I was attracted to her not just for the solace
of romance, but also because we had this exploration in common.

And she was part of "home," since she was the college roommate
of my school and college roommate's wife, a kinship that an anthropologist might have said made us parallel cousins, or obligatory spouses in
some societies. We began a six-year courtship and correspondence, often
interrupted by other attractions, but continuous in its exploration of our
developing goals in life.

The analyst of my fantasy would be saying here: "He resolves the
Oedipal conflict by choosing an intellectual woman as opposite as possible to his mother, thus denying the incestuous wish and, in one sense,
winning the competition with his father." My version would be that, encouraged by Margaret to think of my new career of gradual learning as
a lifetime project, I went back to the only part of my undergraduate devotions that had a clear personal, intellectual, and (not least) economic

future. Once I had decided on a lifetime of learning, analysis seemed large enough to fill that space.

And, as far as "home" was concerned, if the new career required a four-year exile to medical school at the University of Rochester, that now seemed little enough in view of my family's extensive travels in the furtherance of career. Intellectually, I was prepared to leave again.

Some books from my parents' library in Tulsa also influenced my conscious attitude toward exile. Popular psychoanalytic ideas defined Home and Mother as the place, in the culture of success, where psychological damage was done. Philip Wylie wrote, in *Generation of Vipers*, that American Moms, clinging to their sons, castrated them and made them unfit for the struggle to the top. Sinclair Lewis, in *Babbit* and *Dodsworth,* defined the small towns from which we all came as the places we had to get away from or lose our essential rebelliousness in conformity. As a boy in Tulsa, I had read these works with approval, even though I had a hard time connecting Wylie's castrating Mom with my own anxious and apologetic mother. When it came time to leave "home" (which had now dwindled to the playing fields of St. George's) and start my solo journey toward moving up, I thought of it as moving on — a part of growing up that required leaving home.

Psychoanalysis, by confining its attention to the first five years of life, and by taking such an instinctual view of them, raised no questions about these cultural dictates. The class system, we believed, provided equal opportunities to all through education, and we were as uninterested in the dislocation that that education caused for the educated as we were in the damage that the system did to the poor, who could not migrate for better opportunity. We had just fought a war for this Way of Life, and we were getting ready to fight another one against Communism, a form of collectivity that gave all others a bad name. In our society, with such an enemy, but also such rewards for individual ambition, it was easy to see as subversive the claims of community, home, and family against moving up and moving on.

The important question was: What portable armor could the traveler take with him? Analysis could make him proof against fear and failure, undo the castrating influence of Mom, and define his worries as figments of his sexual anxieties, not evidence that there was something wrong with the system. It provided a religion without a church or congregation, without a community obligation that might hold him back. My father, in many ways an ideal representative of the culture, traveled light and far

and became, before he died in 1959, a member of the American–British–
Dutch consortium located in London that directed the workings of the
Abadan Island refinery in Iran. It was a very good position, the culmina-
tion of a lifetime of moving on.

I got a different perspective one day in 1960 at medical school when
I learned that the intern with whom I was making rounds was an Iranian,
and by way of conversation I mentioned, in all innocence, my father's
job. The intern turned to me and explained evenly that the control of
that refinery, its oil fields, and its port had been the main prize for which
the CIA had brought down the elected nationalist premier of Iran, Mu-
hammad Mossadegh, and placed the former shah back on the throne as
a Western collaborator (Risen, 2000). I was stunned. My education up
to that point had protected me from any personal encounters with refugees from the communities that our system had destroyed. It didn't occur
to me that I was myself, in a sense, a refugee from the same system.

I met some refugees of another kind in medical school. Rochester,
New York, is in the middle of Monroe County, which had one of the
best public welfare and public health systems in the United States. Many
black people migrated from the South to northern cities for the opportunities and relief that their own communities denied them. Rochester
was one of the best destinations for this migration. They found health
services and welfare, but not places to live or jobs. We met them in the
hospital's emergency rooms and clinics long before the first race riots of
the new era erupted, to everyone's amazement, in Rochester in 1964, a
city and time of otherwise total white middle-class complacency.

I had some quarrels with the system that produced this indifference
to the claims of equality and community, but like Wylie and Lewis, I had
no alternative to suggest, and I had grown up with it. Perhaps, I thought,
by setting out to be a psychoanalyst, I would be trying to fix some of the
ailments that came from the system's operation. But even in that idea, I
was accepting the individualistic terms — the terms of American moving
and striving — in which the problem was presented. Only my half-year
course in anthropology had suggested that there was a world elsewhere.

CHAPTER TWO
From Monastery to Marketplace

My JOURNEY FROM PSYCHOANALYSIS to public psychiatry had three stages: two disappointments in analysis followed by an inspiration in the public sphere. Of the disappointments, the first was personal; it came from being an analytic patient myself.

At medical school in Rochester, I felt keenly the waste of learning so much medicine that I would never use. I tried to console myself with what I could learn about psychotherapy in the psychiatry department. In the first year, the lectures focused on the biological basis of psychiatry, including the Freudian instincts, drives, and conflicts. Sometimes that material was embarrassing. On one occasion, we were introduced to a mother with her newborn baby. With the mother's permission, the professor, in a long white coat, put a latex finger-cot on his pinkie finger and, lifting up the baby, solemnly put his finger into the baby's mouth to suck, and thus demonstrated to us the instinctual nature of the sucking reflex. This was sort of a laboratory demonstration of "orality." How would they have demonstrated anality and genitality?[1]

In psychiatry courses, I wrote papers based on my reading in anthropology, raising questions about the culture-bound assumptions of psychoanalytic orthodoxy. I got medium grades and no comment. On the other hand, the classrooms had one-way windows through which we could watch interviews and therapy sessions, and I found this thrilling. Through

---

[1] There was a lot of interest in orifices and their instincts at that time. Margaret wrote to me that the distinguished Harvard psychologist Gilbert Murray, for whom she was writing her senior paper, was trying to exploit an orifice unclaimed by the Freudian system: he thought he saw a urethral urge in the imagery of male as opposed to female poets and wanted her to take up the research on this.

such a window, I watched the work of Dr. W., one of the young stars of the department. I admired him greatly for his skill as a therapist and his clarity as a teacher.

Sometime in my third year, I asked him to take me on as a patient in psychotherapy. I thought my boredom, depression, and distraction in medical school might represent a return of my old ailment. Moreover, I had experienced a recurrence of my most agonizing symptom: I had inveigled one of the two women in our class into a romantic relationship, had convinced both her and myself that I was in love with her, and had proposed marriage. She accepted. Celebrations and telephone calls to families were under way before I realized that this relationship was even more wrong — for both of us — than the one that had gotten me through college, and I broke it off. A member of the psychiatry department recommended that I seek help, and I asked Dr. W. if he could see me.

To my dismay, I discovered that he wanted me to lie down on the couch and free-associate. He was going to do classical analysis! "What about all that empathic and understanding face-to-face exploration I saw you do with the clinic patients behind the one-way window?" I asked him. "What about just sitting and talking?" He said, "We'll see about that; let's start this way." I didn't want to be suspected of resistance, and I was, after all, a co-religionist. I lay down, and for two years I talked, dozed, dreamed, and cursed on his couch.

It is such a peculiar experience — lying on a couch talking to the ceiling while your consultant sits silently behind you — that particularly vivid metaphors from common experience seem necessary in order to convey what is supposed to be going on. One of the images of psychoanalysis current at that time was the "mirror": the analyst was supposed to remain as featureless as possible in order to provide a blank reflecting screen on which the patient saw the shadows of her own desire. I tried to see myself projected onto this blank relationship with Dr. W., while he lurked in his corner. I gazed at the ceiling or closed my eyes, listening to myself talk. The deprivation of feedback brought me into a world of dream mixed with a curious reality, where I had all the lines and the analyst silently played all the other parts. His rare utterances drove me deeper into a mirrored search for other selves, *doppelgänger*, that seemed at different times to be posturing heroes, depressed victims, or mean, vicious little sneaks who should never be allowed out beyond that office door into the social daylight. We had to encounter these demons in the

mirror, I knew, if we were to get through the hard crust of my resistance, down to the deeper, hidden sources of my problem.

Archaeological digging was another favorite metaphor for analysis;
getting down into the oldest, most primitive chamber of the mind, finding there the tomb where love or work or freedom had been sealed off
long ago in childhood. Once inside the chamber, what dreams and fantasies could our flashlights make out in the faded frescoes on the walls?
Were those naked figures my parents, locked in an embrace of love or
combat? Which was it? How could I tell? Or perhaps they were a pair
of Egyptian or Greek gods, like the figures Freud kept on his desk to
gaze at as his patients talked.

But after a while, the novelty of these fantastic adventures palled,
and I lost interest in Dr. W.'s rare comments about my resistance. The
original problems didn't come up again, since, as time passed, I accepted
the boredom of having to get a medical degree to be a psychiatrist, and
I had learned not to go around asking people to marry me. Maybe I was
growing up. Medical school may have seemed professionally off course,
but it did bring me into living and working relationships with some very
interesting, and very non-Harvard, people. Margaret and I went through
close encounters with other partners, wrote each other long letters about
them, got together for reunions in New York, and even lived together
for a summer in Rochester.

What really upset me during those years was the fact that on the
other side of the world my father was dying of a chronic kidney disease,
and there was nothing I could do about it. For some reason, neither
Dr. W. nor I had much to say about that. I did pass out one day on
rounds as we stood at the bedside of a man my age who was dying of
kidney disease, but the cause of that symptom didn't seem too hard to
figure out. At the next session with Dr. W., I remarked on my identification with my father's plight and received a silent assent from behind
the couch. Medical students are always short of sleep, the sessions were
in the afternoon, and I slept a lot. Apparently the rules prevented him
from waking me.

We did talk about whether we were getting anywhere, and we
agreed that I should take an extra year of fellowship (in biostatistics, for
which I have always been grateful) to lengthen the time for the analysis.
The possibility of doing my internship in Rochester to add yet another
year was also discussed. One day, in my final year of medical school,

gossip in the dining room let out that Dr. W. was a candidate in the Chicago Psychoanalytic Institute. He and other young instructors in the psychiatry department were commuting to Chicago by plane every week to attend classes, and they were being analyzed by senior members of the department in Rochester. It dawned on me that I was a control case! Someone in Chicago was supervising him on his classically abstemious responses to my problems. Whatever he and his supervisor thought those problems were, they weren't letting me in on it. I announced that I was going back to New York to an internship there and a wedding with Margaret. She and I had been discussing it off and on for six years and I now had had enough experience with other people that I felt sure this proposal was not another one of my desperate moves. Dr. W. had no comment except, "I thought you were going to stay here and finish the analysis."

He went on to a very distinguished career in the psychoanalytic profession, and in later years, I looked at his papers, marveling at how orthodox his opinions were. But I also noted with pleasure his continued devotion to teaching, the quality for which I had originally chosen him. Looking back on it, I don't blame him really. He was a devotee of a monastic system that I understood better later on when I watched my friends go through it. I was part of his training ritual. The psychoanalysts of that time were very intelligent people, some of them brilliant, but they were devotees in a brotherhood that was stuck with its rituals and its sacred texts.

But the analysis with Dr. W. was my first great disappointment with my chosen profession.

§

The second disappointment came from my early attempts to use psychoanalytic ideas to treat patients. In 1961, after my internship, I entered psychiatric training as a resident at the Albert Einstein College of Medicine's department of psychiatry in the Bronx. There I was introduced to the difference between supportive and psychodynamic psychotherapy. Supportive therapy was what social workers gave to demoralized people who needed encouragement and a shoulder to cry on. It was also what we fledgling psychiatrists offered to our Jewish and Italian women patients in the clinic at the Bronx Municipal Hospital, both because we didn't yet know how to do better than the social workers, and because, even if we did, our brief and infrequent contacts with our patients would not allow us to move to greater depths. Supportive therapy was rather like what these same women gave in times of trouble to their children and grandchildren, a resemblance they sometimes pointed out to us: "Doctor, don't take offense, but you're sounding like my grandmother, may she rest in peace."

Psychodynamic therapy, the deep kind, was something else entirely. It was modeled on psychoanalysis, which almost all of us planned to learn. We were now within the outer courts of the psychoanalytic temple, where we were able to study the methods of the department faculty. Most of them were graduate psychoanalysts, and some were even training analysts of the inner sanctum, the New York Psychoanalytic Institute.

Our goal at this point was to get a "good supervisor," and receive his (usually his, not her) supervision of our treatment of a "good case." A good case was a patient who could come to the clinic more than once a week. The difference between once and twice a week was the minimum threshold for going deeper than mere support. It was understood that few citizens of the Bronx could afford to come for the three or four times a week that real psychoanalysis required, and, of course, our own time and skills were limited. We had not yet received the training for that ideal therapy, the combination of frequency and abstinent silence that I had attempted with Dr. W.

A good patient also had to have a particular kind of problem, ideally, a neurotic problem out of the canon of psychoanalytic cases that we studied — the cases of the masters, Freud (both Sigmund and his daughter Anna), Otto Fenichel, and other Europeans, and some of the American greats, like Heinz Hartmann, Ernst Kris, and Allard Loewenstein. The psychotic patients we saw in our first year of work on the hospital ward were definitely *not* good cases. If any of them could tolerate a return from the hospital to their homes and families, and the hazards of the Bronx, they were relegated to medication and supportive therapy in the clinic. Or, if they could not survive, they went to a rural state hospital for a longer stay.

When I arrived on the first day of my training at the hospital and met the patients assigned to me, I was the envy of my fellows because there, among my handful of depressed and raving old people and slumbering alcoholics, was a truly good case. She was a young homemaker, a second-generation Irish woman, whom I shall call Grace (because she looked like Grace Kelly). She had been married for about a year and had many vague and fearful feelings about her inadequacy as a wife. But most important to the psychiatrist who had interviewed her and admitted her to the hospital, she had a hysterical anesthesia and paralysis of the lower half of her body.

Symptoms like these, common in Freud's Viennese practice of the late nineteenth century, were extremely rare in 1961 in the Bronx, and I was keenly aware of a special responsibility as the nurses wheeled Grace into the ward's consulting room. The neurologist's examination had shown that her symptoms were inconsistent with any known physical cause. To my exploratory questions about her illness, she responded with a respectful smile and little feeling. I was gratified to recall that Freud's teacher, Charcot, had called this reaction *la belle indifference* of the hysteric. I performed a cursory physical examination — cursory because I wanted to avoid emphasizing any physical explanation for her illness, and also because I remembered that Freud's hysterical patients fell in love with him as part of the distortion of the therapeutic relationship he called "transference." I was afraid that even the professional intimacy of the physical examination could be misunderstood by such a patient. And then I brought our first encounter to a close, because I didn't know what to do next.

I did not lack for advice. My colleagues and supervisors were, of course, enormously interested in the case, pointing out the sexual significance of the leg paralysis, clearly an unconscious avoidance of intercourse. But did the avoidance stem from an unwillingness to open her legs, or from a denial of the desire to do so? Points like these could be cleared up through careful attention to her speech and were the subject of much discussion. I learned that her father, an alcoholic, had frightened her when she was a girl by lurching about the house, threatening to beat her, and sometimes actually beating her mother. She had gladly married and moved out of that house, only to find that her husband also was an alcoholic whose behavior scared her the way her father's had. My supervisor pointed out the repetition compulsion here, the need to reenact the story of earlier childhood experience. His complete formulation was: In childhood she had repressed her sexual feelings toward her father, and experienced them as fear of attack by him; these forbidden sexual feelings were now reawakened by similar feelings and conflicts in her relationship with her husband. The symptoms of paralysis were the only way she could repress the conflict left over from childhood, and, at the same time, express it by neurotically embodying it in the avoidance of sex.

Was she able to achieve orgasm? In my next interview, I found a suitably medical-professional way of asking her this and when I reported back her wide-eyed response — "I don't think so!" — my supervisor pronounced this the clincher to his formulation: an arrest and inhibition at the genital stage of childhood development. He warned me not to broach any interpretations prematurely until I had established a solid therapeutic relationship with her.

Somehow, in the next weeks, Grace got better. The nurses encouraged her to walk, and she gradually started to do so unaided. Her family visited and appeared solicitous and concerned. I kept my contact with her husband to a minimum, so as not to "interfere with the transference." She seemed comfortable talking to me, answering my questions. She went home, and started visiting me twice a week as an outpatient.

The therapy was not a success. Grace brought me, along with her terrifying childhood memories of her father, some horrendous dreams and plenty of complaints about her husband's violent and abusive behavior. I did my best to connect all these in some schematic and nonthreatening way, and she responded by missing appointments. My supervisor drew a complex diagram explaining how I was now a target of her wish to castrate and/or close out or deny the intrusion of men (these all seemed to be the same to him), so, of course, she was shutting me out of her life. That was her form of resistance in the transference. I decided this was, at best, a premature interpretation, and that if I ever saw Grace again, I would not say anything about it.

I did hear from her: a message reached me that she had been brought to the emergency room in a kind of fugue state of semiconsciousness by her husband, who was drunk. They had been sent home with the advice that she return to her sessions with me. As it happened, the attending psychiatrist who had consulted that night in the emergency room was one of my teachers in the Day Hospital, where I was completing the second half of my first year. He had taught me not to see patients with serious disorders without involving their families in the treatment. He had interviewed Grace and her husband together, and in spite of the state both of them were in, he could see that they made more sense together than separately. He suggested that I start seeing them as a couple. I said I didn't know how to do that yet: would he undertake the therapy

and keep me informed? He agreed, and within a few months, he had defined the husband's drinking and violent behavior as the problem and
worked out what Grace and her husband together could do to decrease
those unwelcome presences in their lives. He also talked to Grace about
her father's menacing behavior, with emphasis on the difference rather
than the similarity between her situation then and the current one, between herself as a child and herself as a grown woman of responsibility
and strength. He continued to see them over the next two years, and
their progress was good. Her symptoms did not reappear.

The point of this story is not the success of the supportive couples
treatment[2] or the failure of my bungled venture into psychodynamics.
At that point in my career, my teacher would probably have done better
than I regardless of method. What impressed me about the experience,
and about similar ones over the years of my training there, was the severely limiting assumptions that the psychodynamic approach made concerning what the problem was and what could be done about it. I mean
here not only the limitations of such crass male assumptions as were typical of that time: that a young and inexperienced woman should, as a sign
of mental health, be orgasmic with her husband regardless of circumstances; that women should welcome male (psychological or physical)
penetration no matter how inept or offensive; and that Grace's significant
conflict with her father involved incestuous fantasies rather than her justified fear of his violence.

But apart from these dated notions, the more fundamental assumptions are that the suitable imagery for understanding the case is sexual,
and that we know this because she is a classical case of hysteria. More
important still, we, the expert therapists, know this, but she does not. It
is our business to know it, and her unawareness of it is the essence of her
problem. The therapy then consists of helping her to discover and conquer her unconscious resistance to what we understand to be the true nature of her problem, one of a limited number of possible scenarios or
plots based on the vicissitudes of childhood instincts.

We searched for these classical plotlines — the Oedipus story, the
Electra story — in the accounts that our "good" patients gave us, which
we presented in turn to our supervisors. The search was difficult, but it

---

[2] Marital therapy for domestic violence is far from a settled matter (Goldner,
Penn, Scheinberg, & Walker, 1990; Serra, 1993).

was not as frustrating as the difficulties we encountered with supportive therapy. There we were stuck with a rather simple mixture of empathy, reassurance, advice, and encouragement: grandmothers indeed. There was even a form of therapy designed by Carl Rogers (1995) that consisted of nothing but empathy. The therapist just sat and reflected empathically — *very* empathically — whatever the patient said. Strange to say, it worked; in fact, in those early days of psychotherapy outcome research, it was one of the kinds of therapy for which success was documented. One investigator, Jerome Frank (1991), wrote that among all the different kinds of therapy, the elements of rapport, support, and alliance were probably what made them work. At least those elements were what they all had in common, and they all worked to some extent.

But supportive therapy was too vague, too general. It merely added the therapist to the patient's failing social world, rather than exploring that world to see what *specific* elements there could be strengthened, and helping the patient to search them out. We did not know how to begin where social psychiatry and family therapy would begin: searching the patient's world and memory for specific experiences of strength to which the patients themselves could lay claim. To do that, we would have had to bring the family and neighbors into the office, or get out of the office and look around to see what was available, or accompany patients on a search for remembered talismans of power against the evils that beset their lives. All that we learned much later. In 1963, the only specifics we had came from the analytic canon of childhood narratives.

In spite of this limitation, the intimations of analytic therapy in which we were indulging with our "good" patients had a little intrigue, a little suspense. We could see that these narratives were sometimes elegant and well formed. In addition to the development of the subconscious plot line, dream analysis provided vivid flashes of poetry, like illustrations in a novel. Dream interpretation was a puzzle exercise that took us back to the undergraduate pleasures of literary criticism. We used to discuss the meanings of our patients' dreams at lunch and compare our exegeses with the models of nuance and complexity that our professors gave us.

Once a month in our last year, the director of residency training, José Barchilon, would treat us to an elegant dinner at his suburban home. Afterward, over coffee, brandy, and cigars, we would have a seminar to analyze characters and plots in world literature, especially the nineteenth-century novel: Tolstoy, Turgenev, Dickens. By the end of the evening's discussion, the grand narratives appeared with the literary symmetry that we hoped to find in our clinic cases, but never did. Of course, it made sense to apply psychoanalysis to nineteenth-century novels: both the novels and the analysis came from the same high culture that we had enjoyed so much in college. It did not occur to us that we were trying to resolve an incongruity between the lives of our patients and our ambitions for ourselves. Most of our patients were struggling with a combination of major mental illness and lower-class status, for which we often felt we had little in the way of help to offer. The characters in the novels lived in another time and place where the family and its disaffections held center stage, and the heroes and heroines were at leisure to engage in those long soliloquies so rich in material for interpretation. Sometimes our joking revealed an awareness of the tension inherent in practicing on the poor in expectation of treating the rich, who would some day pay us for helping them construct those elegant classical narratives.

While we waited for that day, we bolstered our confidence with the medical mystique of the profession. The psychiatric ward was a medical scene in full dress: doctors in white coats, nurses in starchy uniforms and caps. We had heard that downtown at Mt. Sinai, the patients had to wear pajamas and stay in bed so that they knew they were the patients. We were lucky. Apart from the white uniforms, the only such ritual we had to put up with was that our department chairman carried a reflex hammer in the pocket of his long white coat, and we all watched with fascination, when he interviewed our patients, to see if he would ever tap one of them on the knee. These incongruities were small sacrifices in exchange for the reassurance that, when terrible things happened, as they often did, we all knew how to behave because we were doctors.

Psychoanalysis and the medical mystique were brought together in a book, *The Psychoanalytic Situation,* by a famous psychoanalyst, Leo Stone. One of my supervisors recommended it to me, and I read it carefully. Stone said we should go back to our origins, and that analysis originally was carried out by Freud, a neurologist, as a medical treatment for patients with an illness, hysteria. Freud himself had compared this difficult work to surgery, with its discipline of concentrating and ignoring the discomfort of the patient. Stone argued that in order to be a real medical treatment, genuine psychoanalysis should carry no taint of supportive sympathy from the analyst, beyond the minimum required to keep the conversation going. Sympathy and support, I supposed, would be something like germs in an operating room, a contamination interfering with the procedure. The book was widely discussed and much praised, particularly, I think, by fledgling analysts who were in great doubt about how to respond to the tales of human suffering their patients poured out to them. Stone had an answer: if you want to be a real analyst, a really medical-style scientific healer, don't sympathize — just analyze.

I had a hard time connecting that point of view with the lives of the people I saw every week in the emergency room and the ward, and that was the third and final disappointment that turned me away from psychoanalysis; its failure to address the problems of public psychiatry. I had begun to think of my life that first year as going on in two completely different rooms, the emergency room and the classroom.

In the emergency room at the municipal hospital, every unmanageable crisis in the Bronx was brought to us by the police, the relatives, the neighbors, and even by the desperate candidates for asylum themselves. In some cases, we had only an hour or two to think about what to do with these people and their problems. The families and the neighbors and the rest of the Bronx seemed to be out there, ready to bang on the door of the consulting room. Sometimes it made sense to let them in and see if they could help with the problem the patient was describing in such strange language. And what about the police officer who was assigned to bring the patient to the hospital? As an independent observer, the officer often had some useful things to report. As soon as there were more people in the room with the patient and me, more stories to listen to, things took on a new social dimension, and their situation, their predicament, made sense. It was the kind of sense Grace and her husband made when seen together as a couple dealing with alcoholism. The admission, or the discharge, whatever it was to be, was negotiated with the people who would have to suffer the consequences. Soon I learned to save time by doing emergency room evaluations with as many people present as possible.

The other room was the classroom. Barchilon's class was masterful. When you presented a case to him, he would ask for the story of the patient's present illness, a history of previous complaints and mental illnesses or episodes, and a general life history, with as much detail about childhood as possible. As you talked, he drew a long horizontal line dividing the top from the bottom of the blackboard, then wrote certain words and phrases that caught his attention above and below the line. I thought of it as the waterline on the mental seashore. Above it was the realm of the conscious, the air we all breathe together as a common experience. Below it were the contents of the unconscious, the underwater world of dream, of sea monsters. From time to time, but mostly at the end when he was pulling it all together, he would write other words below the line, such as "envy," "murder," "father," or "eat = kill." He drew lines back and forth between the words above and below the line to show the structure of the symptoms, the effort to repress unacceptable impulses.

We were also invited to watch Barchilon treat patients behind the one-way window, a great privilege, and one that few training programs have provided before or since. He was a master of the staging of the transference. In one interview, he sat in silence for half an hour while a woman with whom he had been having a struggle over an issue of dependency waited for him to say something. He was showing her that she was going to have to carry the ball, that he would not do it for her. He could wait. He was turning the drama of their waiting game into a parable of her life, showing her that taking charge of solving her problem was up to her. He made it clear that he had all the time in the world. As for me, I couldn't take it. I left the observation room and took a walk in the hall.

Something about this way of looking at therapy did not agree with my experiences in the emergency room. The people of the Bronx who came there in the middle of the night, having beaten their wives or children, or having found themselves staring at oblivion from the railing of the Bronx–Whitestone Bridge, were not going to sit, even with José Barchilon, and slowly discover the parallels between their relationship with him and their relationship with others. To be sure, the people in the emergency room had problems that demanded immediate response, whereas Dr. Barchilon's patients seemed to be on some leisure-class schedule. But that was not the difference I was thinking about. What got to me was that the emergency room had *life* going on in it, whereas the classroom, the case conference, even the observation of Barchilon's therapy, seemed like an abstraction from life. I felt sure there was something I wasn't learning. In the middle of the first year, I heard that there were places for residents at a new part of the department, the Day Hospital, and I jumped at the chance to go there.

§

The Day Hospital was a place where patients showed up as they would to a job — 9 to 4, Monday through Friday.[3] It was a two-story building on a tree-shaded residential side street of a working-class Italian neighborhood not far from the main hospital. The building had sunny meeting rooms, a kitchen, even a yard in back with a garden, and enough room for the staff and twenty-five patients, who came in to sit in groups of four or five every morning and plan the day's activities. Whatever else they did during the day, they always came together in the kitchen to make lunch. "Feed thyself" was the motto of a day hospital I consulted to many years later,[4] an ideal of minimal but definite self-sufficiency. The Day Hospital brought together the patients I met in the emergency room, the street and family lives those patients were living, and a very different kind of classroom.

The staff got to work at eight in order to have conferences before the patients arrived. The classroom discussion at those early morning conferences was not about childhood experiences or the contents of the unconscious, but about the patient's current life, employment, family, and what we might be able to offer. What appeared on the blackboard was not the waterline, but a diagram of the family, its relationships, its dispersion in space, and its resources. Here you could see the differences between the problems that people faced in different family situations. One morning, we looked at a simple picture: a chronically psychotic 45-year-old son who was living alone with his diabetic, fearful mother in an apartment that her last remaining relative, a rich brother in Connecticut, never visited. Clearly, both the mother and the son needed some additional support, some more open space. The next morning, the diagram was more complicated: a 20-year-old mother, plunged into psychotic depression after the birth of her first child, was expected to visit the homes not only of her parents, but of her three older, married sisters. She experienced this overwhelming support as an intrusion on her new life with

---

[3] The idea of the day hospital had been tried out first in England. I understood that the one we had on Westchester Square in the Bronx was the first in this country, but in fact the Veteran's Hospital in Brooklyn had started one earlier (Winn & Lesser, 1966).

[4] At Roosevelt Hospital in Manhattan.

her baby, and needed help to organize it, and perhaps even to protect herself from it. Maybe she could bring the baby to the Day Hospital and look after it in a quiet room behind the nurses' office.

The idea of looking at the family as a social field where different possible futures were hidden was different from looking for the childhood origins of the unconscious below the waterline. I began to see that the Day Hospital, like other parts of public psychiatry, was interested in prevention rather than repair. We were trying to keep people from getting into the hospital again, keep them from relapsing, by building social structures as stages for possible action.

The work at the Day Hospital was more like theater than literature. It was an improvised stage where new roles could be tried out. The doctors, nurses, and patients met together in groups and talked, not about the patient's introspections, but about what to do that day. Should they paint the walls, repair furniture, bake cookies, perhaps weed the garden? Working together offered the patients an opportunity to act a different part from the central role of crazy person that the script of their recent experience required. Here was a new way of thinking about narrative. In order to carry it forward, it needed new characters, at least for a curtain raiser, a prologue to the next act in life.

Patients who had just been admitted in the emergency room came, with their families, to the Day Hospital, and it was our job to show them around and answer their questions. By the end of the day, we had to reach an agreement with them and their families about whether they should come back. The difference between this approach and talking to individual patients who were locked up in the hospital struck me immediately. We were not authorities with police power, we were a community agency trying to offer something helpful at this difficult point in a family's life. We had to look as if we knew what we were doing. And we had to be very nice to the families, since we were asking *them* for help, and they knew it. We *had* to work with families in a very supportive way, because if they didn't feel they were getting something out of having the patient at the Day Hospital (often a very inconvenient arrangement) they stopped getting the patient up in the morning to come to us. They took their business elsewhere, and we lost the case. So our version of family therapy was the practical heart of the program, and it was based on a very positive attitude toward the family as a source of help.

Further, the Day Hospital had a research program, to test whether it worked as well as did the regular hospital.[5] Randomly selected pa-tients, on their way from the emergency room to the locked ward, were intercepted, and they and their families were offered an opportunity to go to the Day Hospital instead. If they accepted, the outcome of their treatment was compared with that of a similar group of patients who had been admitted to the ward. The whole idea of testing results in psychi-atry was a novelty, not only to me, but, as I later discovered, to the field as a whole.

At the Day Hospital, there wasn't a white coat in sight, and every-one was very friendly. The staff and patients made lunch and ate it to-gether. It was the first time I had felt part of a group with a purpose since I was the drama coach at St. George's, rehearsing and building scen-ery. The director, Israel Zwerling (who subsequently became my boss as the director of Bronx State Hospital), was a family therapist, and part of the fascination of being there was to watch him talk to families behind the window. From watching him, I learned how to listen to people with the aim of being immediately helpful to them. Being respectful brings out the best in people, especially if they are terrified and "crazy out of their minds," as they say in the Bronx. If people in a family interview are humiliated by their symptoms, it is important not to just let them go on in front of everyone, because they will be ashamed and won't want to come back. One young man's way of breaking the tension in the meeting was to sing popular songs. So Zwerling sang with him until he settled down. Everyone enjoyed it, and it didn't take long. One of my favorite memories of the Day Hospital is Zwerling and that young man singing "Moon River" to his large Italian family.

Since family therapy was the essential skill, Zwerling and others watched me work behind that same one-way mirror and supervised my first (terrifying) family interviews. Harris Peck, another of my supervisors, met with me weekly to review my cases. One day, he and I discussed what to do about a very frightened and suspicious man who lived with his mother in a nearby housing project and who had stopped attending the Day Hospital the month before. His mother had telephoned me a few times, explaining that she was worried about him, and that he sat in

---

[5] The research did demonstrate that it was a successful treatment, and one pre-ferred by patients and families (Zwerling & Mendelsohn, 1965).

his room, slept little, and said nothing. Peck said, "Why don't you go see him?" Such a change in my role, from doctor to guest, seemed awkward, but we rehearsed it. I went to their little apartment, and had a cup of tea with my patient and his mother. "Look," I said, "We would really like to start working with you again. If you're too frightened to come back by yourself, I've asked a police officer to drive us back over there. He and I will guarantee that nothing will harm you." He looked out of the window and saw the police car. "No," he said, "I can take the bus." I realized at that moment that the police car was actually for me. He did come back and later said to me, as he rejoined the life of the Day Hospital, "I didn't realize you cared — that you wanted me to come back." I don't know what José Barchilon would have thought about this approach, but I began to see that it was the right way to work with psychosis.

§

What about problems *other* than psychosis? Why wouldn't this kind of external exploration of social possibilities in the immediate future work with the problems for which psychoanalysis prescribed digging down into inner space and the distant past? That was the question I took with me as I graduated from residency training in 1964 and set out into the world. Because of my experience with families at the Day Hospital, I went on to a fellowship as an associate at the federal government's research hospital, the National Institute of Mental Health (NIMH) in Bethesda. That enormous building (the largest red-brick structure in the world, we were told) in the middle of the rolling Maryland hills certainly had its monastic — not to mention military — aspect, but for me it was also a tower from which to survey the landscape. Clinical associates came from all over the country to assist in the care of patients admitted to the wards, and some of the psychiatrists I met there — all of us just out of residency — were very different lunch companions from those in the Bronx. Even though many of them were entering psychoanalytic training at the Washington Institute, they had other interests as well, interests that would take them on to become chairs of departments, editors, research directors, and, in one case, head of the NIMH itself.

My job from 1964 to 1967 was to direct the clinical care of the patients on the ward where Lyman Wynne and his colleagues were studying the communication styles that patients with schizophrenia shared with members of their families. As part of the free treatment they were given in exchange, their families were offered whatever help we could think of, including family therapy. Visitors from throughout the world came to consult on our project, many from the adventurous edges of psychotherapy.

What a time it was for adventure: not only at the NIMH, but everywhere in the country, things were happening. If medical school and residency had been monasteries, this 1960s boom in psychotherapy was certainly more like the marketplace outside the castle walls. It was a therapy fair. A varied assortment of merchants and mountebanks pitched their tents and displayed their wares. Here were encounter groups from California, sitting in a circle for days on end, spilling their confessions of rage, lust, and terror. Here were acid heads like Timothy Leary and Baba Ram Dass, selling peyote buttons to children in the crowd. And all around us danced the half-naked painted and beaded bodies of the local populace (some of them our friends and neighbors), joining in a weekend snake dance that seemed about to become an orgy at any moment.

In a quieter corner of the market stood behaviorist psychologists with clipboards on which they wrote check lists of the fears described by their patients. These they ranked in order of least to greatest, and then they wrote plans for systematic confrontation, starting with the easy ones first. They seemed less than glamourous in their neat lab coats, but as they said in their handouts, they had the statistics to prove that their methods worked. Nearby, the medical hypnotists were demonstrating, to the amazement of the crowd, that a dental extraction could be done using only a trance for anesthesia. Among the onlookers, an acupuncturist from China offered to provide the anesthesia for an appendectomy, with the patient awake, and only a few needles in just the right places. The crowd hooted him down, but some travelers from overseas declared that they had seen such miracles, and more.

My colleagues at NIMH had a booth advertising the newly discovered benefits of lithium for the treatment of mania. And in a very large tent, a family therapy conference was in progress. Inside, people were milling about, talking in groups, in beads and daishikis, the men in beards and the women in long hair, flowing free. But some of each wearing the dark suits that were the livery of service in university departments of psychiatry, psychology and social work. Here and there on platforms, video monitors were showing tapes, or families were being interviewed before a hushed and watchful audience.[6]

All these people were visitors from the family therapy clinics and institutes that were springing up all over the United States. These were small emergency-treatment stations, hastily established in child guidance centers, Day Hospitals, and programs for the study of schizophrenia. Operating outside psychoanalysis and the medical profession, family therapists dealt with the casualties of modern life that psychoanalysts either regarded as untreatable or tried to treat, but with little success: psychosis (especially schizophrenia), marital difficulties, conduct disorders in children, the multiple problems of the addicted, and the family consequences of poverty.

The family institutes were a new type of school. The teaching was done with videotape and direct observation, either in the room with the therapist or from another room through a one-way window. The students watched both the faculty and each other at work, and then had group discussions about strategies, replaying and analyzing minute segments of communication from the videotapes. This was an exciting (and egalitarian) exchange, based on observable data. Even though many of the institutes were dominated by founders with charismatic, often autocratic, personalities, and graduates of the programs tended to act and think like their teachers, it was possible to watch the videotapes and come to your own conclusions. It was easy to meet and talk with other students whose views were different from those of the master. People traveled from place to place, looking for different opinions.

While still working at NIMH, I teamed up with a colleague I had met at the Day Hospital, Andrew Ferber, and we went to visit these institutes, interviewing and observing, collecting observations for a paper about the development of family therapy (Beels & Ferber, 1969). It was clear to us that the institutes and the periodic conferences that brought them together formed a sort of invisible university. But no degrees were given, and there was no set curriculum, an arrangement that produced new ways of working on problems, new theories and models, at a pace that the academic departments of the visible universities never matched.

---

[6] Scenes very like this one actually took place at meetings of such organizations as the American Orthopsychiatry Association, a collection of teachers and mental health professionals who devised new approaches to the problems of children.

Ferber and I got to know the field and each other well enough that when Zwerling, now the director of the Bronx State Hospital, asked Ferber to form a family institute there in 1966, he invited me to join it. This was a unique offer: a state salary for a teaching position in a family institute that was also part of an academic department of psychiatry. It was the same department where I had been a resident. That was certainly another trip "home," but what a different place it was! It had been transformed, mostly by the energies of Zwerling. Having demonstrated the effectiveness of such institutions as the Day Hospital, he had gone on to become the director of a new Division of Social and Community Psychiatry. That division was one of the earliest signs that the psychiatry profession was waking up from its long psychoanalytic dream and beginning to pay attention to some of its more desperate constituents.

The year I entered medical school, 1955, had been the high-water mark for the hundreds of thousands of Americans locked in state mental hospitals. Most of these inmates would soon be released, in an enormous movement that came to be called "de-institutionalization," to uncertain fates — homelessness for some, but for most an obscure life of gradual recovery.[7] Most lived first with their families, and many returned frequently to acute-care hospitals.

There were three reasons for this exodus from the mental hospitals. The one everyone understood was the invention of drugs, such as thorazine (introduced in 1955), which made it no longer necessary to keep madness behind bars in the interests of safety. The phenothiazine drugs helped patients to manage their symptoms with more restraint.

But more important, and older, was the development, in many parts of the postwar world, of the idea of a society in which the mad could live, a society of membership other than the hospital. In 1955, George Brooks, the director of the Vermont State Hospital, released the last wave

---

[7] In some places, deinstitutionalization of the mentally ill was largely a success. One such state was Vermont, where it was done right, with adequate training of staff and diversion of funds from the hospital budget to the community (Harding, Brooks, Ashikaga, et al., 1987). Elsewhere, in addition to the scandal of underfunding, its effects were obscured by the homelessness produced by the urban middle-class housing boom of the 1970s. An evaluation of the complicated effects of deinstitutionalization can be found in Mechanic (1992), Okin (1985), Kiesler (1982), and Gudeman and Shore (1984).

of patients from its back wards to the towns and villages of Vermont, and trained his staff to follow them and help them find the housing and livelihood they needed to become responsible citizens. This well-supported Vermont version of deinstitutionalization had measurably positive results for the patients' lives (DeSisto, Harding, McCormack, et al., 1995). And George Fairweather in 1955 published the first results of his experiment of putting mental patients from the Veterans' Hospitals in community lodges in California. The Fairweather Lodges were planned communities of mutual support, the first systematic demonstration of membership as a secret ingredient of psychotherapy.

The third reason for the emptying of the state hospitals, the one that ultimately turned it into a disaster of homelessness and neglect rather than the modest success it could have been, was the realization by the politicians who had charge of the money that great savings could be realized by economizing on the support of the mentally ill. They dumped patients into communities without providing support, or turned them over to nursing homes, which were worse than state hospitals, for which Federal programs paid the bill.

Social or community psychiatry began as an effort to organize assistance to those former patients in their move from the asylum to the outside world. It started simultaneously in many countries, organizing psychiatric services to help seriously mentally ill people where they lived, working to settle patients in neighborhoods and families.[8] It began as an antihospital movement, since state hospitals had done so much of the damage by holding these patients in custodial care long beyond the time when, with the help of community psychiatry, they could have returned to a sheltered niche in the world outside.

This population of the oppressed — mental patients both in and out of the hospitals — was made up of the people we had set out to liberate, much as others were marching and protesting in the South against segregation and the poll tax, or joining in protests against Vietnam or nuclear warfare. As director of the Bronx State Hospital in 1965, Zwerling again was ahead of his time. He made the state hospital the headquarters of the social psychiatry division, putting the liberating army in charge of the

---

[8] Community psychiatry had some manifestations as part of the socialist class struggle in Europe, notably the movement called *Psychiatria Democratica* in Italy, but in the United States, it has mostly stayed outside politics.

castle. The state hospital, although it had been built in 1956, was still a building based on the old asylums, with floor after floor of locked wards, huge day rooms where the patients paced, and dormitories (1,800 beds) where they slept. In those days, there were only two good things about a state hospital: it had a large budget for the care of its thousands of inmates, and its director had nearly absolute power. If the director, as in Zwerling's case, was a philosopher-king, great things could be done. As those wards began to empty, Zwerling filled the spaces with clinics, day hospitals, and training fellowships. In the sunny visiting room of the empty nurses' residence, he established a nursery school where mothers from the wards could learn how to return to caring for their children.[9] And in the little rooms where the nurses used to live, Ferber established the Family Studies Section.

We began as a band of three — Ferber, Marilyn Mendelsohn (the social worker who had taught both Ferber and me family therapy at the Day Hospital), and me. We had recruited some colleagues from the department who wanted to learn family therapy, and we demonstrated family interviews in the several rooms with one-way windows that Zwerling had built in different parts of the hospital. We also taught the residents of the municipal hospital, most of whom were still bent on psychoanalysis, but some began to join us in our work.[10] Ferber found more colleagues as he traveled around, and soon there were 14 of us.

One day, Zwerling himself came to our weekly meeting, and asked, "When are you guys going to start doing something for the patients in the hospital?" He didn't say what he had in mind, but his meaning was clear. We were being paid state salaries but we were excused from the burden of direct care of patients in the wards where the rest of his psychiatric staff labored. He wanted us to come up with something more challenging than teaching family therapy to our admiring volunteer students. Apart from needing to justify having us on his payroll, Zwerling always had in mind the words of Hillel, which he displayed on the wall behind his office desk: "If not now, when; if not us, who?" He was reminding us that we were, with respect to the problems that awaited us

---

[9] The director and designer of this service was Dr. Barbara Gordon, and one of the social psychiatry fellows who worked there was William MacFarlane.

[10] The first of these was Fred Sander, with whom I later taught a seminar on literature and the literature of family therapy (Sander & Beels, 1970).

in the Bronx, rich, smart, and privileged, and he expected us to get out there and do something about them. If we wanted to be part of a revolution, we should step up to the barricades. But, like so many of our friends in the 1960s, we were looking not so much for a revolution as for a new community, a way to build Jerusalem in streets of the Bronx, and Zwerling was telling us that we had, for a while at least, the money and the people to do something really constructive.

In 1969, we proposed to move the residency training positions of the hospital to the community, and to move the emergency room to the street corner and the living room. We would teach community psychiatry in its proper place. There was a neighborhood south of the Bronx Zoo called Tremont, which was mostly poor and underserved. By 1970, we were ready to set up a residency training program there that would, from the first year, begin in the neighborhood with the problems of the people living there, responding to their crises in an effort to keep them out of the hospital. It would be called the Tremont Crisis Center.

CHAPTER THREE
The Uses of the Past —
Recovering Trauma

THE DAY WE STARTED THE Tremont Crisis Center, we were a little over-come by the adventure, what Zwerling called the *chutzpah*, of the en-terprise. No one had ever set up a residency training program like this before, and we were not sure we would get away with it. Instead of starting, as all other programs did, with the care of patients safely in the hospital, we were beginning at the other end of the story, treating people who were still free citizens living at home or in the street. That kind of treatment requires humility, diplomacy, and other social graces not taught in medical school, and not easy to teach anywhere. Learning psychiatry in the hospital is easy because if you make a mistake, you can come back the next day and the nurses will have calmed the patient down so you can try again. If you make a mistake on a home visit, the patient disap-pears. Our experience with the Day Hospital told us that it was possible to teach first-year residents the skills of community psychiatry, but it required extraordinary faculty involvement.

The building we rented in the Tremont section of the South Bronx was a former post office. It was certainly enough space to work in, in fact at the beginning it seemed like too much space. The building had been stripped of furniture and partitions when the post office moved out, so that it was something like an empty aircraft hangar, with lights high up in the dark ceiling and tall windows at one end letting in the sky. We brought desks, chairs, and filing cabinets from the hospital and the nurses locked the drugs in the one large closet. We called on neighboring agencies to let them know we were there, and soon we started to see clients, who needed a warm greeting to help them venture past the door into this cavernous space. As they arrived, we arranged clusters of chairs like stage settings here and there in the room. We bent close to listen to the citizens of Tremont confiding their problems to us, and as the room filled with these little murmuring groups of families, consultants, support groups, students and teachers, it gradually became a great therapy hall. Doing psychotherapy in the open was strange at first, but then it began to feel like the natural way to do public psychiatry. It took on an atmosphere of public decorum, like the waiting rooms at Grand Central and the Port Authority bus terminal (the safety of which the homeless and the mad of New York would later discover). The day the first group of residents arrived, one of them discovered in a dumpster a leather mail pouch in very good condition. He adopted it as a briefcase, to everyone's applause. I thought it was an appropriate badge. We were, like mail carriers, public servants delivering to the inhabitants of the tenements and derelict parks the services to which they were entitled.

We took all comers, and provided emergency psychiatric consultation, either at home or at the post office building, and then followed up with group, individual, or family therapy as needed. We had a day hospital in the basement, and if all else failed, we admitted the patient to our own ward at the state hospital. We offered consultation to schools, welfare offices, and especially the police, who began to bring people to us instead of to the hospital emergency room. We traveled to unfamiliar and sometimes threatening parts of the neighborhood to visit families and patients at home, and relied on the street smarts of our nonprofessional colleagues, the nursing aides, to guide us. Since it was clear that in these unfamiliar adventures everyone had something to learn from everyone, professional rank often disappeared. We all taught each other a respectful, friendly style of talk such as I had learned at the Day Hospital. The faculty was a hardy group, chosen for experience and teaching ability rather than credentials. We had to be willing to go wherever the residents were going, spending time with them, doing the work with them, demonstrating and then explaining the invention of social therapies.

The place inspired invention. For example, one of our young faculty members who was supervising outpatient work noticed that some children who were sent to us for truancy or other misconduct came from families where the mothers never went out of the house. He and the residents discovered this because the mothers refused to come to family therapy, and the other family members confided that they didn't go anywhere. So he and his students organized a couples group for this hidden population of agoraphobics, women panicked at leaving home. They and their husbands or other relatives met together with the therapists, at first in each other's homes, to encourage each other to try to go out, and as the parents dealt with this and other problems in the group, the children got better.

Our principal model of courage, flexibility, and resilience was our director, Edward Hornick. An expert in adolescent psychiatry, this psychoanalyst and former orthopedic surgeon saw patients in his private office beginning at four in the morning. He explained that he had to work then because his hypomania kept him from sleeping, and he could find plenty of patients on a similar schedule in Manhattan. After such a night's work, he swept into the post office at eight with a flash of his gold earring and a flourish of his opera cape, and everyone knew that the day was on track.

At the beginning, Hornick asked me to be head of the curriculum committee at Tremont, a position that gave me the opportunity to preside over the planning of the curriculum during the months before the first residents arrived. It was a unique opportunity. Much of what I later taught about community and family psychiatry, I learned first at Tremont. Although those were skills I could have acquired in other places, the intellectual adventure was irreplaceable. I could begin to think about a different way of teaching psychiatry — as history, as a story of social and biographical developments outside of "science." I was drawn to the idea of history as the story of psychiatry, rather than to evidence for the truth of its theories. My college course in the history of science had alerted me to the ephemeral nature of scientific theory.[1]

I had been impressed, during my psychiatric training, by my teachers' reverence for the idea of inevitable scientific progress in the history of psychiatry. Biological psychiatry, with its new drugs, was the culmination of centuries of progress away from psychiatrists' ancient origins as the keepers of dungeons where the mad lay in chains. Some of the new drugs were actually called "chemical restraints," and some — the antidepressants and lithium — looked like effective treatments in themselves, triumphs of modern science. Psychoanalysis was presented as an equally scientific culmination of our progress away from the dark ages

---

[1] Bernard Cohen's full-year survey course on the history of science, 1950–1951.

of exorcism and witch burning. With the greater English and American refinements of psychoanalysis in the previous 50 years, we were beginning to get the right ideas. Social psychiatry, on the other hand, was at the beginning of its history — too soon to talk about right ideas.[2]

It may be difficult today to appreciate what an opening into new territory we had in 1970. The settled medical content of psychiatry — diagnoses and their medication and treatment — was still quite small, and nothing compared with other specialties of medicine, or with the expansion of psychiatry's *Diagnostic and Statistical Manual of Mental Disorders* that accompanied the new drugs and epidemiology of the 1980s. Psychoanalysis still occupied the intellectual attention of most other residency training programs, although some teaching about group and behavioral therapy had begun. Instead of seminars on psychoanalytic theory, what would we present?

At Tremont, we could move in an entirely new conceptual direction. Ours was the third, unheard voice in psychiatry — the social, environmental point of view, in contrast to the somatic medical view of diagnosis and medication, and the psychological view of psychoanalysis. How to present that social point of view, the third voice, was the challenge to which I thought the history of the field was the answer.

The other two traditions, the somatic and the psychoanalytic, seemed most open to criticism when they made claims to have theoretical answers. Maybe psychiatry, especially social psychiatry, we thought, should not have a theory, any more than cooking or architecture or other medical specialties had theories. Another way to teach the intellectual side of psychiatry would be to tell the story of the history of its practice, and to use this approach as a way of asking critical questions about the different ways in which that practice could be understood. We would look at the succession of theories in psychotherapy as just that, a history of ways of thinking. We did not have the word *narrative* for what

---

[2] It was only seven years since President Kennedy had established the "bold new approach" of setting up Community Mental Health Centers with federal funding. Zwerling and the Day Hospital's second director, Jack Wilder, had helped to frame that legislation, and, in fact, that Day Hospital in the Bronx had been one of the first centers funded under the new law. But the idea of these centers was so new that most of them were simply hospital outpatient clinics, renamed to get the federal money, where the same kind of psychotherapy-by-appointment was being done by the same people who had been doing it before. Few such centers had day hospitals.

we were in search of in 1970, but without calling it so, we embarked on a narrative approach to our field, a history of its ideas and practices.

When I told Zwerling and Hornick that we had to hire a historian of psychiatry to help teach the course, they readily agreed. Making it happen was something else: one of my strangest administrative adventures of those days was persuading the Office of Mental Hygiene in Albany that a salary for a historian was a necessary part of our program. When I finally succeeded, the reward was worth many times the effort. Jan Goldstein and Hannah Decker, graduate students at Columbia at that time, each occupied that position for two years, and together taught the faculty and the residents the spirit and substance of historical inquiry.[3]

Thinking about history had a calming effect on our partisan involvement in social psychiatry. Even though we were inspired by the possibility of introducing a third voice into the discussion, it was important that this voice not simply present another heroic simplification to counter the other two. Our approach, rather, would be to introduce a way of looking at simplifications in general, examining them for hidden complexities. I had just read Michel Foucault's "Madness and Civilization," an essay about the early history of psychiatry that emphasized the political and cultural forces that had shaped the profession in its beginnings. It also examined the impact of the profession on the social class of others, the patients. Here, I thought, was a start on psychiatry as history.

According to Foucault, psychiatry began in the seventeenth century when the great leprosy hospitals of Europe had begun to empty, perhaps because of a decline in that disease. The new centralized state of Louis XIII took over these buildings and changed them from refuges tended by religious orders into places of confinement operated by the French crown. This Great Confinement, as Foucault called it, occurred not only in France; the confined populations sometimes reached unmanageable numbers, with the overflow going to "ships of fools" on the rivers and off the coasts of England and Germany.

Foucault's thesis was that our profession could be traced back to when the central governments began to lock up the mad, the indolent, the sick, the fractious, and sometimes the merely poor — anyone who was not able to participate in the new order of productivity required by

---

[3] Goldstein is now a professor of history at the University of Chicago; Decker is an associate professor of history at the University of Houston.

the mercantile state — and then recruited doctors to become the administrators of these enclosures, to classify and treat the lunatic and demented who were brought there. Ever since, there has been a branch of medicine whose irreducible function is to protect society from the mad by excluding and confining them and, sometimes, in the more humane enclosures, to protect the mad from themselves and each other. Here was certainly the dark side of public practice. If, indeed, our profession had begun (and continued) with such a statist commission, then our determination to find alternatives to confinement as the only relationship between mental patients and productive society was confirmed. Day hospitals, home support, and sheltered workshops not only were demonstrably helpful in the rehabilitation of patients, but were a kind of historical redemption.

However, Foucault also had a deeper message: professional practice created realities of power whose existence it ignored or denied. In "Madness and Civilization," he began to examine the history of confinement, which he continued in his other works over the next decade. He described the Panopticon, an eighteenth-century prison where every inmate's cell could be constantly observed from a central office. The Panopticon became a metaphor for professional scrutiny in general, for practices that were officially intended to be efficient, scientific, and even benevolent, but that their objects, the prisoners, experienced as an exercise of power. Foucault looked at institutions from the point of view of those objects: the mental patients, prisoners, women, children, homosexuals, and sinners whose acts were diagnosed, stared down, silenced, disciplined, confined, interpreted, and classified by doctors, guards, men, parents, teachers, confessors, and other expert authorities. The explanation was always benign, just as when parents say they interrogate or punish their children for their own good, or as when the Chinese during the Cultural Revolution said they sent intellectuals to the countryside in order to rehabilitate them.

Elsewhere, writing about the history of sexuality, Foucault described the newly strengthened institution of the confessional, from which the priests of the Counter-reformation scrutinized the minutiae of penitents' private lives, including such practices as masturbation, homosexual acts, and the refusal of sex to a spouse. All of these acquired new significance because of their classification as sins. Soon even impure thoughts required repentance and, therefore, had to be confessed in detail.

This was the cultural environment in which the profession of psychiatry had grown to exercise its own authority and power through the centuries, and some of its practices could be subjected to a similar analysis. Using Foucault as a model of searching out the unintended consequences of professional dogmatism, we asked: Is there a way of questioning our own assumptions as practitioners of social psychiatry?

We knew that some of our work concealed oppression behind apparent benevolence. What about our assumption that the community was a better place for patients to be in than the hospital? One of the researchers at Bronx State had shown, for example, that a large group of patients who had tried both hospital and community clearly preferred the hospital, for good reasons.[4] Some parts of the Bronx are even harder to live in, more isolating and alienating, than Bronx State Hospital. The changes in New York housing that were evident by 1975 (gentrification, expansion, and higher rents) led to homelessness for the people we were trying to locate in the community. And clearly for some combinations of patients and families, neither family life nor independent living was possible. We had to admit that we did not know how to predict these outcomes or the misery caused by our attempts at liberation.

And what about our own doctrinaire preference for therapy that addressed the present and the future rather than the past? In the practice of family therapy, for example, freely exploring the childhood memories and private fantasies of each person in the family not only was impractical, it led to trouble. The members disagreed about both the facts of history and their interpretation. Social psychiatry's group and milieu approaches to most treatment problems were present- and future-oriented rather than explorations of the past. A short-range future of small manageable improvements, a present of concrete accomplishment in concert with the other members of the group, these seemed a better source of hope than raking over past miseries. And we were in a hurry. We were looking for rapid resolutions of problems that came to us as crises in the lives of our clients, and we didn't want to wait to explore the past with each individual patient. It not only would slow things down; but it would make the patient feel burdened with responsibility for the problem. Such "blaming the victim" was against our belief that crises and relapses were caused by the "system" of social influences that surrounded the patient

---

[4] Rosenblatt (1974) is a critique of the public psychiatry agenda by a senior social worker also at Bronx State Hospital in the 1970s.

in the present. So we made a virtue of our necessity — and of these present-oriented beliefs — and took pride in our ability to invent therapies that did not depend on exploring the past.

§

By keeping to this professional agenda, were we also doing some unintended damage? What were we missing? To examine this question, we wanted to take another look at the contribution of psychoanalysis. A member of our residency training faculty, Fred Sander, who was a candidate at the New York Psychoanalytic Institute, volunteered to teach a part of the first-year course called "Freud's Great Cases." Freud had written the stories of Anna O., Dora, the Wolf Man, the Rat Man, Little Hans, and Schreber as teaching tales to illustrate his most fundamental discoveries. Here again, without saying so, we were attracted to the narrative part of psychoanalysis — the case histories. We looked to them, rather than to the theoretical refinements of Freud's successors, to tell us what the psychoanalytic discovery had really been about, and what classical analysis might have to say to us about the unconsidered consequences of our own practice.

Looking back, I realize that I was also looking for something more personal than self-criticism. We were barely old enough to be a psychiatry faculty. I was just 40. Our common intellectual experience could be measured in months. We were preparing to induct the next generation of psychiatrists into a profession whose outlines were not really established in our own minds, let alone in our experience. We were feeling out of our depth. An academic generation is 10 years from graduation to professorship, and the responsibility for teaching feels — and is — much greater than the knowledge and wisdom that can be compiled in that time. So, in looking for a tradition that went back further than 10 years, we were looking for ancestors.

Freud was a good place to start. His writing was a model not only of style, but of a consciousness of large-scale history, especially ancient history. And on the small scale, his method itself was a peculiar exchange of autobiography by the patient and revisionist biography by the therapist, a struggle over the problems of interpretation, of "whose story is it anyway?"

In the years since 1970, Freud's stories have been further revised and retold, taking into account the cultural and family backgrounds of the characters, and, more important, putting Freud himself into the stories as an even more complex character than he had described himself.[5] This narrative-historical research shows Freud, the originator of the idea that as the teller of the tale, one should search one's own motives, moving in the straits of circumstances and motives unsearchable in his time and place.

§

His first, and most important, subject was a journey into the past to find the traumatic experiences of childhood. In 1970, childhood trauma was one of the problems for which social psychiatry, particularly family therapy, seemed to have nothing to offer. It was a blind spot. There was something about Freud's early cases that did not fit our simple optimistic model. They were dark and difficult, like the similar cases of our own clinic that did not easily reward our efforts to help. Freud's experiences seemed to have involved similar frustrations. Difficult, angry people who resent their helpers and do not easily reward the efforts of treatment appeared to be a great exception to psychotherapy's history of progress. At the same time, psychoanalysts continued to claim a special expertise in dealing with just such problems. Their theory assumed the universality of certain kinds of traumatic experience. This question, of whether to look for trauma as a universal childhood experience — the Oedipus complex, the "castration" discovery of little girls — or to think of it as something more obvious and specific, like childhood sexual abuse, and to see it as specific to certain kinds of illness, was a subject we were only beginning to think about at that time. It has continued to present obstacles to our own desire to oversimplify and make grand theories, and its history is, in that way, a great cautionary tale.[6]

---

[5] I have read with particular interest Forrester (1997), Crews (1994), Malcolm (1984), Goodheart (1995), and others. But the most important have been three women: Hannah Decker wrote a valuable imaginative reconstruction of the world in which Freud and Dora lived, an outside-in historical study of consciousness that supplied many of the motivations missing in earlier accounts (Decker, 1991). Gloria Steinem retold the story with the genders reversed, to illuminating effect (Steinem, 1994). And most important of all, Judith Herman retold it as one of three origins of the modern science of trauma and recovery (Herman, 1992).

[6] For an overview of the present state of this complicated field, see Shephard (1999) and Sluzki (1993).

§

Freud was 40 years old in 1896 when he published the first paper he hoped would make his reputation: "The Etiology of Hysteria." In this report on 18 cases of hysteria, he announced that "at the bottom of every case of hysteria there are one or more cases of premature sexual experience, experiences which belong to the earliest years of childhood, but which can be reproduced through the work of psychoanalysis in spite of the intervening decades" (Freud, 1896, p. 203). Early childhood seduction resulted in hysterical symptoms, but in treatment the symptoms vanished as the story of the traumatic seduction was told. Here was a double use of personal narration: the telling was the treatment.

Freud had arrived at this remarkable discovery by working with two important mentors. Josef Breuer, a close friend, was a medical consultant with a reputation for dealing with difficult cases. He saw many hysterical women in his practice and had told Freud in detail about one, codenamed Anna O. This young woman had suffered symptoms of coughing and interference with speech, breathing, and eating, after nursing her father through a long illness that ended with his death. It was she who had revealed to the attentive Breuer the phenomenon that symptom removal would follow a rambling recollection of painful events. Freud, writing years later, tried out many scientific names for this process, and finally called it "psychoanalysis." Anna O. called it "chimney-sweeping" and "the talking cure."

Freud's other mentor was Jean-Martin Charcot. Early in his career, Freud had traveled to Paris to study hysteria at the Salpêtrière. This collection of buildings in the middle of the city was a hospital for women. It was also something like a walled village with a population of 5,000, under a medical government. Originally one of the squalid seventeenth-century places of confinement described by Foucault, it had been reformed by the enlightened policies of the eighteenth-century Revolution, and by the nineteenth century, it was a place of refuge, a model of medical efficiency, a center of Republican debate, a teaching hospital, and a demonstration theater for the intellectuals of Paris, all under the rule of the charismatic Charcot. The hysterical patients were the stars of well-attended demonstrations, where episodes of swooning, convulsions, crises, and recoveries were accompanied by Charcot's lectures and running commentary to the audience. While living in this place may have perpetuated a woman's illness by rewarding it, it also made it possible for the woman to contribute to research, and to have, for that time, a kind of authorship, a rudimentary Foucauldian authority.

Although the theatrical side of Charcot's demonstrations has often been described (and once painted), Freud understood well their serious and deeply respectful purpose. Charcot was the first to insist that hysteria was neither an affliction of an unsatisfied womb nor a malingering, manipulative deception on the part of the patient. Rather, it was a genuine medical phenomenon, worthy of serious study as "The Grand Neurosis." These women, whether former prostitutes, as were many at the Salpêtrière, or middle-class women like Freud's patients in Vienna, all had suffered traumatic experiences. Charcot taught that the symptoms had something to do with reexperiencing or remembering those traumatic experiences, and that they could be produced by altering the patient's mental state through processes identical to those that produced hypnotic trance. Charcot's idea of hysteria was quite neurological. He thought of the traumatic experience as producing a sensitive place, a weakness in the nervous system, from which the symptoms proceeded, somewhat like the way in which a seizure emanates from a lesion in the brain.

It remained for Charcot's principal student and successor at the Salpêtrière, Pierre Janet, to refine these ideas into a coherent psychological description similar to the one we have of trauma and recovery today. Freud and Janet were contemporaries, and in the beginning, their ideas were quite similar. Both thought that the pain of traumatic experience leads to an altered state of mind in which consciousness is split into two compartments, with the painful experience imperfectly sealed out of awareness in the compartment that is less conscious. Janet gave this phenomenon one of its modern names, "dissociation." Freud and Breuer originally called it "double consciousness," an early version of Freud's "conscious and unconscious." Breuer and Janet both described the recovery of memories and associations, and Janet named it "abreaction." Later, Freud elaborated this process into the technique he called "psychoanalysis," making the unconscious conscious. Where Freud parted company with both Janet and Breuer was in his insistence on the sexual basis of the traumatic experience, and even more in his searching into childhood for its earliest manifestations.

Freud made a second trip to France in 1886, this time to the other great center for the study of hypnosis, Nancy. There he studied with Hippolyte Bernheim and Ambroise Auguste Liébault, and came back to Vienna with an agreement to translate Bernheim's textbook into German.

But first he finished his collection of case histories, and published his *Etiology of Hysteria*. While waiting for the world's reaction, he put the finishing touches on his first long book, *The Interpretation of Dreams,* a true magnum opus that he was convinced would make his reputation as a discoverer of not only the cause, but the cure for psychopathology. Historians differ as to whether these publications were as little noticed as Freud felt they were, but we know from his correspondence that he was disappointed by their reception. In some quarters, his seduction theory of hysteria was ridiculed. But he decided that this was the sort of rejection one could expect for discoveries that, like those of Copernicus and Galileo, "disturbed the sleep of humankind."

A year after the publication of the *Etiology,* he changed his mind about the seduction theory, deciding that he had not followed the stream of memory far enough back to its true source. The stories of childhood sexual trauma were not true after all, but fantasies that derived from the urgings of infantile sexuality. The experiences were not memories of sexual molestation by real adults, he came to believe, but stories the patients made up to conceal the traces of their own hidden childhood desire for sexual contact with the parent of the opposite sex, or even of the same sex. The memories may have been provoked by the intimacies of the nursery, but they were neither innocent nor passive experiences of trauma; they were projections of forbidden desire. What had brought about this famous change in Freud's thinking, so pivotal for the development of classical analysis?

At this point in his work, we know from his correspondence with his friend Wilhelm Fliess that Freud was feeling alone and unsupported. Breuer disagreed with his exclusively sexual emphasis in the *Etiology.* And he himself was having trouble imagining its implications for society. If hysteria was so widespread among his middle-class Viennese patients, what did that say about the prevalence of child molestation in these respectable homes?

We know from the *Dreams* book and subsequent writings that he had an interest in the contrariness of appearances, believing that in matters of psychopathology, things are not what they seem, and that what is presented as an explanation, especially one offered by a patient in analysis, usually has another twist. This interest in the lurking contrary animates the whole edifice of his view of psychopathology and treatment — a structure of *defenses* that must constantly be erected against the unacceptable. Pushing aside the stories of seduction to find desire hidden behind them began the construction of this edifice.

We also know, from the course of the rest of his career, that Freud was preoccupied with his ambition to found a general theory of the mind. If he had left the *Etiology* and his seduction theory as it was — an epidemiological finding based on 18 cases that explained one illness — he would be remembered only for that. But he wanted to found a total system of psychology, and he was prepared for it to be one that would disturb the sleep of humankind. As Judith Herman says, Freud constructed classical psychoanalysis out of the ruins of the seduction theory of hysteria (Herman, 1982, p. 14).

That Freud's ambition had an impact on his work can be seen in the case of Dora. Here it is possible to follow the Foucauldian twist of perspective, from that of the great man bent on discovery to that of the patient under his gaze. In his treatment of Dora, Freud was in the position of the professional as described by Foucault, who, having a clear idea about what was good for the patient, was determined to see that she got it.

Having published *The Interpretation of Dreams* and his new theory of childhood sexual trauma as the basis of hysteria, Freud was hoping to link the two with a case history showing clearly how dream interpretation led to childhood sexuality, and thence to successful treatment of hysteria. In October 1900, when the 17-year-old girl whom he named Dora came to his office with "a case of petite hysterie," he seized upon it as an opportunity to "subject certain assumptions to a rigorous test" (Decker, 1991, p. 237).

Two years earlier, Dora's father had brought her to see Freud, but she had refused the talking cure. Now, after two years of more unpleasant treatments by other specialists, she reluctantly consented to see him. The fact that her father brought her did not seem remarkable to Freud; in fact he treated all the power relationships in Dora's family as incidental to the main business: analyzing her dreams and associations and discovering the sexual impulses at the bottom of them.

But Freud did give, by way of description, a clear picture of the dynamics of Dora's intimate circle. For many years, her father had been sexually alienated from her mother, who suffered a chronic case of gonorrhea he had given her. Because of this "catarrh" of the female organs, her mother constantly visited cleansing spas for her health, and, incidentally, would clean the house over and over again and lock its rooms against dirt and contamination. This locking-up preoccupation included her husband's cigars and brandy. Rather than spend time with this unyielding wife, Dora's father preferred the company of his mistress,

Frau K., a close friend of the family. The father, although a vigorous businessman, was himself invalided with syphilis and chronically recurring tuberculosis. As Dora negotiated the discoveries of adolescence, the whole group — Dora, her parents, Frau K. and her husband Herr K., plus other family members, servants and tutors — would stay at mountain spas to enable the healing of the parents' illnesses. No wonder Dora developed a "catarrh," a cough and other respiratory problems, of her own, plus headaches, depression, plus various other physical symptoms with no obvious organic cause that Freud diagnosed as "petite hysterie." She was also a moody, sometimes contrary, young woman given to episodes of profound discouragement and depression, and she had a very low opinion of doctors.

Dora was quite attached to Frau K., in spite of her awareness of the woman's intimacy with her father. Frau K. and a woman tutor were the only people who paid any attention to her curiosity about sex and other adult matters. And so Dora was very upset when Herr K. made overtures to her one day during a walk in the woods. She slapped him and ran away.

As Dora and Freud reviewed these events, it became clear to both of them that her father, Herr K., and Frau K. all thought — on some level of shared consciousness — that a romance between Dora and Herr K. would balance the sexual dynamics of the group. Everyone would have a partner, except Dora's mother, who didn't seem to want one. But all three wished these relations to remain secret. Dora insisted to Freud that she wanted no part of this imbroglio. What she did want was his support in confronting her father and Herr and Frau K., naming the deceptions for what they were, and thus declaring her independence from them all. She had tried at least one such confrontation on her own, denouncing Herr K.'s sexual advances to her father and to Frau K., but Herr K. and the others all denied that such a thing could have occurred.

Instead of coming to her aid with this confrontation, Freud produced evidence from her dreams that she secretly desired Herr K., and that her attraction to Frau K. was not the interest of an adolescent girl in a lively and worldly older woman, but a homoerotic residue of her earlier attachment to her own mother. Indeed, at one point, he suggested that a good outcome would be for her father to divorce her mother and marry Frau K., and for her to marry Herr K., legitimizing the very situation by which she felt victimized! Dora was shocked. After debating these conclusions with Freud and continuing to experience symptoms,

Dora took matters into her own hands. She terminated her treatment with him after only three months, far short of his goals for her and for his theory, and went to live separately from her family for a while. Then she chose a moment when their guard was down; they were sitting in mourning for a death in the family. She came into the apartment and once more confronted them all with what everyone knew had been going on. This time they admitted she was right, and her symptoms abated.

Freud heard about this sequel from Dora's father and Herr K., both of whom were acquaintances and former neurological patients of Freud's, a fact that did not inspire Dora to be more receptive to his advice. Freud, nursing his resentment at her sudden absconding from the treatment, changed the name of his case report from "Dream Analysis in the Treatment of Hysteria" to "Fragment of an Analysis of a Case of Hysteria," and did not publish it until four years later. When he did, the lesson that he drew from the experience was that he had become too personally involved in the case and had not noticed that Dora resented his pushing his interpretations at her (like Herr K.'s pushing of a more physical kind).

The published paper was in part an essay on the need to pay attention to the patient's transference to the analyst of feelings that interfere with treatment, and to analyze such feelings to obtain a clearer picture of the sexual and defensive aspects of the relationship between patient and analyst. If he had been able to analyze Dora's feelings about him successfully, he concluded, he could have prevented her "acting out" of the transference by leaving treatment and confronting her family.

In the classical psychoanalytic canon, then, the case of Dora is about the analysis of transference and countertransference. Many analysts, rereading this story over the years, derive the lesson that Freud could have been a better analyst and managed the case with less prescription and more self-awareness. But they give him credit for having the courage to publish a case that he bungled, and they admire him for using the occasion to contribute one of his most important ideas — the analysis of the transference.

There have been many other readings of Dora's story. Feminists think he could have been a better advocate of Dora's own perceptions of her situation and should have backed her in the confrontation that she finally accomplished in spite of him (Decker, 1991, pp. 169–210). In fact, the modern trauma-oriented treatment for such a patient would be to help her decide how ready she is for such a confrontation, and what she wants to do about the timing and its consequences (Dinsmore, 1991, esp. pp. 41–42). Family therapists think he could have promoted communication in the family instead of colluding with the adults (Stierlin, 1976; Hare-Mustin, 1994). But these are all ideas from later times and would not have occurred to Freud. I read the story as that of a man struggling in the grip of an idea, a theory that he is trying to prove against the patient's own narrative of her traumatic experience. The "rigorous test" of the theory turned out to be more an effort to make the case fit the theory. Freud was desperate for an audience to understand his ideas and in a hurry to take his case to the literature. In his letters to Fliess from this period, he sounds isolated and depressed, unappreciated, struggling to get a university appointment, and certainly not, like Janet in Paris, the heir apparent to a great clinical establishment. About two years after Dora's departure, he began to attract a small circle of followers who met at his apartment on Wednesday evenings to discuss psychoanalysis, and groups like this, for the rest of his life, became the audience that was most important to him. From then on, he was able to act the role of the head discoverer, the leader of the loyal group of psychoanalysts, and — among them — the arbiter of right ideas.

Still, the story of having to work alone and unappreciated, guarding a truth that others do not understand, was part of his life experience, and it never left him. Indeed, the seeds of this heroic isolation may have been present at the beginning of his work with hysteria. He introduced *The Etiology of Hysteria* with a strikingly confident metaphor: this work was, he suggested to his readers, a *caput Nilum*, a discovery of the head of the Nile. In the mid-1870s, just as Freud was setting out on his exploration of hysteria, Sir Henry Morton Stanley, already famous for finding Dr. David Livingstone, had found the mountains in Central Africa where the southernmost waters of the Nile arise. Not only had the source of the Nile been a mystery for centuries, but the quest for it had given rise to an international competiton among gentlemen explorers. The image of a great discovery that is the reward of pressing ever further back to the source clearly appealed to Freud.

Today, we would say that even in natural history, the evidence of single causes is an illusion. Finding the source of the Nile says nothing about the river's complex course or its relationship to the land it drains and nourishes. Claiming that one of many contributing streams is "the head" is only an arbitrary way of winning a competition. As Judith

Herman says, Freud did well with his hysterical patients as long as he paid attention to what they were telling him. He got into trouble when he left their company — stopped learning from them — and went off hunting for yet another, higher head of the Nile.

§

In our first-year seminars at Tremont, some of Freud's great cases, especially those of patients like Dora, began to seem special instances of the problems of attempting to generalize a theoretical approach to neurosis in general. But apart from my one experience with Grace, hysteria was a rarity in 1970. Who were the "patients like Dora"? What experience in twentieth-century America paralleled the prevalence of hysteria in nineteenth-century Vienna?

In 1970, a comparable mental illness had begun to assume similar epidemic proportions among young Americans: borderline personality disorder (BPD).[7] But whereas hysteria borrows its stigmata from paralyses, faintings, tics, coughs and convulsions (the symptoms of neurological and physical illness that interested nineteenth-century European medicine), BPD takes its forms from depression, rage, plummeting self-esteem and a preoccupation with suicide, the medical psychiatry of the twentieth century.

Borderline personality disorder is characterized by stormy, dramatic reverses in the patient's relations with people close to her. Usually the patient is a woman, since, as in hysteria, men are much less likely to have the classical form of the illness. Borderline patients have low self-esteem, sometimes to the point of suicide, and their relationship with the therapist, like other relationships, tends to be difficult and full of episodes of disappointment, distrust, and distance or counterattack. The vividness and drama with which such persons act out the disappointments of their lives make some of their experiences seem, to psychiatric observers, to border on psychosis, and hence the name.

Like hysteria, BPD seems to condemn its victims to protracted, and generally unsatisfactory, relationships with the healing professions. But difficult as the therapeutic relationship can be for both patient and doctor,

[7] See Herman (1992) for the sense in which hysteria, borderline personality disorder, and other trauma-related disorders are similar and different.

it seemed to us in the 1970s that the best approach to BPD was long-term psychodynamic treatment. Therefore, we had to decide whether we had the stamina to "see borderlines" or not.

My own first encounter with this painful illness had been in 1962, toward the end of my first year of residency training. A graduating resident came to me and asked me if I would continue the treatment he had begun three years earlier with Dolores, a single young woman who suffered from BPD. She was by this stage of the work a very faithful patient — intelligent, and able to attend sessions regularly. Such cases went on and on for years, and this resident could not continue with Dolores himself because he was taking a position in another city. He described the pros and cons of working with her in terms that have since become familiar: "It's very scary work. She's often quite suicidal, and you will get a lot of calls after hours. I have had to work very hard on her attachment to me and both the positive and negative transference has been very intense. But she's getting better slowly, and if you have a good supervisor, I think there's no better way to learn. I've learned a lot about therapy by working with her, and a lot about myself. I hope you can do it, because I think you're one of the people in your class who has the ability and the patience for it." Now, in this description are buried all the traps of work with BPD: the patient's search for the ideal parent, which is infectious for fledgling therapists who hope to be ideal parents themselves; the search for "good" people, a supervisor with a special internal quality; the flattering and idealizing attribution that I was "good" enough myself; the danger of finding out, in the experiences of the therapy, how far from good enough I was.

In my second year of residency, I had "good" supervisors and "good" role models. The director of training, José Barchilon, was a specialist in working with this disorder, as were a number of people with whom I had seminars. One of them referred to working with BPD as "like trying to approach a startled faun." It was indeed skittish work.

In any case, I accepted my colleague's request, or challenge, or burden, whatever it was. Dolores came to see me regularly. She told me nightmarish stories about conflicts between her parents while she was growing up; her feelings of mixed grief, exultation, and guilt at the sudden death of her father; her resentment at now living with her mother, who poured contempt upon her for being unmarried, friendless, and unemployed. The mother's diatribes, however, instead of driving her daughter away, had the opposite effect. She felt bound to the small apartment where the two of them lived, and compelled to listen while her mother projected onto Dolores her own unacknowledged helplessness and loneliness. We talked about separation and survival as tasks in life, her resentment of the necessity to carry them out. In turn, I spent many hours with my supervisor examining my own resentment of her blaming me and my therapy for a large part of her troubles. Then I went back to her and talked about how our relationship was becoming another in her collection of disappointments, and how the pattern of projection was engulfing me as well. I was trying to "analyze the transference."

Dolores made it clear that I was definitely not good enough to help her. In one session she punished me for a misstep by spiking my toes with the heel of her shoe. It hurt for days while we examined what she thought I had meant by whatever it was I had said that had hurt her feelings, injured her delicate self-esteem. I was able to shift the focus of her anger to people and situations in her life that were truly not helping her, and we talked sometimes, warily, about her disappointment in herself, which was so massive that she could scarcely approach the subject.

With my encouragement, Dolores did make a step forward by moving into her own apartment, but it proved to be a very dangerous step indeed: she jumped from its window to her death. I was devastated by this tragedy. I had known she was suicidal. Why had I not seen it coming? What could I have done differently? My supervisor and many others were very sympathetic, assuring me that it had happened to them, and that I wasn't to blame. But for many months afterward, I thought about what could have been done differently, and I did blame myself, since her final judgment on the inadequacy of my work seemed irrefutable.

Dolores and I suffered from a poverty of ideas. Treatment at the Einstein residency was, as elsewhere, focused on childhood and meanings below the "waterline," rather than on real people in the patient's life. As inheritors of the classical analytic school, we thought that in BPD we were faced with something similar to other, analyzable, intrapsychic problems, only more difficult. We were stuck with a language that focused on "good" and "bad" internal objects. Lacking any objective way to anchor our work in the world of real people in Dolores's life, I continually returned to the only real people there seemed to be in her nightmare: her and me. There the myth of an ultimately trustable good doctor who knows how to "treat" a sick patient plagued us again and again.

But BPD patients react negatively to being "treated." For them, relationships with people who claim to know what will help them recalls the experience of childhood, especially of a parent who disqualified, humiliated, and degraded the child. On the other hand, there seemed to be no alternative to the "good doctor" story, even though it might generate anger in the patient, depending on how "good" the doctor is supposed to be. It is an isolating myth, this "good doctor" story. Dora and Dolores chose different escapes from it.

§

It is not surprising that social psychiatrists at Tremont were willing to leave the treatment of BPD to the analysts, in spite of the absence of any solid outcome studies to show that the analysts were succeeding. Our vision of social intervention was limited to family therapy and crisis intervention. The presence of a patient with BPD in one of our family sessions was a signal to cut our losses and bail out. Worse yet was trying to do marital therapy with two people with this kind of problem, and facing the abysmal disappointment on both sides of the marriage when it failed.

Reading Freud's cases at Tremont, we would not have picked out the specific influence of trauma on "this kind of problem." Like Freud, we were more interested in generalizations than in specifics: we were looking for the influence of the present environment, in much the same way as he was looking for childhood sexuality.[8] It was not until the 1980s that the approach to BPD took a new turn —a recognition that indeed it was a kind of problem — one type of response to trauma, comparable to others. The focus changed from psychoanalytic treatment to examining what the experience of such patients had in common with others, turning, as Foucault would have said, to the experience of those who suffered. This new approach was made possible by epidemiology: the study of large numbers of cases, reexamined from different points of view. By grouping together people who had suffered trauma, the profession began to see that this category encompassed victims of domestic violence, victims of rape, incest survivors, survivors of violent accidents and

---

[8] In fact, Freud did reconsider the role of trauma as a unique factor in psychopathology, later in his career when he wrote "Beyond the Pleasure Principle." See Shalev (1999).

other disasters, veterans of combat, and patients with multiple personality syndrome, borderline personality disorder, and hysteria.

All of these patients tend to handle painful experiences or memories with a mental process that Pierre Janet had first identified as *dissociation* (Spiegel, 1994). Dissociation, or passing into an altered state, could be, at first, a painful and uncontrollable reexperiencing of the memory (flashbacks), phobias, panics, or fits of depression, or later, a substitution of symptoms for the painful experience. These symptoms could be physical, as in hysteria; blind rage or blame, as in BPD; or becoming another person, as in multiple personality. Careful epidemiological research on these dissociative disorders has begun to reveal some differences in the type of past trauma experienced by each type of patient, but what is more interesting for us here is the underlying similarity of human responses to painful experiences (Johnson, Cohen, Brown, et al., 1999).

Dissociation is actually a very common response to pain of any kind, present or past. The out-of-body journey I made into the chapel tower at St. Paul's to hide from my feelings about graduating was a mild and transient example. More severe dissociations, psychic numbness, or a retreat into emotional absence or forgetfulness is part of the post-traumatic stress disorder that follows a recent, definite experience, such as a near-fatal injury or rape. Judith Herman, one of the principal investigators in this area, has proposed that the syndromes that follow repeated, prolonged traumas of captivity, such as childhood sexual abuse or combat exposure, should be called "complex posttraumatic stress disorder." Repetition and helplessness make these problems an order of magnitude worse, and contribute to such chronic conditions as the "shell shock" of combat veterans, hysteria, BPD, and multiple personality.

Two social developments, new since the 1970s, enabled this research on dissociative disorders, especially the sifting of the multiple factors predisposing to the different types. One was the development of a large, expensive, nationally funded research establishment, centered in the National Institute of Mental Health, which makes it possible to look carefully at the records of many times Freud's 18 cases. And the second was the influential position of women in that establishment. Judith Herman, for example, is the director of training at the Victims of Violence Program at Cambridge Hospital, associated with the Harvard Medical School. She and her women colleagues, having a different sympathy with the experiences of victims of trauma, have noticed similarities that others have neglected. Whereas Freud in his later work attempted to overgeneralize from his experience with hysteria, Herman and her colleagues focus on the specific effect of traumatic experience on these dissociative disorders. Like Freud in his "Etiology" paper, they are more interested in careful description than in theoretical generalization, and, as a result, their analysis welcomes complexity. For example, although research reveals a high frequency of obvious kinds of childhood trauma, such as physical or sexual abuse, the causes of BPD are more complicated than that. The essential childhood experience in producing BPD seems to be a more subtle damage to the child's developing sense of confidence (Gunderson, 1990). There may also be, as Charcot thought of hysteria, a constitutional vulnerability to such experiences (Stone, 1993). Recent research also suggests that trauma changes brain chemistry, so that the biological basis for these illnesses may not be only constitutional (van der Kolk, 1997).

Herman describes another similarity among dissociative responses to trauma: the best treatment programs contain a similar set of elements, whether the condition follows childhood trauma or more recent traumatic experience, such as rape or domestic violence. Here again, the treatment is not a single elegant procedure, as in psychoanalysis, but a collection of several kinds of experiences. Recovery begins with a healing relationship with a therapist, which can have all the life-and-death difficulties of the treatment of BPD, but is concerned first with protection, calm, and safety, not with revelation. Establishing safety may include providing shelter from the perpetrator of the trauma, if necessary. The effort to remember the traumatic experience, and to mourn its effects on the parts of life lost or damaged, is made only when the patient is ready. Finally comes a reconnection with new life and a commonality of witness with other victims. This last phase is especially interesting because it is the one of which Freud and Breuer — and I in working with Dolores — had no inkling. We could not have imagined this *social phase* of recovery from trauma.

We might have had a clue if, returning to history, we had known about the later life of Breuer's first patient. In the 1880s, Breuer had succeeded in restoring Anna O.'s lost ability to speak by helping her to recall her long and exhausting experience of nursing her father in his final illness. But when her treatment culminated in her becoming intensely dependent upon Breuer's daily visits to her, he stopped it abruptly. She relapsed, had to go to a hospital, and remained ill for a long time. When at length she recovered, she became a champion of her era's women's liberation movement. She founded the social work profession in Germany, directed an orphanage for girls, took up the cause of the treatment of prostitutes, founded a feminist organization for Jewish women, and, in general, converted her negative private experience into a matter of public testimony and public action.

Anna O. (or Bertha Pappenheim as she was known to the world) has become a hero to the feminist critics of psychoanalysis. She survived the patriarchal treatment and by her life made a statement that went beyond it: the way out of such conditions as hysteria lies not only through the private exploration of one's history of personal trauma but also through the social realization of an active response to it. The public witness that Dora was able to carry out within the small society of her family, Bertha Pappenheim carried out on a much larger scale. The question for therapists today has become, after the private counseling and exploration: What arena of public *protest*, of action with a different audience, will be effective? Christine Dinsmore calls this the "survivor mission" (Dinsmore, 1991). Anna O. used her experience as a trauma survivor to "make the trauma a gift that helps her to make the world a better place. In moving on, the survivor recognizes that she was victimized but being a survivor is only one small part of her/him. She/he is complex, and it's time to focus on the other parts that make up the whole" (Dinsmore, personal communication).

One example of this public-witness aspect of recovery from trauma is the work of Marsha Linehan, a psychologist at the University of Washington in Spokane, who has designed a treatment program for BPD (Linehan, Tutak, Heard, and Armstrong, 1994). Clinical trials of her treatment are the only ones so far that demonstrate a superior effectiveness against BPD. Her patients, when matched with comparable patients receiving psychodynamic therapy, do better faster and stay well longer.

Linehan renames BPD "parasuicidal behavior," something that patients can identify and speak about. A condition for membership in her program is participation in group sessions with other women members, meetings that are guided by an educational workbook. The patients learn through exercises in that book, and through homework exercises and group discussion, that they have an objectively describable condition. It can be treated by means that they have at hand in their own minds and experience. Against this background, the individual therapy, which is done by the same members of the clinic staff who run the groups, has the atmosphere of a publicly supported enterprise. The therapists also discuss the treatment in a group of their own, so they get the support and perspective they need.

Linehan's program teaches these suicidal young women: (1) You may have had terrible parenting, but you aren't stuck with it. After you get angry, you can eventually take steps to keep it from dominating your life. (2) You have an objectively describable condition, and as you learn to be objective about it yourself and practice countermeasures against it, you will start to see changes. (3) You are not alone. Everyone in this group, and in other groups, is coping with this problem, and although they all have different lives, you can learn a lot from them, and even teach them something yourself.[9]

These inventions, as I pointed out, would not have been possible without social developments barely visible in 1970, such as the occupation by women of responsible positions in psychiatric services and research. According to Herman (1992, pp. 7–9), the subject of trauma

> provokes such intense controversy that it periodically becomes anathema. To study psychological trauma is to come face to face both with human vulnerability in the natural world and with the capacity for evil in human nature. To study psychological trauma means bearing witness to horrible events.
>
> Three times over the past century, a particular form of psychological trauma has surfaced into public consciousness. Each time the investigation of that trauma has flourished in affiliation with a political movement. The first to emerge was [Charcot's study of] hysteria, the archetypal psychological disorder of women. Its study grew out of [Charcot's participation in] the republican, anti-clerical political movement of the late

---

[9] This idea of adding a social arena to the treatment of trauma is in line with the writings of Ritterman (1987) on the subject of recovery from torture and political terror. She points out that public consciousness, naming the oppressor, knowing the place and location of the traumatic experiences, and sharing solidarity of awareness with others who were also oppressed are important parts of the recovery from torture and terror.

nineteenth century in France. The second was shell shock or combat neurosis. Its study began in England and the United States after the First World War and reached a peak after the Vietnam War. Its political context was the collapse of the cult of war and the growth of an anti-war movement. The last and most recent trauma to come into public awareness is sexual and domestic violence. Its political context is the feminist movement in Western Europe and North America. Our contemporary understanding of psychological trauma is built upon a synthesis of these three lines of investigation.

As compelling as this historical perspective is, it omits one factor that threatened to take over this story: the American ability to turn anything into a religion. Even as Herman was writing in 1992, a therapy cult was forming around childhood sexual abuse. It was fueled by books, magazine articles, and television talk shows, many of which were responding to two particularly powerful publications. One retelling of the story of Freud's desertion of the seduction theory, a book by Jeffrey Masson (1992), attributed a kind of craven connivance to Freud's "coverup" of his original discovery, and implied that revealing "the truth" would destroy psychoanalysis.[10] The other was a best-seller on recovery from childhood sexual abuse, so helpful to the victims and their counselors that it inspired a movement. It suggested that not only dissociative disorders but also "eating disorders, an addiction to drugs or alcohol, suicidal feelings or sexual problems ... may be symptoms of sexual abuse" (Bass & Davis, 1988, p. 349). Therapists began to look for such histories in their patients' childhoods, and found them with remarkable frequency. Other books followed, and as stories of child abuse proliferated, confrontations of parents ensued. Parents who were sure it never happened formed self-help groups, some patients recanted their confrontations, and articles in newspapers and magazines took sides.[11] It was a thoroughly modern

---

[10] See Malcolm (1984) for an illuminating account of this episode from all points of view.

[11] The professional debate about false memory and the recovery of trauma in psychotherapy is elegantly and readably reviewed in *The Family Therapy Networker* of September/October 1993. It includes articles by researchers and therapists of different persuasions, and at least one who hews to the difficult middle.

American media uproar, but out of it came some careful and critical studies. Psychologists were moved to investigate the reliability of memories, especially those appearing for the first time in therapy. The suggestibility of patients and the impact of the therapists' assumptions all came under review. At the same time, it has been important to avoid silencing the inquiry into abuse, to which every therapy must be open.

The problem with the recovered-memories scandal, once again, was overgeneralization from a single idea. That is the lesson I have taken, over the years of reviewing them, from the stories of Freud, Dora, Delores, and others in the annals of trauma, dissociation, and their study and treatment.

When I think about how difficult it is to apply these categories in a dogmatic way to particular cases, I think of Mercedes Vargas. She was suicidal at the beginning, and, in fact, she had almost every kind of symptom at one time or another, including "eating disorders and addictions." But her relationships with those around her, including her family, were intense, steady and enduring; in the case of some of her dependent boyfriends, they verged on the fanatical. I never discussed diagnosis with her psychiatrist, but BPD did not seem to me a good description of her problem. Certainly, at the beginning, she was depressed, but as she got better, all these characteristics seemed to change. I will return in Chapter 5 to the part family therapy played in her getting better, but here I want to focus on the way she dealt with the experience of trauma after most of the family work was over.

Toward the end of her last year in high school, as she was preparing to go away to college, Mercedes requested some meetings between herself and her father, Fausto. She felt they had been living in the same house peacefully, but distantly, for a while, and she wanted to try for a more personal kind of conversation between them. Partly, she wanted to talk about his demanding perfection from her in her schoolwork as a child (her traumatic experience), but more important than that, she wanted to change the distance and tension between them. She wanted to see if they could talk about feelings — particularly his. Fausto acknowledged that she was asking him to move to an area where he was weak and she was strong, the reverse of the situation that prevailed when she was a child. He tried gamely, but after a few meetings, they had to admit that this was only a slow beginning on that project, and Mercedes turned, with some disappointment, to her next venture, going to college.

In spite of how little the relationship had changed, the act of witnessing provided by Fausto and me was a step forward. There were no confrontations or revelations of terrible secrets, but confrontation was not the most important agenda. She took her position and was heard. I should also note here that in college, Mercedes went on to fulfill her survivor mission by becoming a special-education teacher, helping children with learning problems.

Child abuse is a widespread and important problem, but as Mercedes' example illustrates, not every patient is a victim, and not every childhood trauma is sexual. Deciding who is and who is not a victim may be difficult, and therapists may try to overcome the difficulty by leading, rather than following, their patients' memories. At length, the psychotherapy profession has had to recognize that the remembering, forgetting, or misremembering of childhood experience is a very complex matter, one easily affected by the experience of psychotherapy, which is not a research environment. It is, most important, an audience for the patient that has a powerful effect on the patient's memories and reflections, and invariably, to some extent, a rewriting of history.

Trauma is not a subject that yields to political or theoretical philosophizing, and throughout this history, it keeps recurring, presenting exceptions that lead to the rethinking of simple explanations. The professional discussion is now beginning to subside, but the talk shows, the books, and the public arguments between factions of true believers continue.

§

Freud, in his time actually had his own fateful exposure to this kind of American clamor. In 1909, he and two other members of the Wednesday evening group, Carl Jung and Sàndor Ferenczi, were invited to attend the twentieth-anniversary commemoration of the founding of Clark University in Worcester, Massachusetts. The experience turned his isolation inside out. Although he himself was afterward quite skeptical about the future of psychoanalysis in the New World, the United States — its writers, its popular magazines, its psychotherapy profession, and its outlook on the world — has never been the same since his visit.

CHAPTER FOUR
The Uses of the Past —
Discovering Ancestors

AFTER PRESENTING FREUD'S GREAT CASES, the first-year course at Tremont ended with the history of social psychiatry in the United States. We wanted to understand both where social psychiatry came from and why it chose the 1960s to make its appearance. Was our generation really inventing it, or did we have forebears whose vision had waited until now to be realized? We looked to the histories of American psychiatry and social science to cast some light on what we were all doing there in the post office building between the Bronx Zoo and the Grand Concourse. Being claim-stakers in new territory, we were in search of legitimacy, of ancestors.

Again, the story began with Freud, but this time in a different mood. His arrival in America was as much a triumph as his experience in Vienna had been a disappointment. When he arrived at Clark University in Worcester, Massachusetts, in 1909 to give five introductory lectures on psychoanalysis, Freud entered a world that was prepared to hear him. His visit had decisive consequences for the development of psychotherapy, since it was the American audience for those lectures that, more than any other public, established the place of psychoanalysis in the modern world (Freud, 1909).

The New England where Freud arrived was in a crisis of religious belief and institutions. The modern environment of industrialism, commercialism, and scientific materialism challenged religious faith and practice, at least among the professional class. Most people probably continued going to church and believing as before, but those who took the life of the spirit as a calling were more deeply troubled. Outside of traditional

Christianity, transcendentalism was what New England had to offer the passionate believer. And as early as Emerson himself, who left the Unitarian Church because he could not believe in the Eucharist, that doctrine vitiated the belief in ritual in favor of an intellectual individualism. One of Emerson's group, Henry David Thoreau, went off by himself to explore solitude in the midst of Nature at Walden Pond, and confirmed Americans in a form of anticommunity ritual of meditation and retreat that suited our individualist temper. It was the opposite pole of congregational communion.

As the century ended, the bourgeois home, as in Victorian England, developed a cult of childhood and the family (Lasch, 1971) organized around a sentimentalized and idealized mother. The mood of antimodernism in the professional class suggested other ritual forms. Eastern and medieval motifs appeared in art, and — the closest thing to a ritual practice — the Arts and Crafts movement sanctified the work of the un-mechanized hand and eye (Lears, 1981).

Emerson once said that New England was the conscience of America, Boston the conscience of New England, and Harvard the conscience of Boston. If we look past the smug parochialism of this view, rather like a cardinal talking about Rome, it suggests a search for something secular, a visible institution to replace the lost church. And the university to some extent saw itself in that way. In 1869 the Harvard Board of Overseers appointed as their new president a Massachusetts Institute of Technology chemistry professor named Charles Eliot, because they knew that the science faculties were the key to the university's future. But a strong minority of them objected that having a scientist rather than a member of the clergy as president would have a damaging effect on the morals of the undergraduates. Science, as represented by Darwinian evolution and the "dark satanic mills" of industrialism, seemed, at best, amoral, and at worst, a force of evil. Apart from the material goods that came out of its laboratory, science was not self-evidently good for the soul.

Nevertheless, thinkers who took upon themselves the care of society were casting about for new certainties, and science in the new age was one vein they could mine for reality. Could a constructive scientific philosophy of human nature and morals replace what was being lost with the fading of revealed religion? If so, what institutions, what activities would embody that philosophy? For many in Freud's audience, the answer was psychology. American psychology was at that time indistinguishable from philosophy, which, in turn, was only beginning to be distinguishable from religion. Although they were not divines, like the founders of the New England theocracies, for the psychologists and psychiatrists trying to found a new profession, the connection with divinity was still there.

Freud's host, the president of Clark University, G. Stanley Hall, exemplified this connection. He had done graduate work at Union Theological Seminary and thus was in the mold of university presidents of the generation before, almost all of whom were Protestant clergy. He had gone to Harvard to study with William James, and there, in 1878, earned the first Ph.D. in psychology to be given in the United States. Thus the man who invited Freud to America was both the first official psychologist in this country and the first to be a university president. This academic festival over which he presided, the twentieth-anniversary celebration of Clark University, was a convocation of something quite new: a profession in the process of defining itself.

William James was there, although ill with the heart disease of which he would die a year later, and was revered as the senior architect of the new science. William and his brother Henry had grown up under the jealous tutelage of their father, a Swedenborgian with intense religious preoccupations. After much indecision, William had determined to study medicine. He got through medical school with frequent interruptions due to recurrent depressions. For treatment, he consulted spiritist healers and practitioners of American "talking cures," of which there were several in Boston. He also went overseas to study philosophy, picking up what he could learn about psychology as it was developing in the laboratories of such experimentalists as Wilhelm Wundt in Germany. He also studied hysteria with Charcot.

James was determined to unite the experimental physiology of perception and cognition, the ideas of psychiatrists like Freud, Charcot and Janet, with his own emotional struggles to keep his will on course. He received his medical degree, but never practiced. Instead, starting in 1872, he taught anatomy and physiology at Harvard and continued to bring both the physical and spiritual sides of psychology together into the same system. He began work on his *Principles of Psychology*, which he planned as an integration of experimental psychology with experience, accessible and interesting to the common reader, full of practical examples from life, including his own.

Much of James's working life was also devoted to the Society for Psychical Research, which applied scientific tests to the claims of mediums and clairvoyants, hoping to find a place for the spirits of the dead in the natural world. In two of his most popular writings, *The Will to Believe* (1897) and *The Varieties of Religious Experience* (1902), he treated religious faith as a psychological phenomenon, to be studied objectively, but the way he wrote about it showed clearly that he yearned to find it in his own life.

Worldly philosophers such as James were widely read and admired in the 1880s and 1890s. James was in great demand as a speaker, especially at colleges and schools of education. But his message was more like a sermon at church, and did not touch on the personal life and needs of the individual hearer. The psychology of James and others, like the philosophy of Emerson, was well articulated, sophisticated, literate, eclectic, and even enthusiastic and inspired, but it had no compelling central image. It fell short of providing a replacement for the personal religious conviction with which people were accustomed to face their fears. And it provided them with no institution, no congregation, other than the audience at the lecture hall.

Much of the malaise of the time appeared as physical or psychological illness, or as a new and epidemic nervousness, neurasthenia, which seemed to be a combination of the two. At Emanuel Church in Boston, the earliest form of American self-help support group was meeting, chanting in unison, "Not well yet, but perfectly able to get well" (Hale, 1971). The First Church of Christ, Scientist, had been founded by Mary Baker Eddy in Boston in 1879. It asserted the power of faith alone to heal the body's ills. Americans were very consciously troubled in body and spirit, and many among the clamor of healers offered institutions rather like churches (Meyer, 1980).

§

Freud lectured in Worcester on five successive days, in German, on the "talking cure" of hysterical symptoms, dream analysis, childhood sexuality, and the evils of civilization's repression of sexual desire. His lectures were a bravura account of his discoveries as he traced the cause of neurosis "ever further back" to the earliest stirrings of childhood sexuality. He was interviewed by Boston newspaper reporters, who, although they could not print some of his more scandalous observations, found him a fascinating subject for feature articles. He gave advice about child-rearing and sex. These official discussions continued informally as his hosts took him, and his disciples, Jung and Ferenczi, to an outing in an Adirondack wilderness camp. He would never have received this sort of reception at home in Vienna, where as an obscure neurologist, he had struggled to get a university appointment.

In the United States, he was an instant success, and his triumph in Worcester and Boston led to the founding of American and English psychoanalytic societies, the translation of his works into English, and the grounding of a revolutionary profession, much more important in the English-speaking world than it ever became in Europe. It is a story that has been told and retold in many books.[1]

§

What ingredient did he supply that changed the culture of ideas? His contribution had two parts; the first was evangelical, and the second was political.

The evangelical message began with excitement. American psychotherapy, as described (and experienced) by such writers as William James, was eclectic and prosaic. It was not comprehensible in five lectures, and it was, above all, not obviously exciting as a subject of conversation. Freud's theory, that infantile sexuality lay at the root of the life of the unconscious, was, on the other hand, a scandal. It played a great joke on the sanctimonious idealism of religion and philosophy, by which many of the devotees of Emerson were burdened. If one could accommodate to the scandal, if one joined in the joke, Freud's theory had an instant earthy appeal. It was about sex, scatology, and babies — even about jokes themselves. It was an antidote to academic and bourgeois stuffiness and

---

[1] There has been a new version of this story to read every few years since, as a resident, I worked through the worshipful first two volumes of Ernest Jones' biography. Since then the retellings that I have relied on most in this book have been those by Ellenberger (1981), Rieff (1959), Sulloway (1992), Crews (1994), Hale (1971) and Forrester (1997). Cushman (1995), Hale (1995), and Caplan (1998) each describe in different ways the history of American psychotherapy both before and after Freud's impact upon it.

prudery of all kinds. It combined the incandescent elements of science and romance with the thrill of the horrible, as Mary Shelley's *Frankenstein* had previously done. It combined the imagery of Wagnerian myth with (Henry) Jamesian family tension. It was what the intellectual world was looking for: a simplifying scientific vision that, like the Gospels, had a daring revelation.[2] It made the good news of salvation available in an area as small and private as the memories of childhood, an area that, although filled with dragons, was, in some sense, under one's personal control.

And like the Gospels, it had a story. Psychoanalysis was the first narrative therapy. Freud's teacher, Charcot, had scornfully referred to the little details of his patients' stories as "*la psyciatrie de la concierge.*" But Freud and his disciples listened to these stories and fashioned them into a new mythology, in which the child-hero does battle with the giants of the nursery and with her own passions. Like the fading Christian mythology, it was a universal story: a story of Everyman.

The Freudian narrative not only was able to include these exciting elements, but also to exclude difficult alternatives. Under the guarantee of medical science, it could ignore not only the mysteries and yearnings of religion, but also the contradictions of society. Freud wrote with great confidence, and massive simplification, about society and religion, placing them aside as a setting or by-products of the main business (Freud, 1927, 1930). Since the story, "followed ever further back," was played out in the first five years of life and in the privacy of the family, the reimagined childhood could be a place where the social problems of the adult world — such as class, culture and discrimination — could be left out of focus or in the background. The child's world as metaphor for adult distress simply finessed much of the discussion of what some adults, such as the Marxists, thought were other causes of their trouble.

For all these reasons, and especially their union of science, mythic imagery, and *Kulturkritik,* Freud's ideas caught the attention of the intellectuals; Walter Lippman and Lionel Trilling were only two examples. By 1920, artists and writers were being analyzed, whether neurotic or not, as an educational or spiritual pursuit. In London, James Strachey provided the definitive English translation of Freud's collected works, the Standard

---

[2] Paul understood, even better than the authors of the Gospels, what a scandal the Christian revelation was, and how important that quality was to the intensity of the faith (Corinthians I, 1:23–24).

Edition, while he and his friends in Bloomsbury discussed the connections between their childhood experiences and their complex sex lives.
Freudian language began to appear in literary criticism, just as Marxist
language had appeared in social and historical analysis, as a far-ranging ex-
planatory system that seemed to have an answer for everything.

§

But apart from its evangelical inspiration, Freud's political influence
in the newly emerging psychotherapy business was also important. The
most historically fateful members of Freud's audience in Worcester were
the psychiatrists: American leaders such as Adolf Meyer; Freud's American translator, A. A. Brill (who had roomed with Lippman at college);
and the young British disciple, Ernest Jones, who later wrote a biography
of Freud. These people were inventing what proved to be the controlling
party of the new profession.

At the moment of Freud's arrival, the politics and economics of psychological healing were in a crucial and uneasy balance. On the one
hand, there were the medical people, neurologists and physiologically
inclined psychologists, who had not quite jelled into a psychiatry profession. They advocated various cures and treatments under medical supervision, operated asylums, directed state hospitals, and generally inclined to
somatic views of emotional ailments. In addition to the historically familiar
psychoses, they offered such diagnoses as neurasthenia, which was thought
to be due to fatigue plus the strains of modern family life and a weak
constitution. For these patients, they prescribed rest and retreat, sometimes sedation, sometimes exercise under strict professional supervision.

On the other hand, there were the advocates of Christian Science
and New Thought, and the chanters at the Emanuel Church. Related
philosophically to Emerson's transcendentalism, these movements
preached a new freedom from the old restraints of Calvinist religion
(Meyer, 1980). They believed in the ability of the human soul to reach
enlightenment and health of mind and body through its own power to
attain unto higher things.[3] Christian Science recruited believers in yearly
increasing numbers. New Thought retreats and groups met everywhere.

---

[3] Both Christian Science and New Thought were inspired by Mesmerism; see
Chapter 13.

Other groups flirted with spiritist sèances and Eastern practices of meditation. (Henry James in his novel *The Bostonians* describes such a group in its early chapters.) William James managed, by the breadth of his interests and learning, to bestride these conflicts, but the rivalry over what everyone could see was a new ministry, perhaps a new profession, in the making, was considerable.

Freudian theory and practice promised a medical-scientific resolution of this struggle. A group of Boston neurologists, led by James's medical school classmate James Jackson Putnam, seized on it to delineate a clearly medical definition of psychological healing, and founded the American Psychoanalytic Association in 1911. In the next decades, excluding nonmedical practitioners from their training, the association established an elite profession, which, by the 1930s, had institutes in several major cities and, by the 1940s, had recruited most psychiatric residency training programs to its standard. The exile and diaspora of Freud's European colleagues caused by Hitler's persecution of Jews added scholarship and distinction to the new American and English professions. (Freud himself, with his daughter, Anna, sought refuge in London in 1937.) The American doctors succeeded in making a clear, apparently scientific, and definitely medical statement of what mental healing was all about, more clearly under medical supervision than in England, where lay analysts such as Anna Freud were able to assert their leadership.

In the early twentieth century, medical progress was on the march. Epidemics of infectious disease were being prevented by immunization. Aseptic technique inaugurated the miracles of modern surgery. The Flexner Report (1910) inspired reforms that ushered in the scientific reorganization of the medical schools. Psychoanalysts, by taking upon themselves the new mystique of the medical profession, put themselves in a special economic class and relegated all nonmedical nonanalysts to the status of assistants (the social workers who dealt with the patient's outer world, the psychologists who provided the testing of intelligence and the ink-blot fantasies). Those professions were allowed to help, and to charge lower fees for their services. But the nonprofessionals — the survivors of the New Thought movements, the dabblers in spiritual healing — were at last clearly defined as nonscientific charlatans and quacks.

§

As the new profession of psychoanalysis flourished, the practice of seeing patients many times a week made it possible for a large number of practitioners to share in treating a limited clientele. As a professional and literary priesthood, analysts appeared in novels, later in the movies, and especially in jokes and cartoons. The priest in the confessional booth was now replaced by the analyst and his couch. A new folk-figure was born.

The rituals surrounding the analytic couch were, in a religious sense, the most important contribution of Freudian analysis. Here, at last, was a religious institution, a ritual of adult passage perfectly suited to the new American society, and especially to its geographically and spiritually migrant professional class. It was a graduate tutorial in the care of the self-made soul. The analysis, the couch, the hour, the intimate drama of the transference, was a ritual of self-communion without a creed or a congregation to bring up troubling ethical contradictions. Without entangling alliances to place or class, it sped the new American man on his way, usually in the few years between major dislocations in his life. And it turned out to be even more popular with his wife and traveling companion, the woman who had to deal with the frustrations of her subordinate role in furthering his career, keeping his houses, and raising his children.

§

How much of this future was visible to Freud's audience in 1909 is hard to say. William James gave Freud high compliments on his presentation, and told Ernest Jones that the future of psychotherapy "lies with your work." James was only being polite. To a friend, he wrote that Freud suffered from an *idée fixe*, "a regular *haluciné*" and that "obviously 'symbolism' is a most dangerous method" (Simon, 1980, p. 363).

In fact, James had very different ideas from Freud about the future of psychology. Already in place before Freud's arrival was an American discipline that embraced both the mental and the social, but its philosophy was eclipsed for almost 50 years by the dominance of psychoanalysis, and only began to make its return in the 1960s with the appearance of social psychiatry. Its origins were in the philosophy of pragmatism.

William James and John Dewey had a common tutor, Charles Sanders Peirce, the founder of pragmatism. When James first met Peirce as a fellow student at the Lawrence Scientific School in 1861, he did not think of him, only three years his senior, as a mentor. But 10 years later at Harvard as graduate students (Peirce was a physicist), they joined with other nonphilosophers (notably law student Oliver Wendell Holmes, Jr., later Chief Justice of the Supreme Court) to form a discussion group, which they ironically named the Metaphysical Club.[4] This group of anti-metaphysical young men was trying to understand the philosophical consequences of Darwin's vision of evolution, in which brute success determined what became true in the biological world, not what was noble, eternal, or transcendent. At these meetings, James was impressed with the originality of Peirce's assertion that the truth of a philosophical idea could be actively investigated by testing its usefulness — the natural history of its effects in the world — just as a theory in science was tested. As Holmes wrote later, "The life of the law is experience," not abstract principles. The idea that truth is a function of consequences rather than origins was the essence of James' pragmatism. In 1879 Peirce went on to teach philosophy at Johns Hopkins, where John Dewey was one of his students. Dewey, under the influence of his mother's strong Presbyterianism, still began his classes with a little sermon, but he had been searching since his college days for an alternative to traditional beliefs. He recognized Peirce's pragmatism as the comprehensive method that would help him to gather together his eclectic range of interests.

But pragmatism as a philosophical approach to knowledge was only the intellectual side of Dewey's enterprise. His conception of what philosophy could be about, a vision of the philosopher actively exploring the world, was larger than any theory. As the founding chairman of the philosophy department at the University of Chicago beginning in 1894, Dewey was able to turn philosophy into a working organization in a way that James could never have done at Harvard. The Chicago department of philosophy became a formidable organization (Faris, 1967). It took up mind, language, and social relations as a unified study, examining the human organism in all its social extensions, from the microscopic function

---

[4] Intellectual clubs of this kind in eastern cities were the congregations of the new religion. They gathered together like-minded thinkers and their devotees to invent the tools with which the contradictions of life could be faced. The club life of Boston, as William James grew older, was particularly intense, and included country retreats.

of words and sentences to the operation of large institutions. The city of Chicago was their laboratory. Dewey began there the laboratory schools where he brought in children to test his new ideas of progressive education, and his other students went out into the city to discover and test their ideas as well.

W. I. Thomas, who taught sociology at Chicago from 1895 to 1918, took sociology out of the armchair and into the streets of Chicago. There, he and his students, Robert Park and William Burgess, observed what was actually going on in public spaces, schools, parks, and slums. It was the beginning of urban sociology, which, at that time, looked very much like applied anthropology. They interviewed, counted, and measured: they went into newspaper offices to study the operation of the media; and they laid down the methodologies of the survey and the opinion poll. Thomas and Florian Znaniecki also originated the field of American applied anthropology in their study, *The Polish Peasant in Europe and America* (1918–1921), which attempted to understand the Polish immigrant population of Chicago by tracing its folkways to the old country. Dewey and Jane Addams, one of the founders of the social work profession, were close friends. In 1899, Addams had organized Hull House as one of the first neighborhood settlement houses. With her colleague, Jane Lathrop, she visited poor families in Chicago, and together they outlined some of the institutions that have become the foundations of urban social welfare.

At the heart of the philosophy department, Dewey's closest colleague, George Herbert Mead, was the founding philosopher of the communications sciences (Mead, 1962). The two of them wrote about psychology, sociology, the organization of services to the urban poor, the design of schools and the nature of education, the possibility of making social research scientific, and the study of human communication and language — all as interlocking and related subjects. Mead was the first philosopher of psychology to locate mind in the social field. He taught that the origins of thought and language lay in the gestures of animals. Others, including Darwin, had described animal gestures, like the growl or the bared teeth of dogs, as outward expressions of inner emotional states. Mead studied them in temporal sequences, such as meeting, threatening, or playing between dogs, and described animal communication as the expression of patterned immediate social *intentions* of each animal in the group. In this way of thinking, what happens in the "self" is always understood in relation to the "other." The members of Mead's famous trinity, "mind, self, and society," all depend on each other, with society framing and shaping mind and self as much as the other way around. Speech and communication are interlocking sequences of gestures toward the common social future of an interacting group, not an "expression" of the emotionally determined past of an individual member. This was the foundation of a new view of social analysis, and later of social therapy.

James, reading the work of Mead, Dewey, and others coming out of Chicago, hailed "a new school ... a 'Chicago' school," as a particularly American triumph of pragmatism (Ryan, 1995, p. 118). It was American in the sense that its inventors had shaken loose from the scholastic debates of German idealistic psychology, in which all of them had been trained. Its work certainly smacked of frontier practicality and irreverence, the jack-of-all-trades eclecticism and optimism of a country whose response to failure was to move on and start again somewhere else. And the new psychology's interest in environment rather than heredity suited the outlook of a nation of immigrants who had left old social structures behind and had come to America looking for a better place to live, a better environment. This pragmatic psychology turned outward to grapple with the experiences of class, ethnicity, culture, and family life — what Dewey (1930) called "communication and participation" — in a way that psychoanalysis did not.

§

The impact on psychiatry of Dewey's group at the University of Chicago can be seen in the career of Adolf Meyer, the director of the recently founded New York State Psychiatric Institute, and certainly in 1909 the most distinguished American psychiatrist (Hale, 1995; Sicherman, unpublished). Meyer, who gave one of the papers at the Clark conference, discussed the possibility of environmental, as opposed to somatic, factors in the origin of schizophrenia, a radical idea at the time. Events and experiences in the patient's life, he suggested, could reinforce "habit patterns," out of which even such a serious illness as schizophrenia could develop. This made room for an environmental contribution to a condition that at that time was seen as a degenerative brain disease entirely caused by heredity. Meyer thought that the environmental and experiential contribution to mental illness could be traced by taking a careful history of the events in the patient's life, which, in turn, could be related to the changes in habit patterns that caused the illness. He was an originator of the "history of the illness," which is now standard in psychiatric patient records.

Meyer was born in Switzerland. Like Jung, he had studied at the Burghölzli Institute near Zurich. His mentor there was August Forel, a leader both in brain anatomy and in hypnotic therapy. When Meyer's mother became ill with a severe depression and paranoid delusions, Forel was her psychiatrist, and Meyer had an opportunity to observe this most personally important case in some detail. His mother's illness, Meyer was convinced, had something to do with the very harsh treatment she had received from an uncle. And when she recovered, he had at hand a clear example of the variable outcome of serious mental illness — especially the possibility of treatment and recovery.

In 1893, after coming to the United States, Meyer got a job as a neuropathologist at Kankakee State Hospital in Illinois, not far from Chicago. Charged with doing brain autopsies on patients who had died in the hospital, he found that the records of the patients' illness and treatment were so poor that he was unable to relate his autopsy findings to the clinical course, so he began to agitate for changes in the administration. His vigorous and scientific style won him recognition, and soon he became the director of the hospital. The staff began taking and recording detailed histories.

At the University of Chicago, Meyer found a number of people who shared his interest in the impact of social experience on the development of health or illness. He knew both Dewey and Jane Addams and, in fact, married Mary Brooks, one of Addams' students in social work. (Later, when Meyer was director of Manhattan State Hospital on Ward's Island, Mary Brooks Meyer went to visit patients' homes to investigate environmental conditions contributing to their illness and to assess the consequences of their returning home.)

In 1895, Meyer left Illinois for Massachusetts to become the director of the Worcester Insane Hospital, which he attempted to make into a training center for psychiatrists. He also gave lectures at Clark University. His teaching there and later in New York (at the Psychiatric Institute, 1902–1910), inspired an interest among many future psychoanalysts in connecting the life history of the patient to his or her unique form of illness.

Meyer himself remained skeptical of the Freudian system, as he was of all systems. His was an eclectic and pragmatic style, welcoming all facts that might contribute to an understanding of patterns of development. His ideas about illness as a reaction to experience contributed a conceptual background to the first official diagnostic classifications (which eventually became the *Diagnostic and Statistical Manual of Mental Disorders*, the now-famous or -infamous DSM). Under his influence, many of the illnesses classified there were called "reactions," schizophrenic reaction, for example. On the other hand, he remained deeply skeptical of most systems of classification and explanation. As an experienced pathologist with a statistical curiosity, he was interested in exceptions. Why, he wondered, were some illnesses so prevalent in one part of the world and nearly absent in others? Could it be that diagnosticians of different schools saw what their theories told them to see? Or did culture make a difference to the occurrence of illness? His skepticism led him to anticipate many of the questions that are still at the leading edge of the field. He was one of a long, thin line of generalists in psychiatry who excelled equally at teaching, research, and public administration — a good ancestor for the Tremont Crisis Center.

§

Although Dewey's philosophy influenced psychiatrists such as Meyer, it did not produce a new psychotherapy. One man, however, came close (and his story is of special interest to me, since his method was the method of my second and, finally effective, third analysis.) Harry Stack Sullivan, born in 1892, belongs to the generation after the Clark conference, and he had no direct connection with Dewey's influence until later in his career.

He and his followers wrote many books,[5] most of them unread by people who are constantly reinventing his ideas and calling them their own.[6] As the Freudian revolution took hold in the 1920s and 1930s, Sullivan provided the principal alternative by proposing an *interpersonal* basis for both psychological problems and their cures. He moved psychology

---

[5] One of the best is the biography of Sullivan written by his secretary, Helen Swick Perry (1982).

[6] I find, for example, the current generation of "inter-subjective" analysts remarkably insensitive to their debt to Sullivan.

out of the space of inner consciousness into an intimate social space *between* people, the space of what Dewey had called communication and participation. His therapies involved talking actively with the patient, and questioning and investigating the natural history of the patient's characteristic ways of involving other people in the solution of problems. The lack of fit between these learned social strategies and the expectations of others produced anxiety: this was the focus of the therapy.

Sullivan was an Irish-American farm boy who grew up in the loneliness of being an only child in the anti-Catholic poverty of Chenango County, New York. In 1922, at the age of 30, Sullivan set up a therapeutic community that had a characteristic appreciation of the odd and peculiar: a special ward at the Sheppard and Enoch Pratt Hospital in Towson, Maryland, exclusively for acutely ill young men in the grip of a schizophrenic episode. They were cared for by a carefully chosen all-male staff (since he thought female nurses would remind them of their mothers). The patients were sedated with generous but decreasing doses of whiskey[7] and gently calmed and coaxed back to reality by low-pressure activities and sympathetic conversations. Sullivan was interested in studying the social patterns of interaction that produced an effective interview. It often helped, he discovered, when interviewing an acutely psychotic patient, to have one of the attendants present and to keep much of the conversation between the attendant and the doctor, so that the patient could enjoy the position of commentator and not have to bear the burden of being directly interrogated. He was also interested in why the patients he treated on his ward got better there but relapsed after they were discharged. What did this have to do with the social environment? With the family? The expectations of society?

This kind of thinking about the details of the interpersonal field was one of the marks of his practical approach to social psychiatry. It was reflected in the articles he chose for the journal he founded, *Psychiatry*, today still the premier publication connecting social and biological processes. And it was reflected in the beginning of the two training institutions he founded, the William Alanson White Institute in New York and the Washington (D.C.) School of Psychiatry.

One reason I was drawn to Sullivan was his openness to anthropolo-

---

[7] This good Irish remedy must have been available by medical prescription during Prohibition.

gy. He had attended medical school in Chicago, but did not really connect with the social science faculty of the University of Chicago until many years later. That connection came in 1926 from a chance meeting with Edward Sapir, an anthropologist and linguist at the university who specialized in Native American languages.

Sullivan was 34, in the middle of his experiment at Sheppard and Enoch Pratt, and had gone to Chicago to give a lecture. While he was there, Sapir called to ask if he could visit him at his hotel to talk about his ex-wife's mental illness, and Sullivan agreed. The conversation began with this personal consultation, but it soon went on to many other things and lasted all afternoon and half the night. The two men discovered connections between Sullivan's work with psychiatric patients and Sapir's ideas about the impact of culture on personality development. Their partnership continued after that meeting, and their thinking in both specialties took a significant turn.

Sapir, like others at Chicago, had carried forward the ideas of George Herbert Mead, looking at the patterns of interaction between people or animals in communication with each other (Sapir, 1968). As a linguist, he was able to apply methods of analyzing language to the analysis of nonverbal communication patterns. In this process, he saw rules and regularities in communicative behavior, a "language understood by all and spoken by none" (Sapir, 1968, p. 556). A musician, poet, and critic with wide experience in the academic world, Sapir provided what Sullivan was missing in his narrower medical-psychiatric career.

They educated each other. Sapir thereafter introduced psychiatric insights into anthropological fieldwork, laying some of the foundations for the investigation of the relationship between culture and personality. Sullivan, for his part, brought to psychiatry a new understanding of the cultural constraints on the individual patient's life choices. Psychological healing, he saw, must be sought within the vocabulary of those constraints, or else the cultural assumptions of the patient's environment must be questioned directly by the therapist. Sullivan was, for example, one of the first male therapists to attack gender stereotypes in his work with women patients, an idea he may have learned from his friend and analyst Clara Thompson (Havens, 1967, pp. 44–50).

Sullivan himself was not a natural leader in academic psychiatry. He was a facetious, difficult man, and his writing style was so cranky that only his devotees wanted to read him. After his death in 1949, it was left to his disciples, a small but dedicated band, to bring his vision of an interpersonal psychotherapy to life in academic psychology and psychiatry departments. They did not succeed, but the William Alanson White Institute in New York continued to train Sullivanian analysts. And the books were available. At the same time as I was dozing on Dr. W.'s couch in Rochester, getting nowhere, I was devouring the works of Sullivan in the medical school library. I was determined to find a Sullivanian analyst as soon as I got to New York in 1960.

I picked the name of Janet Rioch out of the *Handbook of Psychiatry* and worked with her for two years during my internship and the start of my residency. My work life and her own illness with severe depression prevented us from doing more than dealing with the death of my father, the previous year, and opening my curiosity about myself. She recovered, married at the age of 65, and moved to Washington, referring me to Meyer Mendelson. He would be tough enough to get my attention, she told me. She was right.

The problem with a patient like me has nothing to do with childhood trauma. Quite the opposite. I grew up accustomed to, and comfortable with, a remarkable degree of solitude. Being an only child and moving frequently, I never had to deal with peers on any terms other than my own, and I had plenty to do sitting alone in my room, drawing, writing, constructing things. My parents were either too depressed and guilty, or too absent and preoccupied, to interfere. Except for times of extreme loneliness, such as at medical school, I picked my own friends and activities. I got away with this until the adult worlds of work and marriage confronted me with demands for "participation and communication," to which I had been accustomed to respond by just closing the door. I got into enough trouble with that approach to see that I needed help.

Mendelson was indeed tough and challenging, which was right for someone like me, with my well-organized set of rationalizations for my comfortable position. He confronted my image of myself as an only child in our quiet house in Tulsa: how comfortable I was in the corner of my room, writing and drawing for hours on end with no one disturbing me. Taking my image of becoming an analyst quite literally, he asked me how I had come to see myself as sitting in yet another snug corner behind my patients. He was clearly not in a corner; he sat in front of me, actively questioning, as we struggled with different views of my various encounters in the world. I realized that a life of limited involvement with analytic patients, who had to leave and close the door at the end of the hour, was a continuation of my pattern of living a social life on my own terms. Mendelson prodded me to get out and explore the alternatives.

Working with Mendelson on the choices that faced me, I realized I couldn't stay in a corner all my life. I got out, and pretty much stayed out, with some notable lapses, taking up what Mendelson referred to as my "joyful burden" as we shook hands and I left his office a couple of years later, the therapy ended.

The image of coming out of my protected corner came not from the Freudian canon, nor from the Kleinian, nor from any other card catalog of ideas. It was a straight quotation from me and my recollections, and although it was reflected by Mendelson's strong presentation, it was my story. It also challenged my comfortable interpersonal strategy. In Meyer's terms, it confronted me with the habit patterns that I had made out of the experiences of my life. In Sullivan's or G. H. Mead's terms, it asked, what did this say about my intentions for myself? In narrative terms, it put the question to me: How did I want to write the next chapter, the beginning of a different story?

§

Clearly Sullivan and James, as well as Dewey, Mead, and the others at the University of Chicago, were the intellectual ancestors we were looking for at the Tremont Crisis Center and on the streets of the South Bronx. The philosophical environment in which psychotherapy was being developed at the beginning of the century, the work of these ancestors in that environment, provided all the ideas needed for the development of a therapy that actually stepped into the social field. The Chicago social workers and anthropologists had gone out into the city, to see what could be understood, what could be changed. Dewey's ideas about education were being tried out all over the world, as a result of his teachers' classroom experiments, which, in turn, invited their pupils to go out into the laboratory of real life.

In psychotherapy, those ideas lay dormant, not part of practice. The theory proposed by Sullivan may have been interpersonal, but the setting and action, and hence the therapeutic experience, was individual. Like Freud, Sullivan made special use of the only relationship in the room —

that between the therapist and the patient.[8] Sullivan was ingenious at making sharp observations about what went on in that relationship and its distortions and misunderstandings (what the analysts called "transference," and Sullivan insisted on calling by his own word, "parataxes"). That was, and still is, the heart of Sullivanian therapy. But psychotherapy as an institution was stuck with its traditional form, the individual interview.

The problem with the individual interview, as I experienced it with even so skillful and reflexive a Sullivanian as Mendelson, was that it tends to box the therapy into the space of the office and the relationship with the therapist: it can be dissociated between meetings, kept in a special state confined to the relationship with the therapist, and *not practiced*, not acted upon, not carried forward into the world of social action. I noticed, for example, that I could keep my conversations with Mendelson out of my thoughts for the entire time between sessions. And even in the sessions, I could duck and weave, covering my tracks.

Family therapy addressed that problem by dealing with the family interactions directly. It brought the entire interacting group into the office and rehearsed them in conversations, action patterns, and gesture exchanges that they then took home with them. Rather than looking at what might be supposed about their motives, it offered, as Mead would have said, a way to change their intentions toward each other in future interactions. As a social institution, it provided a new experience with durable, continuing family life. It was the keystone of practice in social psychiatry.[9]

---

[8] For Sullivan's disagreement with Freud about techniques of psychotherapy and the use of the therapeutic relationship, see Chapman (1976, pp. 230–235).

[9] See Zwerling's Stecker Lecture (1965).

CHAPTER FIVE
Family Therapy

BETWEEN THE BEGINNINGS OF SOCIAL PSYCHOLOGY at the University of Chicago at the turn of the century and the later development of family therapy lay the 50-year detour of psychoanalysis. Blocking the development of social therapy was a cultural artifact that psychoanalysis had left in the middle of the road: the confidential one-to-one interview. Until family therapists decided to step around it into a new practice, it was accepted as the "natural" locus of psychotherapy. The opening up of the secret relationship of patient and therapist allowed the admission of many other stories and metaphors to the therapeutic discourse, eventually turning it inside out.

Consulting with members of the family together seems like such an obvious activity — an extension of the kinds of informal but serious discussions that happen in families without professional intervention. Nevertheless its advent in psychotherapy in the middle of the twentieth century produced an explosion of new ideas for the treatment of many problems. It introduced the therapist into the midst of the family in action, as a person who was willing to tolerate the family's disagreements, the clash between different members' interpretations of events — different stories — and help them find a way forward toward some common, immediate future. The therapist helped them write a next episode of their several stories, one they could support and perhaps even agree on.

Family therapy had many inventors, most of them unknown. It arose independently in many places, in response to many different challenges — juvenile delinquency, childhood problems, marriage counseling, and the management of psychosis. I encountered it first at the Day Hospital, where it was a part of the treatment of relapse in psychosis. I used it, along with a number of other approaches at the NIMH, with families in research projects on depression and schizophrenia.

Schizophrenia is an extreme prototype of the failure of communication in which different interpretations of experience — different stories — drive peope apart. A family in which one member has begun to develop schizophrenia, usually a young person on the threshold of adult life, is repelled and disorganized by what is happening to them, by the blighting of unfolding intellect and purpose, of the promise of youth. The illness attacks the very abilities of perception by which the victim might save himself. He considers the possibility that he might be crazy, but rejects it in favor of more miraculous explanations, since his life seems to bring him miracles every day. Consulting with his family seems impossible, since they are as mystified as he is by what is taking place.

The family members urge him to "see a doctor" (for what illness?); keep their own diagnosis ("he is crazy!") a secret, and try to maintain a pretense of normality. The chances are that no one in the family knows a story that began this way and yet had a good outcome, and so both family and patient begin to ponder how it happened that they have been uniquely singled out for catastrophe.

How to help people in this predicament was one of the earliest concerns of family therapy. The family therapy of schizophrenia is an example both of the ingenuity of the new therapy, and of the reckless invention of explanations that it fostered. Even more than the family members, we needed a theory to explain what we were doing. We interviewed the families, who seemed grateful to have someone with whom to talk. At NIMH, the psychiatrists tried to educate each other by engaging in an exercise called a family case conference: since the NIMH was a Mecca of theory and research, we were able to entertain experts from all over the world and watch them work. The expert interviewed the family while we watched through the one-way mirror, and then we all discussed the interview afterward, without the family.

§

Most of our consultants at the NIMH started from the common American (and analytic) assumption that parents control the way children grow up: they are responsible for their turning out well and happy, and, in particular, they are able to damage innocent children. Freud was actually quite modest in his position on parental repressiveness. He suggested in *Civilization and Its Discontents* that growing up necessarily requires the subjugation of the instincts, and that its results are both neurotic and creative. But some Americans in the 1960s went far beyond this, developing a romantic view of children, and turning parental repression into a conspiracy. The idea of the counterculture was that adult society ruins young people by oppressing them with child rearing and education. Summerhill in England was an experimental school, an anarchist society, that attempted to raise children without such oppressive influences. And Scottish psychiatrist Ronald Laing (one of our visitors at NIMH) singled out schizophrenia as a particular case of how middle-class families do their children in.

Laing was the most famous proponent of these ideas, but he was joined by many others. The anthropologist Jules Henry wrote popular books describing his sojourns as an observer in the homes of "crazy-making" families (Henry, 1971). Although Europeans, following the great German psychiatrist Emil Kraepelin, tended to see schizophrenia as a degenerative and chronic brain disease, some British and American radicals were determined to find a social or psychological cause — and cure — for this most difficult challenge. I use the word *radical* not only because, like Sullivan, they held maverick positions within psychiatry, but also because, like Laing, they considered what ailed the schizophrenic patient to be a reflection of what ailed the society, for which they proposed radical cures. Like William Burroughs' heroin addict, the madman was seen as a lonely prophet, the holy beggar at our gates, whose rantings revealed the evils of the society of which he was only the most obvious and mortifying victim. And although the evil was pervasive throughout the culture, the microsociety of the family was the place where the deed was done.

§

The man who connected this notion of schizophrenia with behavioral science was the British anthropologist Gregory Bateson, who, in the 1960s, was studying the family relations of schizophrenia at the Palo Alto Veterans Hospital in California. Bateson and Margaret Mead, husband and wife during the years when both were writing their popular books, were together responsible for my cohort's anthropological enlightenment. The son of William Bateson, a famous naturalist, and educated at Oxford,

Bateson met Mead when the two of them were doing their fieldwork in New Guinea just before the start of World War II, and he returned with her to the United States. Of all of their books, his *Steps to an Ecology of Mind* (1972) was the fundamental text of the invisible university to which my generation of social therapists belonged. I picture dog-eared copies of its paperback edition in all of our canvas schoolbags.

What Bateson wrote with such angelic clarity was a philosophy of mind inhering in relationships — not only between people, as Sullivan had suggested, but also between living beings in evolving biological fields, such as the prairie or the redwood forest. Mind has an "ecology," he wrote, a set of lawful external relations. This ecology was inherent in relatedness, in communication among parts of a biological system, much the same way that bison and prairie grass evolved together, mutually responding to changes in each other. The "mind" lies in the system of mutual responses. The system can have steady states — the grass feeding the bison, the bison cutting and fertilizing the grass — that would resist change borne in from the outside. A system could undergo runaway escalations of change if its regulatory dynamics went wrong (humans hunting the bison or turning the grass into farms); or it might slowly evolve in adaptation to change. According to Bateson, a biological system's responses to change are in many ways similar to the way in which an individual person's "inner" mental processes respond to information coming from the environment. Thus conceived, mind is "out there" among the members of a family, in the dealings between groups, as well as inside an individual's head (Bateson, 1979). To put it another way, what we call the inner mind is only a subset of the mutually regulating reactions among parts of biological nature.

Bateson's examples of the systemic mutual responses among living things came from studying a great range of natural history. He found them in his father's embryology and in evolutionary biology; as well as by studying several types of learning, schizophrenia, alcoholism and Alcoholics Anonymous, Balinese art, children and animals at play, morale and national character in wartime, the process of ethnographic observation, communication among dolphins, ecology and urban civilization, and the nature of poetry, to name just a few. Bateson saw himself in the philosophical tradition of Bertrand Russell and Alfred North Whitehead, the semioticist and semanticist Alfred Korzybski, and the cyberneticist Norbert Weiner. But the American therapy culture of the 1960s also took him up as a spiritual descendant of Emerson and the transcendentalist New Thought movement of a century before.

The schizophrenia project at Palo Alto was an example of Bateson at his most original (Bateson, Jackson, Haley, & Weakland, 1956). He set out to analyze patterns of communication between patients and family members visiting them and studied letters from mothers to their schizophrenic children. For his team of observers, Bateson recruited an analyst named Don Jackson, who had just completed a fellowship at Chestnut Lodge, the foremost hospital in the country for the psychoanalytic treatment of schizophrenia. The other members of the team were Jay Haley, a specialist in the communication arts, and John Weakland, an engineer turned anthropologist.

One of the puzzles in schizophrenia at that time was: why is it a disorder of *thinking* — delusions, hallucinations, paranoid misperceptions, and failures of reasoning — when most of the other major and minor mental illnesses manifest themselves as disturbances of *feeling* (depression, anxiety, fear, worry), disturbances that leave reason more or less intact? That the key symptom of schizophrenia was a thought disorder made it seem less like a response to stress and more like a dementing brain disease due to injury or age. Kraepelin had called it *dementia praecox* — early dementia.

Bateson proposed a social origin for thought disorder. Schizophrenic patients, he suggested, were suffering from a kind of socially negotiated suspension of reason that had arisen in response to transactions in the family of which all its members were essentially unaware. Taking leave of rational discourse, in other words, could be an adaptation on the part of the patient to a set of communications by other family members. This explanation was called the "double bind" hypothesis, and it went like this: Suppose a person receives a primary negative *communication* (such as criticism), along with a simultaneous *command* concerning that communication (such as behavior that subtly commands "do not notice this criticism"). The result will be a confusing dissonance between the communication and the accompanying command. If the communication and the command are made by a parent to a child, and if they occur in a situation from which there is no escape (such as in an isolated family), then a psychotic response might result. The psychosis could be the child's adaptation to the *system*, because it preserves the relationship with the parent by simultaneously being a response (to the criticism) and not a response (since it does not confront the conflict exactly). The child's psychosis could thus be a contribution to the homeostatic balance, the steady state, of the family system, an avoidance of differentiation from the critical parent, replacing direct confrontation with a crazy compliance. Bateson's double-bind hypothesis was a great hit, coming as it did on a rising wave of optimism about family therapy and other new treatments. It was an outstanding example of systems thinking. And it provided family therapists with a mechanism to explain how the small society of the family could drive a patient crazy.[1]

§

They had been searching for it for some time. In the late 1950s, the recently founded National Institute of Mental Health began a scientific study of the relationships between genes and the environment in schizophrenia (Rosenthal, 1956). They had located a family with quadruplet daughters, all of whom suffered from different forms and degrees of the illness. Since the quadruplets had identical genes, their case represented an opportunity to study the contribution of the environment to variations in the illness.

The family and the daughters were moved into the institute, and, sparing no expense, the NIMH not only gave everyone in the family psychological testing, it also assigned each of the children and each parent his or her own therapist. At the large staff meetings for this project, the therapists all reported the conflicting views of their informants, and arguments flared. The staff meetings began to reproduce the family tensions by proxy. It occurred to someone that it might be better just to have one or two therapists sit down with the family as a group and see what their concerns were. Thus, the family therapy of schizophrenia was born (Irving Ryckoff, personal communication).

The part of NIMH where I spent three years as a clinical associate was the part where the quadruplets had been studied a decade before. Partly because of my training in family therapy, I was allowed to join a project there investigating the environmental, and especially the family,

---

[1] Carlos Sluzki edited a book called *Double Bind* (Sluzki & Veron, 1976), in which he and other reviewers of this concept demonstrated that it was useful as a general description of communication pathology, but not necessarily in the treatment of schizophrenia.

problems of patients with schizophrenia. The idea of family treatment for schizophrenia was beginning to be formulated by my mentors: Lyman Wynne, who directed the project; Joanna Day; Carol Hoover; and Sydney Ryckoff.

This early version of family therapy attempted to incorporate the psychoanalytic ideas that had preceded it. Many of our supervisors were analysts from Chestnut Lodge, which was just up the road. Harold Searles, a leading analyst at the Lodge, joined Lyman Wynne to treat and consult with families while we watched through the mirror. He and others at the Lodge were still trying to cure schizophrenia with individual analytic treatment. The evidence that it worked was slim, except in popular books like *I Never Promised You a Rose Garden* and other anecdotes.

Freud himself had been almost silent on the subject of schizophrenia. He rarely saw schizophrenic patients in his private practice in Vienna. Nevertheless, he tried to make a scholarly connection between his theories of sexuality and the phenomenon of psychosis. In 1910, he came upon a book by a middle-aged judge named Daniel Paul Schreber who had had an acute psychosis, probably what we would today call a depressive disorder of middle life with paranoid delusions, in 1894–1902. Schreber had written a diary, which he published after his recovery, describing these delusions of persecution and torture by a god-like being whose name was the same as the asylum director's. Several years later, Freud wrote a commentary in which he demonstrated that the cause of the judge's psychosis was the repression of homosexual impulses. The Schreber case was the only case study in the Freudian canon that was about anything remotely like schizophrenia, and we all had to read it (Freud, 1911).

By the 1960s, several historians and one analyst had pointed out that Schreber's father had been a famous German authority on the rearing of children, who had written an illustrated manual showing how to make children sit up straight at the table by strapping them into body trusses (Niederland, 1959; Schatzman, 1971). Schreber's delusions of torture and persecution were so similar to what had happened to him as a child that his case may throw some light on the phenomena of trauma and recovery, but its connection of homosexual impulses with psychosis is fanciful. Nobody I knew could connect this idea with a treatment for schizophrenia.

Following Freud's example, however, many of my teachers in residency and at NIMH recommended exploring the significance of schizophrenic delusions. They regarded them as "the primary process of the unconscious," the stuff that would come pouring out of everyone's id if the ego and superego weren't editing it for public consumption. I had even been told as a resident that I should listen to what schizophrenic patients said about their delusional world, the primary process, because it would teach me what was going on in the unconscious mind, my own included. I soon realized that this kind of academic exploitation was not helping the patients or me. I turned my attention to family therapy in the hope that it would at least address some of the real problems of communicating with people with this disorder — real problems that occur in the homes where the patients live, mostly with their families.

Clearly, from a social standpoint, the families of schizophrenics suffered a terrible sense of social isolation. Embarrassed or frightened by the behavior of the patient, hesitant about going out to social events with or without the company of this child — too old in any case to be considered a child at all — and unable even to participate in the favorite middle-aged pastime of talking about the career exploits of "the children," parents stayed at home. The crucial issue is whether this isolation is to be perceived as a cause or as an effect of the illness.

The analysts at Chestnut Lodge, most famously Frieda Fromm-Reichmann, the doctor in *I Never Promised You a Rose Garden*, saw isolation as an effect, not of the illness, but of the parents' behavior. They thought that one of the causes of schizophrenia was the mother's overly close, alternately intrusive and rejecting behavior toward the patient. The mother somehow caused the isolation, or contributed to it, by intrusively taking over the child's life and thought, rendering him or her unfit for going out and exploring the world. She drove the patient crazy, a prisoner in the madhouse of the family. This notion was medicalized as "the schizophrenogenic mother."[2]

Ronald Laing called what such parents did to their children "mystification" (Laing & Esterson, 1964; Laing, 1965). Harold Searles (1959) wrote about it in a paper called, candidly, "Driving the Other Person Crazy." In this theory of transactional psychosis, the parents were responsible for driving the patient crazy, but Searles at least had the grace to

---

[2] Hartwell (1997) presents an excellent historical discussion of the theory of maternal responsibility for schizophrenia in the context of midcentury attitudes toward women and mothers.

admit that it could be a two-way process, and he sympathized with the mother because his patients sometimes drove *him* crazy.

The idea of schizophrenia as a transactional thought disorder had the advantage of taking the blame off the patient (or the patient's impulses, as in the Schreber explanation), but it transferred the blame to the family, especially the mother. Accordingly, early family therapists tried to educate parents, particularly mothers, in clearer, more straightforward styles of communication and gave them exercises in turning the patient loose from their supposedly intrusive grasp. Moving the pathology from the patient to the mother seemed like a tactical improvement, since the mother might try for a while to cooperate with these recommendations. After all, she most likely had supposed, or feared, that she was responsible for her child's tragic collapse and would be grateful for professional guidance.

During my three years at NIMH, I watched some of the world's most distinguished psychoanalytic consultants interview patients and families behind the window, and I listened in supervision sessions to my mentors from the Chestnut Lodge. It all made me deeply uneasy. It seemed to me that it was bad enough to have schizophrenia, with frightening voices shouting in your head and the world giving away under your feet, without also having to cope with the idea that something your mother or your father did to you when you were a child had caused it all.

Some patients found the idea upsetting or puzzling, but others grasped it with single-minded relief, feeling that at last they had someone to blame for their misery. The story of the ruined childhood now became a stereotyped feature of our sessions. Yet what was the evidence for it? Unlike Schreber's father, these parents were not sadistic tyrants. They were confused and frightened by what their children were going through, and they were coming to the hospital once a week for family meetings, hoping to learn something. They were trying to be helpful but did not know how, any more than I did. What were we all supposed to talk about? I tried giving the mothers lessons, demonstrating nonintrusiveness in my own conversations with patients. They were not impressed.

I was in charge of teaching family therapy techniques in my last year at NIMH, and in my discussions with colleagues, some new ideas began to percolate.[3] We tried organizing family meetings in which the patholo-

---

[3] Loren Mosher, John Strauss, David Reiss, Jan Fawcett, John Davis, and John Zinner were in that group of clinical associates.

gizing finger was pointed at each person in turn, so that everyone had a chance to be "it." We tried locating the problem in communication patterns, a sort of disembodied Batesonian "it." Developing ideas about how to talk with families about their experience with schizophrenia is something I have been working on throughout the rest of my career in psychiatry. What fascinates me in retrospect is that a solution did not occur to me until I faced the families and patients in a completely different setting, one where I had to see the problem from their point of view.

§

The different setting was Bronx State Hospital, to which I returned in 1967. I had a chance for the first time, without an institutional agenda, to think through the question: What do these families and patients really need from us? In addition to medication, hospital care, and psychotherapy, did they need family therapy as well? If so, what kind did they need, and what was the family's experience of being helped? No one had the answers to these questions, but there was a general sentiment in favor of family case conferences as a way of learning more for ourselves and teaching the staff. And now it was my turn to be the visiting expert, to conduct those conferences.

At their invitation, I would arrive on the ward for a two-hour meeting with the staff members. For the first half hour, I would listen to the history of a patient's illness, the chronology of symptoms, presented by the patient's therapist with as much dispassion and emphasis on facts as possible. Then the patient and the family would be ushered in, and while the staff listened, I would interview them for three-quarters of an hour. Here the clash of stories could be especially dramatic. After the patient and family had left, I tried to do some teaching with the staff, but they needed a discussion and catharsis as well, since they were usually bursting with their reactions to the interview, their versions of the story — medical, psychiatric, or social. Afterward the family had a private conference with me, where they asked questions and poured out feelings they had had to inhibit while in the presence of the patient. What did I think? Whose story did I believe? If this was an illness, did I have a treatment to recommend? I generally tried to say something positive and noncommittal, and it generally disappointed the family. They had come all this way for this? I, too, was dissatisfied with the ritual.

One of the problems I faced was that the story in which the staff was interested differed from the medical plan the family wanted to hear. The staff expected me to talk about ways in which "the psychopathology" was caused by "the family dynamics." At the very least, I was expected to demonstrate this in the interview and describe it in my discussion. This part of American folk wisdom — that parents are responsible for what goes wrong with children — was as well known to the families as to the staff. It was what the families were afraid of, that they had somehow contributed to their child's collapse, and that the interview was a demonstration of this. Otherwise, why had they been asked to come?

But demonstrating their "guilt" did not lead to a treatment either. If the family caused the problem, what kind of an illness was it? Who was the patient, the child or the parents? Was a scene of reconciliation after childhood trauma expected to take place? It sounded uncomfortably similar to some of the patients' assertions of a conspiracy against them. Or was psychosis a kind of social-educational problem? A misunderstanding that could be resolved by clarifying everyone's good intentions?

As the person responsible for these interview sessions, I decided that frankness about the real situation would help. First, I explained to the family at the beginning that its purpose was to educate the staff, and me, on what they had learned from their experience. I asked if they had had to leave work to attend our meeting, thanked them for taking the time and trouble, and invited them to be critical of the help they had been given so far. I asked what had been helpful to them as they went through this terrible experience. So framing the conference as a review of our performance rather than of theirs shifted the moral balance in the room a little. At the end of the interview, I again asked what they had found helpful in the discussion and what more they were hoping for. But I knew there was a problem with the basic design of the exercise that I had not solved. I was only chipping away at it, taking the edges off. This group of people needed to participate in some collaborative educational activity that would have a better outcome.

§

Unsatisfying as these experiences were, they apparently captured the interest of the staff at the Bronx State Hospital. After a year or so of family case conferences, some of the people working on the wards met with me to hatch an ambitious plan. What about running a service, an entire part of the hospital, in collaboration with the families? The two wards that served the area immediately around and north of the hospital were soon to change directors; if I would agree to be the director of that service, they would volunteer to join me. I was elated by this proposal, but quite daunted at the prospect of being a director of service. It was a job for a more experienced person, and in 1971, I already had my hands full with my work at Tremont. Still, these were people with whom I wanted to work, the political moment would not come again, and when I talked to Zwerling about it, he was enthusiastic. He agreed to our most important conditions: one ward would be an inpatient ward with the usual twenty-five beds, but the other would be a day hospital. Following the Tremont experiment, we would cut the bed use in half by an active, preventive outpatient operation with three mobile crisis teams and the use of the day hospital. It would be called the Family Service.

At this time, both city and state hospitals were admitting only patients who lived in their assigned "catchment areas," and Zwerling continued this policy down to the wards of the hospital. It was a way of eliminating the competition between hospitals and wards for holding on to preferred patients, while dumping others. You had to treat the patients in your area, and if you had special problems, you asked for extra help. This was one of the ethical foundations of social psychiatry. The population of the catchment area for which the Family Service was responsible was, on the average, better off economically than the people of Tremont. The neighborhoods of Baychester and Morris Park, around the hospital, were mostly blocks of small apartment houses and row houses with working-class Irish, Jewish, and Italian families. To the north rose the massive towers of Co-op City, where young middle-class families had bought apartments because of the schools, the parking garages, and the security. Some of them had gone on to the suburbs and had turned their apartments over to their parents and their chronically psychotic brother or sister. This was a constellation we came to recognize as the Co-op City family, as the brother or sister was admitted to our ward shortly after the stress of the move.

By choosing an area where the families had some means and greater flexibility, and where travel to the hospital for day programs and meetings required taking only one bus, we knew we were giving ourselves a better chance of success. Some families had cars. But as I walked around the ward to meet the patients for whom we were about to become responsible, I saw many who did not fit into this category. There were aging, hallucinating people who had been on the ward for years and whose family contacts were completely unknown. One Asian man of uncertain age who had been there for 10 years would allow his clothes to be changed occasionally, but he always carried a smelly brown bundle of rags and papers, and no one had been able to find a language that he could understand. He smiled, hugged his bundle, and was silent.

But most of the patients did have families living in the area, and we started to plan how we were going to work with them. We knew how to run a day hospital and crisis teams, and we recruited a good head nurse who knew how to run a ward. What we didn't know was how to begin to involve the families of the patients in noncrisis long-term preparation for the goals of discharge from the hospital, placement in the community, and prevention of relapse. Well, someone suggested, why don't we invite them to a meeting and see what they would like from us? It required some research and telephoning, but we located a family member for almost everyone, and we invited all the families of all the patients on the ward to a meeting the same night.

To my alarm, they all came, and many brought everyone at home with them. We located chairs for about 70 people, and I made my welcoming speech, wondering what to do next. We started to introduce ourselves, and then, quite spontaneously, the stories began. There were stories of first episodes, breakdowns on the eve of marriage or success, efforts to find treatment, heartless hospital administrators, incompetent therapists, failed efforts to live together in the family — all the stories we had heard at the case conferences but here poured out to an audience of others who answered, "Yes, that's what happened to us." The meeting went on for hours; no one wanted to leave, and no one expected answers to their questions. Afterward, as people were milling around and talking in small groups, a nurse came up to me, leading the man with the bundle. He was smiling broadly, surrounded by his niece and her family, who were chatting with him in his own language. They explained in halting English that the bundle contained the names and addresses of his family members, only no one had been able to read it. They were glad to have found him and wanted to help him find a place to live.

That was the first time I felt the power that comes to a group of families when they are given a chance to tell their stories of undergoing

a common life experience. The *size* of the group also had several unexpected effects. Since they outnumbered us, the families were not so much
asking our professional advice as telling us what they needed. They
needed to be listened to and respected. And as this was a large public
meeting, each family was careful what they said about the patient. The
histories of psychotic breakdown and retreat from the world were told
sympathetically, with a minimum of embarrassment for the patients, who
sat listening, adding corrections. The patients felt reassured by finding
themselves for the first time in a society of people who regarded their experience as typical. And finally, since they were a large majority, the
families felt entitled to set some terms for the discussion. They wanted
a common language. Many knew this was an illness, or more likely, several illnesses, but they wanted to know from us what to call them, what
the words meant, how to become experts themselves. They recognized
in each other the rudiments of a society in which psychosis, if not a de-
sirable goal, was at least a livable life, a story with many possible endings.

After this experience, we could begin to imagine building the work
of the service around family groups. We set aside one night a week,
Thursday, to run groups of up to five families each, led by two-person
teams of staff people from different parts of the service. Other outpatient
business, crisis meetings, and medication discussions were scheduled before
or after the group meetings. Meanwhile, on the ward, a group of patients
who had no contact with their families began their own Thursday night
meetings, to talk about how, or whether, to try to resume the contact.
Some did, and moved into the family groups as they were discharged
from the ward. Others had to face the fact that that tie was gone, and
they would have to get on with their lives with other companions.

The Family Service lasted many years after I left the Bronx for my
next job in 1975, and the multifamily groups lasted as well, quite independent of the fortunes of the service. They seemed to have a life of
their own, an energy that came from the real concerns of the families and
patients rather than from a professional agenda being inflicted on them.
In these groups, we soon learned that guilt over having contributed to
the illness was not a useful conclusion to the family's story, at least not
after the first telling.

For us, the center of the service moved out into the community,
into the world inhabited by these families. And for me, the shift in perspective from the case conference, where the family was seen as a part of

the problem, to the family group, where it was seen as part of the solution, was a change that characterized the development of family therapy as a whole.

It was a shift from searching for the story of a traumatic childhood or family influence, thought to be at the base of all pathology, to a prospective social view of mental or emotional suffering. It was a search for an improved social world where these lives could be better lived. How could we build a small model of such a world within the family? What small improvements in the management of this condition would be helpful? What had other families discovered that made it all bearable? This was an enormous change in point of view for family therapy, and it took at least a generation to be fully realized.

In these groups it became evident that we all — staff, patients, families — had to be on the same side, fighting against the illness. The illness, with its accompanying isolation, and stigma, social disorientation, was *it*. What really worked was putting the problem *in the problem*: externalizing schizophrenia as an affliction that had come upon the patient through nobody's fault, and had to be dealt with as a medical problem, like diabetes, or a social problem, like unemployment. Looking at it this way mobilizes the resources of the family, because the members of that family understand that isolation is the *cause*, not the result, of the mother's taking over her child's life. Nobody else but a mother will put up with so much misery for the sake of her child: what left her isolated with that child, preoccupied and obsessed, was that everyone else — especially other relatives, neighbors, and friends — wanted to have nothing to do with this crazy person. The other families in the group could testify to this from their own experience. It became clear to the professionals as well, as soon as we ourselves entered that community of experience.

What was helpful in producing new ideas was a change in the *practice*. We started to think differently when we were confronted — outnumbered, actually — by the families in a large group in a place where we were responsible to them. The group of families supplied the missing ingredient, the image of a society larger than the family, in which the conflicting stories of some family members could be dissolved or held in suspension while they listened to others tell theirs. It led to a buildup of experience and a decrease in isolation. The theories, even the most elegant such as Bateson's double-bind, were more of a hindrance than a help. Thinking of parents as driving patients crazy in an elegant way was no better than thinking that they did it crudely, as in the case of Schreber's father.

The same idea was occurring to many people working with this illness in other centers, and the clearest and most developed programs of treatment were published and tested as the "psychoeducational approach to the family treatment of schizophrenia" (Anderson, Hogarty, & Reiss, 1981; Falloon, Boyd, McGill, et al., 1982). This family and family-group approach, treating the illness as an external affliction rather than as an internal family problem, has been repeatedly demonstrated in clinical trials to be more effective than any other approach to therapy. The idea of the parental cause of schizophrenic disorder, however interesting it was to researchers,[4] ultimately proved to be without pragmatic value in helping patients and families. Both do better when they are regarded not as the source of the problem, but as an important part of the solution.

The ultimate historical development of this realization was the rise of the National Alliance for the Mentally Ill, an organization made up mainly of the parents of patients with schizophrenia, but lately also including the patients themselves, which has become an important political power. It lobbies both state and national legislators for the improvement of services and promotes and publicizes outcome research. Its meetings at all levels of organization, large and small, have some of that extraordinarily moving sense of purpose and power that I experienced for the first time on the Family Service.

The National Alliance for the Mentally Ill is the political side of a community I began to see as necessary for the progress that individuals and families afflicted with schizophrenia could make throughout their lives. All of us in the urban and suburban world of late capitalism live in invisible villages, social networks we construct out of the opportunities our work and influence send our way. The effect of schizophrenia on our ability to build those fragile networks in such a competitive environment is devastating, and needs to be countered by a social organization much stronger than what is implied by "therapy" and "services." It needs

---

[4] The reseach in this area (Tienari, 1991) yields complex results. Adoption studies make it possible to separate rearing from genetics. Rearing, as reflected in the pathology of biological parents, to some extent does predict the occurrence of schizophrenia in adoptees, but even more, adoptive family health protects genetically vulnerable adoptees from developing symptoms.

an invisible village of its own — a community with some values explicitly counter to those of the dominant culture, and such a "community" and "values" require a scale and level of organization larger than an office or even a community mental health center (Beels, 1989). The successes and frustrations of the Family Service gave me my first sense of what that scale might be.

§

I think it was lucky for me that I got into family therapy by way of schizophrenia. It taught me again to be suspicious of grand schemes, such as Bateson's. Some problems are system problems, but some are not. Still, since people with schizophrenia make up only a 1 percent minority of the population, and a shunned minority at that, the family approach to that illness did not take center stage in the awareness of either the psychiatry profession or of the public. More interesting — and more widely discussed — was the work with children and with couples.[5] Nathan Ackerman, a child psychiatrist and analyst in New York City, was the pioneer of the family approach to the problems of children (Ackerman, 1966).

Before Ackerman, the classical analytic child therapy had been a "play therapy," in which the analyst encouraged the child to tell fantasy stories or to act them out by playing with dolls or puppets. The sessions with the child were governed by a rule of confidentiality similar to that of adult analysis, but the child's analyst did meet periodically with the parents, especially the mother, to "gather information" and give some cautious advice. The full-dress treatment, if the family could afford it, was psychodynamic therapy for each of the parents as well, perhaps with social workers who conferred discreetly with the child's analyst.

Ackerman had been trained this way in the 1930s, but early in his career, he began to see families together in joint sessions — everyone in-

---

[5] The first known formal description of family therapy with children was a paper given by John E. Bell in 1953 (Bell, 1967). He had picked up the idea when he was a fellow at the Tavistock Institute in London in 1951. John Sutherland had told him that John Bowlby often met with the family as a group to resolve a problem. Supposedly, when Bowlby heard that Americans were using family group treatment as the principal method of treatment, he said, "I didn't mean *that*."

cluding the brothers and sisters and the baby. He sat with the whole family and joked with them in the style of a rascally Jewish grandpa, teasing them out of their inhibitions with an affectionate presence that they found hard to resist. His view was: "If one person in the family's got a problem, everybody's got a problem." He founded the Ackerman Family Institute, the first of its kind, which still operates in the original house on 78th Street in Manhattan where I am one of the faculty.

From this center, Ackerman distributed movies of family sessions as teaching aids. The atmosphere of these sessions was shocking to many observers: if you were not in the room with him, he seemed outrageously intrusive and presumptuous. But he was effective in helping people, and his institution succeeded as well. Ackerman introduced family therapy with children into a number of departments of psychiatry in New York, and into the practices of the Jewish Board of Guardians, which later, as Jewish Family Services, founded one of the largest training programs.

The early child-family therapists were analysts, with analytic ideas about their work. Ackerman, for example, described what he did as "tickling the defenses." But family institutes were different from analytic institutes, and this difference in organization was critical. Because of the way in which they were designed, family institutes impelled change as vigorously as psychoanalytic institutes resisted it.

The institutes were fed by an informal system of regional and national conferences that had small beginnings, but grew rapidly. One of the earliest and most original teachers to appear at these conferences was Virginia Satir, a social worker who taught herself to see families when she was in private practice in Chicago (Satir, 1964). Possessed of a wonderful eloquence and presence, Satir more than anyone originated an open style of talking about intimate matters in such a positive way that families did not mind appearing before an audience of several hundred strangers as she coached them lovingly through an improvement in their ability to communicate with one another.

Satir developed a unique training format: a series of two-week retreats at places such as Esalen in Big Sur, attended by therapists with their spouses. She demonstrated her techniques by treating each couple at the conference while the others watched. These people then went home and started study groups where they taught others.

§

The family therapy institute that we developed at the Bronx State Hospital was called the Family Studies Section. In the several rooms with one-way windows that Israel Zwerling had built in different parts of the hospital, we demonstrated family interviews to all comers and our trainees watched each other do them. The blackboards had a different image: an extended kinship diagram, borrowed from anthropology, called a genogram. This diagram, a map of family relationships with horizontal ranks of generations and marriages and vertical connections of descent, was a hallmark of family therapy training and thinking. It showed ancestors, deaths, legends, interesting uncles who substituted for absent fathers, nurses and grandmothers who were always home, and sequences of birth order (one's place in line among siblings). The genogram provided a number of ways to locate the problem of a family in a two-dimensional space, showing relationships moving through time. This map of outer family space rather than inner individual space is an example of externalization in therapy, of putting the problem out there so that we can all work on it, rather than leaving it inside one of the members of the group.

Birth order is one bit of family structure that can be seen easily from looking at the genogram. The idea that birth order can help explain family interaction goes all the way back to Freud's colleague, Alfred Adler (Sulloway, 1996). To take my own case, for example, my father was the oldest of three sons, and was accustomed to command, to being on top in a competition. But my mother was by 10 years the youngest of three sisters and an invalid brother. She was accustomed to being criticized and bossed because she was the baby. I was an only son, which gave me a position of removed entitlement and detachment from which I watched my father patronize my mother, and my mother try, and usually fail, to get it right from his point of view. This kinship diagram was a useful externalization, not only of the tensions in my original family, but of the position from which I could consider changing my distant ways with my wife or my leadership style at work.

One of the originators of this way of thinking was Murray Bowen, director of the Family Institute at Georgetown University Medical School in Washington, D.C., and a frequent visitor to our group in the Bronx, both in person and on videotape (Bowen, 1978). We spent many hours watching videotapes of Bowen and others doing therapy. Bowen clearly liked to talk to people about their family constellation, not only their birth order, but also patterns of two-against-one triangles. He saw one of life's goals as the successful negotiation of change in the shape and quality of the relationships spread out on that family landscape. He was especially interested in triangles, which he called "the most stable form of social group," and their resolution into dyads or couples, which he regarded as the most difficult relationship, because in a couple it is so hard to balance closeness and distance, flight and pursuit.

If he had looked at my situation, he would have noted the alliance between me and my father, our apparent closeness, and then he would have questioned its triangular structure: one of the main things my father and I were close about was our disapproval of my mother, out there on the far end of the triangle. I can imagine him saying, in his southern drawl, "Well, did you and your dad ever have a close personal conversation that was not about your mom? Hmm — now, what would you have wanted to talk with him about of a personal nature, if you just talked one to one? Do you think your dad would disapprove if you spent some time getting to know your mom better?" Such an inquiry would have started me thinking about the unique contributions my mother made to my life when she was not operating under my father's disapproval, our cooking together and listening to music, for example, not to mention her habit of giving me a hug or a squeeze for just being there.

This way of thinking about the structure of family relationships was carried a step further by Salvador Minuchin, who bent the structures of the genogram into a different shape (Minuchin, 1974). He looked at the collusions and alliances, the enactment of gender roles, the age-grading of the children, searching for things that were out of line. He saw these as structural faults, to be corrected by action. If Minuchin had been working with my family, he would have reinforced the generation boundary. He would have sent me out of the room. "Go take care of your own business for a while," he would have said to me. "It's time for you to grow up. I'm going to meet with your parents and see if I can get your mom to stand up to your dad. Don't worry about him; he can take it."

Minuchin's was a good example of the authoritative voice in family therapy. We family therapists had learned that we had to speak up. If we didn't exercise leadership in the meeting but just sat there, the family, with its powerful organization of customs and assumptions would do its thing and recruit us into a collusive role in their process. But in order to know what we were doing, we needed a theory, a model.

Family therapy has countless models like Bowen's and Minuchin's, each with a different way of defining problems, a different idea of how to look at the genogram, to divine the hidden anatomy of the family (in triangles, parental alliances, secret or buried allegiances to grandparents). Each model had its own view of what constituted a healthy family life, a healthy functioning of this anatomy that might require the therapist to prescribe more or less correction. Minuchin called his model of family pathology "enmeshment," which was a little different from Bowen's "fusion," but they both served to indicate an unhealthy degree of involvement or projection or interference or reactivity to one another on the part of family members. Bowen even had a scale of the opposite healthy tendency, "differentiation," which he claimed to be able to measure on a scale of 1 to 100.

Amid all the models and theories, family therapists held to one common belief: we were systems thinkers. The Bateson system metaphor was at a high enough level of generalization that everyone could believe in it. It suggested a mechanism within the family that would explain both resistance to change and change itself. Systems thinking explained why straightforward advice usually didn't work: the system of the family's organization was stronger than the reasonable intentions of the individuals who constituted it, and, therefore, change had to be approached in an indirect and strategic manner. We couldn't just throw a wrench at the delicate machinery of the family system to get it started again. It needed deft and profoundly intuitive adjustment, as in that other favorite image of the time, "Zen and the Art of Motorcycle Maintenance" (Pirsig, 1974). Systems were attractive to family therapists because they provided a picture of what was going on in there that the therapist could "work on."

These many models were externalizing discourses, at least by comparison with the internalizing view of analysis. Yet they were also a way of pointing the finger at a problem in the family, seeing the family as enmeshed, undifferentiated, collusive, mystifying, and so on, and in need of some kind of master reorganization work. It was very similar to pointing the finger at the "schizophrenogenic mother" and saying that she needed to be restrained from her intrusiveness, redirected, shaped up.

In fact, the treatment of children's problems somewhat paralleled the schizophrenia story and its solution. In the early days of family therapy, it was axiomatic from systems theory that if a child was having problems, it was because there was a problem "at another level" — probably some miscommunication between the parents. The miscommunication did not even need to be about the child's problem, but could be in another area altogether, and the idea was still that the symptomatic child was somehow responding to the parental "schism or skew" (to use a favorite distinction now lost to us: secret skews were more crazy-making than open schisms) (Lidz, Cornelison, Fleck, & Terry, 1957). And that old favorite pathological pattern, the distant father and the overintrusive mother, might lie at the bottom, it seemed, of almost any kind of trouble. (All of these ideas were variations on the theme of parents ruining children, without focusing on the specific effects of trauma that later studies would reveal; see Chapter 3.)

Sometimes these ideas were useful for dealing with episodes of child misconduct or making some short-term changes. But in the absence of trauma, a better approach clearly was to move the child's problem out of the emotional system of the family and describe it as an interaction of the child's temperament and the parenting tactics. This idea came from the research of a team of child psychiatrists: Stella Chess, Alexander Thomas, and Herbert Birch (1963). Stella Chess wrote a book about this long-term prospective research on the interaction of children's temperament and the expectations of parents, *Your Child Makes Sense,* in which she pointed out that different strategies of child rearing are not inherently right or wrong — they work for different kinds (temperaments) of children. Your second child is not necessarily like your first, and this is something you can study, and with which you can experiment. One parent may be better than the other at picking up on these things. Parents were greatly helped by this approach, and family therapists finally adopted it as well. It was a very usable externalization, and it had the advantage of being based on careful natural-history research.

§

As it matured, American family therapy was becoming more diverse, open, active, and experimental, full of ingenuity and the imagery of many disciplines — just what William James would have been proud of. By moving other people into the consulting room, it had broken up the analytic assumptions about privacy, neutrality, and abstinence in therapy and instead had substituted an ethic of openness, activity, and enthusiastic advocacy. Once that process began, many new models of helping people became possible.

But in spite of these advances, family therapy was ultimately moralistic and prescriptive. The therapist was trying to get the family to improve according to a theory of healthy/unhealthy functioning that he or she understood better than did the family. It was up to the therapist to devise the enactments, assign the behavioral homework, script the better and more constructive fights, negotiate the sexual rapprochement, and show the parents how to talk to the children.

Therapists took this active stance naturally, not only because clients came to them for advice, but also because their vision of what was wrong required it. Their "structural" model of the family was akin to the psychoanalyst's model of the mind — an organism with dynamic structure, with functions and dysfunctions, concerning which the therapist was expert. At his famous case conferences, Minuchin needed only five minutes of observation through a one-way mirror to figure out what was wrong, go into the room with the family and student therapist, and produce one of his masterful stage directions.

Systemic family therapy considered itself a match for any problem, and in order to fulfill this ambitious purpose, it made some simplifying assumptions in theory and practice. One assumption was that the atoms of individuals jiggling around in those systemic relationships were all of equal weight and valence. The only inequality that systems thinkers recognized was that between parents and children. In the diagram, they were on opposite sides of a generation line, but even this inequality implied a certain ultimate parity since it would be compensated for later when the children created families of their own. This abstract linking of generational patterns led to such scientific-sounding theories as the "Three-Generation Hypothesis" of schizophrenia, which Murray Bowen (1960) took up with enthusiasm.

This picture left out some very important factors. As later critics pointed out, the cultural inflections of gender make some of these atoms unequal to others, and that requires new theories and practices, in which fathers and mothers participate in the system balance in very different ways.[6] I would add two other inequalities: The specific problems of traumatic experience create differences I described in Chapter 3. And schizophrenia is an example of a psychiatric illness (Chapter 13) that renders one person in the family profoundly unequal. Ignoring such inequal-

---

[6] See especially the feminist critics, Goldner (1985) and Luepnitz (1988).

ities has a high price: in the case of schizophrenia, regarding the person as a victim of mystification or a genius in disguise is no help either to the person or to the supposed persecutors.

Summing up, I would say that, on the one hand, this period (1960–1980) of family therapy's development produced ideas of critical importance. Minuchin's "structural" interventions were intended to get families to *enact* patterns of behavior that were different from the unhealthy ones they had brought to the consultation and repeated under his diagnostic eye. Minuchin's idea that a family changed its story by acting it differently, not just understanding it differently, had a counterpart in Bowen's "coaching" approach. Bowen would prepare members of the younger generation, seeking greater differentiation from their parents, for visits home, and then on how to take a walk with the parent to whom they had never talked, or how to guide the relationship actively in the direction the child preferred.

§

On the other hand, the work of family therapy was always more complicated than these grand schemes suggested. In my work with the Vargas family, I began by framing what we were doing as rehearsal for action. Following a Minuchin approach, the wild fights that broke out between Mercedes and Fausto were reviewed as interactions that needed a better script or different timing. Although Mercedes was suffering from an illness that interfered with her effectiveness in these exchanges, it was also clear that Fausto's approach to parenting was in a style that made the encounters worse. His passion for control met her emotional vulnerability in a combustible mixture. He turned arguments into power struggles instead of appealing to Mercedes' ability to come up with better solutions after she had calmed down. Medication and therapy might help to fight Mercedes' depression, which was certainly one word for what she had, but, in addition, the family needed a better way of thinking about what they were doing in response to it. I suggested a cognitive-behavioral handbook for treating depression (Burns, 1998). They read it, and used it, reinforcing their sense of independent mastery of these technical difficulties without my help.

Mercedes was also searching for different audiences. She dropped out of her high school, not only because of her failing grades, but also because, as she said, "I've been a failure at school and I want to be a success somewhere." She joined an Alcoholics Anonymous group to get control of her drinking and other addictions, finding this a better way to bring them into the open than was possible in her family. In short, we welcomed and used every model that had any prospect of making a contribution; cognitive therapy, behavior modification, AA, psychopharmacology, psychotherapy.

Gradually, the family was able to back off from behaving like the hospital staff and to return to a more normal definition of their lives. Mercedes joined a volunteer program helping out at a children's shelter. Maria, relieved of having to be available for long walks and talks with Mercedes, went back to part-time work as a social worker. Mercedes' doctor and I conferred less often on coordinating our suggestions and plans. After a year's productive detour, Mercedes went to a different high school to complete her last year.

We succeeded in revising Mercedes' story of failure by finding ways to pick out the thread of success that ran through it. We did not succeed in changing the story of Fausto and Maria, a stereotype of the difficult husband and the sainted wife. Work on that seemed to be constantly postponed.

Mercedes tried to change the asymmetry of her relationship with her father. I described in Chapter 3 the effort she made in that year before going to college to meet with him in my office and talk about their history together, her attempt to lay the groundwork for becoming an adult in his eyes. I felt that the success of this attempt was not so much in the immediate effect on the relationship — which was small — but more in the attempt itself, the effort to make a statement about herself, to take a position. Murray Bowen would have approved.

Once family therapy had substituted this kind of eclectic practice for the theoretical preoccupations of analysis, there was no limit to what else it could become. For techniques, we turned to behavior and learning experts in psychology. For models, we turned to sociology, seeing the family as a small community. How do its members resolve their differences, share power, delegate responsibility? Even more, we turned to the larger storehouse of anthropology for ideas of how folk healers in other societies, working with other kinds of families, do their work with ritual and pilgrimage. In one such adventure, I stumbled on the answer to the problem of the family case conference.

CHAPTER SIX
Anthropology

THERE ARE SOME ILLNESSES that are unique to their own culture. In the American cultural empire, which now extends to much of Europe, and even to parts of the Pacific, such as Australia and Japan, our special proprietary illness is anorexia nervosa (Brumberg, 1988; Gremillion, 1992). This disorder is supported by our cultural assumptions about the value of thinness in women and of individualistic self-discipline in general. Awareness of these cultural assumptions has helped us to design a counter-culture of women's support groups promoting contrary beliefs.[1]

Studying culture-specific illnesses with the help of medical anthropology gives psychiatrists a chance to look into the dark mirror of the parallel healing practices of another culture and see, not our own practice confirmed, but something different, something new, reflected. Early in my experience at the Tremont Crisis Center, I had a chance to learn about one of these culture-specific illnesses, the *ataque de nervios,* a dramatic trance- or seizure-like affliction of some Latino patients.[2] Vivian Garrison, a medical anthropologist who was studying folk-healing practices called *espiritismo* and *santería,* explained that *ataque* victims are sometimes seen as possessed by spirits. After they disappeared from our emergency rooms, dissatisfied with the medical explanations given or not

---

[1] See the discussion of David Epston's Anti-Anorexia League in Chapter 10.

[2] I use "Latino" to refer to Spanish-speaking peoples of the northeastern United States. At the time Garrison wrote, the word was "Hispanic," but that seems to be less favored now, and "Chicano" clearly refers to Mexican and South American immigrants in the Southwest. Among themselves, Latinos use the name of their immediate place of emigration. In that sense, all the people in this story are *Puertorriquiños.*

given, they and their families frequently consulted healers, *espiritistas*, or *santeros*. To study the way *espiritismo* worked, Garrison observed and interviewed consecutive samples of clients in *esperitismo* centros, *santeria* "houses," and psychiatric outpatient clinics, including Tremont. She compared the diagnoses and treatment processes in the medical services with those in the folk-healing settings.

One day she asked me about a family she was studying, several members of which had psychiatric histories, including a suicide. A woman with healing powers had married into this family, and in her attempts to use her powers to cure her new relatives, she was becoming unhinged herself. She said, "This family is driving me crazy." Garrison asked me if this could be true. Here was a puzzle in interpretation. Spiritist: Were the family's spirits taking revenge on her for intruding? Psychiatric: Was she responding with symptoms to a dislocating life crisis, her marriage into a difficult family? Family systems: Was she adjusting to the family equilibrium, which was set at a "crazy" level of interactive response? I didn't have a ready answer, but I was fascinated by the question. This was a new twist on the phenomenon of family members driving each other crazy.

Thus began a collaboration with Garrison that has lasted until this day. Over the years, she has taught Margaret and me about folk healing, and we have worked on her projects as psychiatric and family consultants. Garrison taught us that *espiritismo* is a blend of several elements. One is nineteenth-century European spiritism (spirit possession, with the spirits of the dead interrogated through a medium in trance, the phenomenon that interested William James and the Society for Psychical Research). Another is *santería*, the Hispanic version of voodoo religion brought to the Caribbean by African slaves. Many of the healing powers to which *espiritistas* appeal for help are *santería* gods, sometimes bearing the attributes of Catholic saints. *Espiritismo* is similar to *curanderismo* in Mexico, and also has some pre-Columbian Central American elements. Garrison had immersed herself in this culture. She lived in the Bronx apartment of an *espiritista* and *santéra* whom she named Rosa in her writings, and following her as she went about the community, receiving people for individual or family consultations, or holding group séances or *reuniones* in a basement room for a self-selected walk-in clientele.

About a third of our patients at the Tremont Crisis Center came from one of the Caribbean islands. Their Spanish language and customs distinguished them, and their religion was Roman Catholic, which, apart from the objections of the priests, did not conflict with their practice of *santería* and *esperitismo*. Indeed, in the *botanicas* or shops where they bought candles, herbs, and images of saints for curing purposes, one could see Christian and African images blended together.

Another place where the imagery was combined was in the exorcism of spirits. I once watched an *espiritista* casting out a tormenting spirit from the body of one of our patients writhing on the floor. Placing her foot on him, she looked around and called, "Has anybody got a crucifix?" much in the manner of an emergency room intern calling for a syringe of adrenaline. From the spiritist's point of view, the cultures of spiritism and Catholicism, or even of religion and medicine, were not inconsistent. But, as we learned from Garrison, their practitioners were expected to keep a respectful distance from each other.

Garrison helped us at the Crisis Center to understand our Latino patients' expectations concerning this distance. We were the medical consultants, she explained; psychotherapy was not expected from us. When a patient appeared in the emergency room in the throes of an *ataque*, our job was to declare whether there was a physical cause for the problem. If we could find nothing, no *causa material*, the family was likely to take the problem to an *espiritista* for consultation because she would be the one to cure a *causa espiritual*. We were the partners of a professional whom we never met, and our own version of nonmedical help, psychotherapy, was merely confusing to devotees of *espiritismo*. Garrison helped to make some cautious introductions to spiritists in the neighborhood, and we were able to see some videotapes of their work, but, by and large, the patients and families expected us to let them keep their beliefs to themselves.

One of the reasons that insight-oriented North American psychotherapy is confusing to participants in *espiritismo* is that they are philosophical opposites: the mirror image here is really a reversal. Psychotherapy looks for problems and solutions inside the patient, buried in memory or in the unconscious. Spiritism looks outside. The fundamental belief underlying spiritist practice is that human troubles, if not the result of physical disease, may be caused by a troubling spirit from the world of the dead, or a conflict with one's own spirit guides. An *espiritista* first determines in consultation that a patient is suffering from the affliction of a *causa espiritual*, a molestation by a wandering spirit of the dead, perhaps someone holding a grudge from a past life experience that the patient does not know about; or from a *brujeria*, the working of ill through a spirit called upon by a witch at the instigation of some unknown enemy. The medium then summons her *protecciones*, her good tutelary spirits and powers, to protect her from her coming encounter with the malignant dead, and she goes into a deep trance, where she is inhabited by the offending spirit. An associate, at the same table, interrogates this spirit sharply, and the medium responds in the voice of the spirit.

The interrogator may ask, "Why are you bothering this person? Why don't you go back where you belong?" The possessed medium replies reluctantly and with annoyance, but eventually, after much cajoling from the "president," the voice of the errant spirit tells the story, the cause, of the affliction. The president scolds the spirit for being a party to such "unenlightened" and "unevolved" mischief, causing such pain to the suffering patient. Sometimes this rebuke, repeated often and loudly, is enough to make the spirit repent. Sometimes, in addition, a reparation or ritual is needed, or a votive task must be promised, but eventually the negotiation is completed, the spirit departs, and the possessed medium slowly awakens with a shudder, and with no memory of her possession.

It struck me that although, as Garrison pointed out, skills of interviewing and diagnosis are involved in *espiritismo*, the medium's journey is into another world. The difference between the medical and the spiritual consultation is reflected in the difference between the knowledge of the medium and that of the doctor. The doctor is an expert. Her knowledge comes from the authority of medical science.

The medium, on the other hand, is an adept, tutored by her experience, her guiding spirits, and apprenticeship with other mediums. She discovered her calling to participate in these mysteries because she herself was once afflicted with a *causa espiritual*. In the course of her deliverance, she has discovered that she was in need of "the development of faculties." She was called to develop the ability to help others by apprenticing herself to adepts, such as those from whom she had received help. But in developing faculties, she did not become an "expert" in the sense of knowledge, as in medical training. She learned to commune with the dead, but she is literally the *medium* of that communion; when she awakens from her trance, she says, "I only know what the spirits give me."

As people enter this calling, they enter something other than a worldly profession. Unlike students of medicine or nursing, they do not expect to make a living out of it. They already have a job, a function in the structure of the regular society. Garrison's *espiritista/santéra*, Rosa, owned and managed three apartment houses and was active in the political life of the Bronx Puerto Rican community.

Relationships in the spiritist community are familial and spiritual, rather than collegial and professional. Rosa formally adopted Garrison as her spiritual goddaughter in *santería*, and her student in *espiritismo*. A godparent is responsible for spiritual development, and in their beneficent relationship, the contradictions of real parenting could be discussed in a different way. Relationships such as this, a network of fictive kinship based at the shrine at the house of the godparent, are the organizational principle of *santería*.

As for the *protecciones,* these are saints, sometimes deities of the *santería* cult or strong spirits of healing presences, and sometimes departed teachers of the adepts, who are summoned to assist in the work. Once when Garrison arranged for Rosa and me to explain our differing methods of therapy to an anthropological colloquium, Rosa said that everybody who does healing has *protecciones*. "I can see yours right now," she said, looking over my shoulder. "He is a nice old man with a white beard." I felt a thrill of recognition — Freud, coming back to be supportive after all. There he was in the middle of my *cuadro espiritual,* my ghostly support group, my collection of ancestors and teachers whom I could summon to help me to struggle with the forces of evil.

How could I learn more? Only, Garrison insisted, by looking at clinical details, as perceived and treated by both physicians and folk healers. The special contribution of anthropology was to seek the truth, not through psychological or sociological generalizations, but through a focus on cases, on behavior in context. As William Blake said of love, clinical and anthropological truths are conveyed only in minute particulars. Garrison's cases were full of particulars. One such case, centering on a young man she called Roberto Maldonado, is described at length in her study of support systems of psychiatric patients (Garrison, 1982). I read it with great care and used a synopsis of it in my teaching for years afterward. It provides an approach to comparing spiritist healing with psychiatric, the mythology of the world of the dead with the neuromythology of the brain or the system mythology of family therapy.

Here is the cast of characters.

The **Maldonado** family: **Roberto** (16), who broke his leg jumping out of a second-story window during a fire; **Teresa** (14), his sister; and **Juanito** (13), his brother.

Joy, the mother of these three, lives in another apartment with **Juana**, her lover. Joy and Juana work in the same factory. Juana, who was nicknamed *la loca* (the crazy one) in her hometown, had a psychiatric hospital stay at the age of 9, and still suffers from seizures. Currently she has a cyst in her breast and an abdominal mass for which she is consulting a surgeon. Juana also has a child by a man with whom she had a short liaison, and that child is in a home for mentally disabled children.

Consuelo, mother of Joy and grandmother of Roberto, Teresa, and Juanito, has the three grandchildren living in her apartment. Joy was her second child, born shortly after her first infant daughter died. Like most of the women in this story, Consuelo is separated from the father of her children, and he, as well as the two fathers of Joy's children, lives in Puerto Rico. Little was known about them at the time of Garrison's account, except that Roberto's father was said to be "a rich man." Consuelo has a brother and sister living in the neighborhood who help her to look after her aged, blind mother in another apartment.

Among Consuelo's neighbors are the **Rivera** family: **Agustina**, the mother, who is the superintendent of Consuelo's mother's building; **Cirillo**, Agustina's alcoholic husband; and their children.

Dolores Nieves, another neighbor, is depressed and has many somatic ailments. Her arthritis impairs her work as a beautician. She has diabetes and recently suffered three heavy losses: she lost her beauty shop; her husband left her for another woman, taking with him the money they had made running a small grocery; and her son moved to another city, taking her grandchildren with him.

Ricardo Fuentes, another neighbor, is a gay man who lives alone, having recently lost his long-term lover and only intimate friend.

Consuelo wants to consult an *espiritista* about her family's troubles. Roberto sits at home with his broken leg, "blocked in his projects," depressed, not going back to school. The circumstances in which he broke the leg worry her: the small fire that caused him to jump out of the window was quickly brought under control, and was not something from which he had to escape to save his life. He is avoiding his mother, Joy, who, for her part, is not supplying the money she agreed to give Consuelo for the support of the children. Teresa is behaving defiantly and disrespectfully, and even Juanito is having trouble sleeping. There are, as Consuelo tells Agustina, "bad things happening in the house."

This is not the first time Consuelo has consulted an *espiritista*. Some years earlier, one told her that a male spirit was bothering her. She had "dreamed" with this spirit, felt his presence, and smelled his odor, but since the medium banished him, she has stopped having these sensations. The departing spirit cut off the possibility of desire or happiness with any man, and Consuelo is just as happy this way, because now she can devote herself to her grandchildren.

The interpretation of this story as read in the psychiatric mirror would be that Consuelo is a woman perhaps approaching menopause, or at least that time of life when she must reconcile herself to her sexual history and experience. Regret, depression, and anxiety all might be expected as she faces these issues. But even granting some validity to that psychiatric description, what would psychiatry or psychotherapy have to offer her — the consolation that others have the same experience, the relief of knowing that her hormones rather than her self is at fault? How would this externalization compare with the one offered by the spiritist?

Consuelo's grandchildren are on her mind when she goes to talk to Agustina, a frequent devotee of the *centros espiritistas* in the neighborhood. She asks Agustina who would be the best one to consult. Agustina immediately recommends Rosa, who helped Agustina's widowed sister-in-law to escape pursuit by her husband's departed spirit. She also calls in Dolores, who tells Consuelo that since she has been attending Rosa's *centro* in the last few weeks, she feels better. Rosa has massaged Dolores's arthritic joints with oil blessed by San Lazaro and has identified a spirit that "wanted to see me in a wheelchair, useless, maimed, so crippled I can't even lift a comb to my own head." This spirit has not yet been "worked" and is still bothering her.

The next week, Consuelo, Agustina, and Dolores go to Rosa's *centro,* early enough so that Consuelo can have a *consulta* before the *reunión* These consultations are individual diagnostic sessions, usually done with the aid of spirit communication, in which the problem is explained and defined. Rosa finds that Consuelo's difficulties are material, not spiritual. Chief among them is her distress over her daughter's lesbian relationship and her consequent burden of having to raise the grandchildren by herself. Rosa agrees to come to the house, meet Roberto, and see what she can do for him.

Afterward, at the *reunión,* a number of the spirits that are bothering Dolores are addressed, including one brought on by the witchcraft of the woman who is keeping her husband away from her. At the end of the meeting, Rosa gives Dolores some of her wigs to dress, saying they might be easier for her to work with than the live heads of customers who are in a hurry.

The stage is now set for the four very different spiritual treatments of Roberto, Joy, Juana and Dolores. I have abstracted them from Garrison's chronological account to show how specific they are to each person's case, but it is important to remember that these transactions occur in the midst of a busy scene of meetings, visits, consultations, and *reuniones,* often involving many others, an audience of people who are praying, singing, going into trance, being counseled, being "worked," at the same time. The *reunión* in particular, is a group of perhaps 10 or more people, with two or three mediums at the table, and others apprenticed or in development assisting them. These four experiences are orchestrated parts of larger group and family relationships, dances with a very present audience and chorus.

Roberto. Rosa comes to Consuelo's apartment, to which she administers a ritual cleansing. This takes a while and permits her to chat with Roberto. She then does a "work" with him to secure the aid of the "saints" in the healing of his leg, and he promises to come to the *centro* to pay his respects and give thanks if it heals quickly and well. She also tells him that he has a dragging spirit that is holding him back. She regards him as being in a process of spiritual development and promises to discuss this with him when he visits.

Concerning his broken leg, Rosa tells Roberto that one of the spirits in his *cuadro espiritual,* a Congo guiding spirit who likes fire, gave him the impulse to jump out of the window in the fire to try to save the children in the apartment below; and that he was a hero, not a coward, in what he did. Roberto acknowledges that he was thinking about those children at the time. He goes to the doctor the next week and finds that his leg is healing. The cast is removed. The next week he goes to the *centro* to pay his respects and give thanks to the saints.

Rosa does not immediately begin a ritual treatment with him, but instead hires him to do some repairs in her apartment building and asks him to paint a mural on the wall of the *centro* to honor the saints that have helped him. As he works on these assignments, Rosa talks with him about his family and his spiritual guides and protectors. When at length he does appear at a *reunión,* he is introduced as the painter of the mural, to much appreciation, and that evening, he approaches the table for a conversation with Rosa and the spirits that are dragging, testing, and challenging him. Concerning his treatment, Rosa told Garrison (1982):

> The boy can be helped. He comes in spiritual development. [he] has a complex because he never knew his father, and he was raised by his grandmother because his mother is a lesbian. This affects him deeply in his intimate life. I will insist that he go to school and I will consult with him with reference to his complexes regarding his mother.

In psychiatric terms, Roberto would be a good candidate for psychotherapy, an adolescent presenting with depression. He responds well to what a psychiatrist would call behavioral treatment (assignment of tasks, focus on success) and some empathic exploration of his family situation, but whether he will undertake long-term therapy (spiritual development) is left up to him.

Joy. Depressed over an attempt by Juana to end her life with an overdose of pills, and upset about her children's troubles and their lack of respect for her mother, Joy goes to Rosa for a *consulta.* As she emerges from it, she is so filled with the importance of what she has learned that she tells Garrison (the first person she finds in the apartment) about it.

> Rosa had told her that she was supposed to have been born a male, but when her older sister died, while her mother was pregnant with her, her mother had wanted another girl so badly and had prayed so hard for a girl, that her sex had been changed in the womb. Consuelo later said to me, "It is true — she should have been a man. She looks like a man. It is true that I wanted a girl so badly that — [it is] a misfortune for us both." (Garrison, 1982, p. 70)

In family therapy terms, Rosa reframed Joy's sexual orientation in such a way that the mother and daughter can talk about it with mutual sympathy and understanding, which leads, in turn, to their being able to talk about other things. Rosa takes the position that Joy's homosexuality is a material condition ("in the blood, in the desire") and in no way blameworthy. It is something for her mother and her son to understand.

Juana. Joy, Consuelo, and Agustina bring Juana to the *centro* before her next medical appointment, and she is "worked" for the spirits that want her to get an infection in the hospital, to die on the operating table, to be the victim of botched surgery — all summoned, allowed to repent and beg her pardon, and retreat. The protection of the Archangel Michael, the Holy Trinity, and the anointment of a special palm juice, all are secured to ensure that the surgery will go well. Finally, she is asked to come to Rosa's house to receive necklaces blessed by the saints of *santería*. This is an all-night ceremony, the first of a series, in which she becomes Rosa's spiritual godchild for life.

Juana is seen as someone not in a process of development, but in need of protection. A psychiatrist might say that her many symptoms and psychiatric history show that she has a constitutional vulnerability to stress and the threat of loss. Therefore, the proper treatment is the reinforcement of her external social supports. But Rosa's interventions also relieve the family system of which Juana, Joy, and Consuelo are members. Supporting and adopting Juana relieves Joy of her preoccupation with being Juana's sole support and helps her to move more freely onto the path that has been cleared for her in restoring her relations with her mother and son.

Dolores. At the *reunión*, Rosa wears one of the wigs Dolores dressed and asks everyone to admire it, recommending Dolores' services. During the day, she takes Dolores with her on her rounds as she visits people in need of *caridad* and assistance, and she involves her in the work of the *centro*. Dolores brings Ricardo to one of the sessions because he is depressed and in need of Rosa's evaluation. Ricardo is relieved when she finds nothing spiritual, only natural grief from the loss of his lover. After that, Ricardo and Dolores begin to cook for each other.

A psychiatrist would say that, buffeted by illness and loss, Dolores finds relief in changing her role from that of victim to helper of others, and the activities of the *centro* provide her with the place where she can make this change. It also promotes the enlargement of her circle of social support in her relationship with Ricardo.

§

As I read this and other cases of Garrison's, I began to think of Rosa as a combination family therapist, hypnotist, and one-woman community mental health center. But of course this was a misunderstanding arising from my solo model of practice. She did not, as she would have been the first to say, do any of this by herself. She practiced in concert with a whole world of local and historical institutions, and the study of those institutions was what Garrison's anthropology was all about. This led me to think about the institutions that underlie and support the practice of psychotherapy on my side of the mirror.

Two questions immediately arise. The first has to do with effectiveness. Does it matter that the patient got better? Of course, it does. After two years, Garrison went back to see how the Maldonado family and their neighbors were doing, and she found a level of improvement, especially for Roberto, that the Tremont psychiatrists would have been happy to see in their patients. Whether either Rosa and her *protecciones* or the Tremont doctors should be credited with the improvement is another matter. Rosa would have given credit to the saints, as she directed Roberto to do, and I think that such humility would also be good for the doctors. The whole question of effectiveness and the ways in which its measurement may inform the design of psychotherapy is a subject to which I return in Chapter 13. A strict pragmatist would say it is the only question really worth asking.

The other question has to do with belief. What does this look into the mirror show about the place of belief in healing? Clearly, the world of the spirits was something in which Rosa's petitioners believed, but they were not naïve about it. Roberto and his friends often asked Garrison about her researches, especially questioning whether she had discovered any truth to the existence of spirits or the effectiveness of spiritual work.

And on my supposedly scientific side of the mirror, do we psychiatrists believe in the reality of our ideas? We certainly do not proceed on the basis of strict scientific evidence: We construct beliefs *with* the help of our audience. A successful psychotherapy is a piece of negotiated truth, involving contact between an illness as a patient experiences it and the powers of healing provided by the patient's culture.

I found an illustration of that point in an essay by anthropologist Claude Lévi-Strauss (1963) called "The Sorcerer and His Magic," which I subsequently assigned to every class of graduating residents before they escaped my classroom. In it, he describes an inquest by a group of Native American shamans and elders who are trying to determine whether a boy who has been accused of witchcraft is really a witch (for which the penalty would be death). The boy is terrified, and the elders clearly want to let him off, but he has to make the right confession. They help him to plead, so to speak, to a lesser offense so that the culture's beliefs about the diagnosis of witchcraft and its penalty can be preserved.

In the same essay, Lévi-Strauss also tells the story, first collected by Franz Boas, of Quesalid, a Northwest Coast Native American shaman. As a young man, Quesalid believed that the shamans were charlatans who used trickery to achieve their cures, and he apprenticed himself to them to learn their arts and expose them. He found that indeed he was right, that the evil things they appeared to suck from the bodies of the sick were actually hidden first in their mouths. But by the time he learned this, so many people had been cured, and there was such demand for his help, that he realized that he had no choice but to continue in his profession and study its effectiveness. Most residents have recognized in this story the way in which their clinical work forms their beliefs about psychotherapy, rather than the other way around. We all learn to work in traditions of practice larger and older than our theoretical doubts.

§

I did find one kind of anthropological theory helpful, however. After comparing *espiritismo* and psychiatry, and family therapy, I searched for the next step in the dialectic, the fruit of the comparison in a further idea. I found it in the writings of Victor Turner. Turner's work began with the conceptions of Arnold van Gennep, whose *The Rites of Passage* (1908) brought into anthropology the idea that, as individuals go through the life cycle from birth to death, they pass through a series of natural personal and social crises of membership. The progress of the person through life brings conflict, at each age, between these changes, occurring in the lives of individuals, and the stability of the group, the family, the village. In this view, life is a series of individual passages from group to group, while the groups — children, youths, married couples, parents, the old and the dead — remain stable, like standing waves, while the life stories flow through them. The enterings and leavings of the first family, and then the second family, are marked by rituals at the crisis points, birth, adolescence, marriage, parenting, and death. In addition, a more or less formal *training* goes on during those uncertain in-between periods, the preparations for passage which are the continual occupation of the human psychological career. Family and school are the most obvious institutions managing these changes; psychotherapy is less so, because it is less public and less universal.

Writing a half century after van Gennep, Turner (1969) further described the rituals that mark these passages. Rituals marking change, growth, and passage, he pointed out, are set off from the ordinary workings of the community. Community and its structure of daily work are the foreground, whereas rituals of passage are the background. Turner emphasized that ritual is set apart from the functioning community, in which people behave and think as if the social world were set and finished.

Turner had previously studied the "set and finished" vision of society as a student of the British school of anthropology. That school traditionally saw society as a collection of such "structures" as kinship, government, and economy, corresponding to the idea of "organization" in sociology. These organizational structures all have "functions." Some structures are obvious, such as the division of labor between the sexes in securing food (men hunt, women gather, and both farm, but in different ways). Such structures have functions such as preventing conflict, maximizing efficiency, and promoting mutual dependency in the marriage relationship. Some functions are less obvious, such as the way in which certain rules for marriage between cousins keep property from leaving the family through dowries and inheritances.

The work of the British School was to figure out the hidden functions of structures, justifying the ways of humans to a concept of anthropological "design." This view of society is relatively static, with all of its citizens standing still and doing their part in organizations, both formal and informal. In this view, the *community* is an ingeniously functioning mechanism, or an English village (gentry, clergy, shopkeepers, tenant farmers, all with their functions), or — more to the point of applied anthropology in the early twentieth century — a sensitively administered, "indirectly governed" British African colony, the actual subject of study by A. R. Radcliffe-Brown, the founder of the school.

Turner emphasized that this view of community as structure and function was only partial, especially if one is interested in healing. Taking van Gennep's description of the rites of passage a step further, he located those rituals in a different phase of social organization, "anti-structure." The experience in this more fluid phase of the group's life he called *communitas,* to distinguish it from *community,* the view of people as inhabiting structures with functions.

Again, concrete particulars are the only way to understand these anthropological ideas. Turner's earliest examples of *communitas* involved a healing ceremony among the Ndembu people of Zambia, from which we can begin to see the relevance of these ideas to psychotherapy. Healing rituals, he noted, have many elements in common with initiation rituals. In the healing of sick and infertile women in the society, and in the initiation of boys and girls at puberty, we can see ritual oases in the social order where something very different from that order is going on. Both the candidates for initiation and the sufferers from illness are ritually separated from the rest of society. In both rituals, work stops, medicines and herbs are found, ancestors are summoned, and sacred powers are invoked. In *communitas,* the structures and functions of the daily community are suspended in favor of a ritual recognition that some members of the group have not yet come into their powers, are sick and in need of healing, or are not yet ready to function in the next stage in life. They are in a *liminal* state (van Gennep's word) on the threshold of responsibility, or still in recovery, and require the help of those whose task it is to teach the children, heal the sick, comfort the afflicted, and bury the dead. These healing, recovering, and learning functions have been separate in our culture as well, ever since in medieval European society, they were the work of priests and women, in a sphere of service that stood apart from society's structural (and patriarchal) concerns with trade and warfare.

Communitas is similar to the ethos of the spirit world envisioned by *espiritismo,* where all beings are in a slowly ascending, transmigratory state of liminality. Explaining Roberto's candidacy for spiritual development, Garrison (1982) says:

> In spiritist theory, certain people were born in this lifetime with the "spiritual and material mission" to "develop spiritual faculties" and learn to help themselves and help others through the use of these faculties. In this way they are believed to "advance" in their "spiritual mission" toward the state of a "pure spirit" that need not be incarnated again. All beings were created gross, ignorant, dominated by material impulses, and it is the mission of every [being] living or dead, to develop towards greater light and understanding, formality, wisdom, and the replacement of material impulses by refined sentiments.

It is for this spiritual development that each person has her *cuadro espiritual,* her guides and guardian angel, her testing and tutelary sponsors in development. Here is the imagery of Turner's antistructure, of child rearing, teaching, learning, healing and transformation throughout the stages of a life history.

§

In our society, under the intellectual dominion of Marx and Freud, ritual got a bad name as a part of religion, the opiate of the people. One of the few books for which Freud wrote a preface was Theodor Reik's *Ritual,* which described rituals such as circumcision as defenses against unacceptable impulses, a sort of societywide symptom formation, the need for which should disappear when correctly understood. In college, I was a fan of Freud's other book along these lines, *The Future of an Illusion,* but reading anthropology, such as that of Garrison and Turner, turned me toward viewing the institutions around me, especially those connected with psychotherapy, with an anthropological eye. I began to see their ritual side.

Turner (1982) defines ritual as "prescribed formal behavior for occasions not given over to technological routine, having reference to beliefs, invisible beings or powers regarded as the first and final causes of all effects." Even in a society such as ours, where belief in supernatural powers is mostly absent, ritual plays a role. As Turner's student Barbara Myerhoff has pointed out, rituals are not performed only by religious believers. Moreover, even when performed in religious societies, they are not naïvely magical. "No primitive society," Myerhoff says (1992, p. 183), "is so unempirical as to expect to cause rain by dancing a rain dance. A rain dance is, in Burke's felicitous phrase, a dance *with* the rain."

In that same sense, even our secular society has transformative rituals that *make a difference,* not by changing the world, but by changing our experience. A baseball game is a ritual of bravery, skill, and virtue. It changes our experience of the world by enacting for our reverent attention a performance in which courage and skill are rewarded in a contest carried out according to visible rules of fairness. For a short while, the structured powers of our society, which often repel us as sleazy and unfair, are revoked, and we are able to believe in virtue. The world is transformed.

Myerhoff makes a distinction between ritual and ceremony that is useful in secular society. Both add definition and meaning to life, but ritual transforms, whereas ceremony indicates. Thus, there are ceremonies, such as the forms of hospitality and greeting that manage encounters between different degrees of acquaintance, and those that manage as well as indicate reassuring behavior. As Erving Goffman's works show so well, these face- or impression-management ceremonies are very important in stabilizing *community*, but they do not set aside its structures. Indeed, they may preserve and protect those structures. And ceremony does not signify change. That is the task of ritual, which may even challenge or break up structure — or at least suspend it — and brings with that suspension a sense of *communitas*.

Consider a familiar secular ritual, the birthday party. The participants may be so worldly that they insist it has no significance for them ("I don't go in for birthdays — I just like the party"). But even for such scoffers, a brief moment — the toast, the cake with candles, the song, or the joke about "feeling a year older" — is transformative, compressing a year into a moment, making all the participants, whoever they are in the structured world, at that moment equal votaries in a ritual of passage, and changing the celebrant for that moment into a favored brother or sister whose secret wish will be granted. After the moment passes, the secular spectator goes back to her disenchanted position if she likes, but the ritual and its audience has brought her an instant of altered belief.

Clearly here, *communitas* is a *feeling* state as well as an occasion, a performance. Turner compares it to the sense of brotherhood and sisterhood in a religious congregation, a sense of equality before a higher order, or the kind of personal relationship that Martin Buber described as the I-Thou relationship, a relationship of personal regard, of *caritas*. This feeling can be intensified by taking it out of the structured sense of time. Ritual has a different sense of time, apart from dailiness. Community runs on secular time: deadlines, work periods, appointments, efficiency defined as production within a time frame. Ritual is psychologically outside of time, as participants in a *shabat* supper or at Sunday church can understand. The day of rest marked off from the work week begins with a ritual of celebration in which the obligations of structure and function are set aside, and in the midst of the ritual, the celebrants are both suspended and united in a sense of *communitas* whose timelessness is enhanced by the communion of saints or of ancestors stretching back into the past.

Rituals of passage, on the other hand, address the experience of liminality, of being in transition, for specific persons at specific times of crisis or celebration. The most intense experience of liminality is childhood, where we awaken from the dream of infancy to find ourselves children in a family. This is why metaphors of childhood appeal to healers all over the world, the Ndembu as well as the Freudians. But childhood is not the only liminal institution. Many others preside over other passages of life and provide other metaphors. All our lives, in fact, we are preparing to move on to the next challenge, the next transition.

Suppose we reverse the fields and put liminality, antistructure, in the foreground and structure in the background. We would see then that the in-between preparations, the rehearsals, are more interesting and continuous than the performances. Looking at life as more or less continual liminality, we would see the occasions when we do stand still and assert ourselves in our roles, our functions in social structure, as a kind of pretense, a performance for which we have long rehearsed, and of whose outcome we are never as sure as we appear. Performance then would be an altered state, the trance of battle, in which we know what we are doing as soldiers, attorneys, doctors, parents, and therapists. We give a good accounting of ourselves when we are "on," standing at our station in the community.

But liminality, a relief from that pretense, in this view may feel like a more "natural" state. We are not "on" yet; we are unfinished, unsure, imperfect, and in need of a different kind of membership, one less demanding than the structures of community, one that helps, supports, teaches, heals. The two ways of experience — the uncertain rehearsal and the finished performance — alternate throughout life, sometimes in the course of a single hour or day. Sometimes liminality takes over completely, as in the experience of illness, either physical or emotional. Then we know again how it feels to be uncertain and in need of care. Finally, our ending is as liminal as our infant beginning. By the time we face death, we may see it as a last preparation to join our ancestors, family, and friends, the ultimate *communitas*, where there are no more structures and functions, and all our strivings cease.

Turner was especially interested in a case of lifelong liminality, the vows of poverty and the abjuring of secular power that distinguished the brotherhood of St. Francis from other orders. It was this placing themselves outside the hierarchy and power of the church that gave the Franciscans their mysterious authority to preach reform. Our own time and culture seem so opposite to the outlook of St. Francis. We embrace the "rationality" of structured, accomplishing society, as well as the functioning within it of a radically individual self-expression, which we think of as "authentic" if it seems to come from the inside. If we think about ritual at all (church attendance, family gatherings), it seems irrelevant to both the society and the authentic self because it is formally prescribed, external in the sense of imposed from outside. The heroes of our novels and movies do their thing regardless of circumstances, especially the circumstances of family, education and class, the home ground of ritual. But in spite of this prejudice, we have a secular religion that is full of ritual. We have reinvented ritual in the form of pilgrimages to shrines of health, nature, and art and put considerable time and energy into their contrivance, since we think of them as selections we have made from the inside, expressions of individual taste.

I am reminded of John Ruskin, the first professor of art history at Oxford and in that sense the founder of one of the most envied roles in the professional class, the modern arts and letters professional, the self-made man or woman of taste and discernment (Kemp, 1990). A critic of society and a philosopher of the place of art in that society, Ruskin was able to turn his avocation into a career, getting paid for what he loved to do. But his eminently expressive life was centered on ritual. His family's annual pilgrimage to the Stones of Venice, taking the same routes each time, stopping in the same hotels, was a prototype of the Victorian family vacation. And he recorded, before it might be lost, the art that was the precious residue, the essence, of Medieval and Renaissance ritual expression. Today, others of his class undertake scuba diving, or visits to Florence or the Museo del Prado or the Rolling Stones or the National Open, with a similar joy, reverence, and seriousness.

These occasions, which we think of as communing with our souls or with our truly authentic, personally chosen interests, in art or exercise, are only the most excursive examples of modern ritual. The backyard garden we tend on the weekend, the barbecue and swimming pool with which we recreate the simple pleasures of Neolithic family life, are suburban ritual destinations, shrines at the end of a pilgrimage, far from the job we hold in the structured world. Our daily escape from structure is so well traveled that we hardly notice the trip, except to feel a lifting of the spirit in anticipation of our arrival. Only because we believe that what is emotionally real must come from the heart rather than be imposed upon it by convention do we ignore the highly conventional and ritual nature of these enactments.

Victor Turner, interested in pilgrimage as modern secular ritual, collected a number of modern and historical examples, noting that each of the Abrahamic religions has made a major place for this affirmation of the religious self: the Islamic hajj to Mecca, the Jewish return to Jerusalem, and the many Christian journeys, to Canterbury, Campostella, Lourdes, and so on (Turner & Turner, 1995). If our secular society has turned all this into "travel," and if our destinations are, like Ruskin's, stones rather than saints, we are no less involved in the experience of life as a journey, and the transformations we are looking for on these vacation pilgrimages are no less genuine, the company we journey with no less essential to the outcome.

Pilgrimage is a good metaphor for therapy, one of many ways of focusing on the purpose of the journey, although, like the journey to Lourdes, its effect may reside as much in the decision to set out as in the arrival at the destination. The guides who conduct us on these journeys, the psychotherapists, may believe, because of their individualistic assumptions, that they have escaped the original audience, the community that validated the ritual, the crowd of villagers praying at the mysterious spring. But they are only ignoring that part of their experience. The cloud of witnesses is there, even in the analyst's office: the patients who occupy the other hours, the teachers hidden behind the diploma on the wall, the friends and family, real and imagined.

§

Family therapists have been more hospitable to ritual as something to be incorporated into life rather than explained away, especially since they have been interested in the social location of mind and have found it natural to include an audience, the family, in their description of the individual's problems and their solutions. This step was natural: having brought the family members together as each other's audience, some just kept adding people until they had something that looked like a tribal group.

Ross Speck was the first family therapist to add more audience. When consulted by a mother who lived with her schizophrenic son, Speck replied, "Not enough people. You have to bring someone with you the next time" (Speck & Attneave, 1973). They couldn't think of anyone, but in order to comply with his request, they brought along the couple from whom they rented their apartment. The interview went better, but Speck asked for still more people, and as the meetings went on and the discussions expanded, a large neighborhood support group developed. The original patient got a job driving a cab with the help of one of the participants, but many others took advantage of this forum as well.

This was the birth of "network therapy," the idea that many illnesses and cures need to be embedded in a social field larger than the family. Edgar Auerswald's "ecological" therapy convened committees of the family and people from the agencies responsible for dealing with a wide variety of problems (Auerswald, 1968). This strategic recruitment of social support continues in many public agencies today. And just a little beyond network therapy is the familiar territory of "group," "activity," and "arts" therapy. There is dance therapy, art therapy, psychodrama, music therapy, even sports therapy. The last is a particularly good way in which to reach young people: baseball followed by a locker-room rehash of the game with the coach-psychologist (Ian Canino, personal communication).

Within family therapy itself, the foremost proponents of ritual are Evan Imber-Black and Janine Roberts (1992), authors of *Rituals for Our Times,* a widely read and much used collection of practice models.[3] They present ritual as a natural way to approach life crises and resolve conflicts between opposites.. They help families organize dinner parties, for example, to celebrate transitions, or they help to choose a gift to express a change in a relationship. My favorite of Imber-Black's ideas is a ritual for dealing with rejection, separation, and loss. The client lists on a deck of note cards all the characteristics and qualities of the person she has lost, and then separates the cards into two piles: things in her experience of the person she wants to keep, and things she is happy to be rid of. Then the client and the therapist burn the second pile.

Many of the life transitions for which therapy is needed, Imber-Black and Roberts note, are the ones without prescribed rituals; indeed they involve transitions between states that society would rather not recognize at all. Two of these unscheduled and unrecognized crises of transition are recovery from alcohol addiction and the acceptance and

---

[3] Roberts, in her historical chapter introducing the first edition (Imber-Black, Roberts, & Whiting, 1988), makes special reference to Victor Turner as a forerunner of this thinking.

management of long-term mental illness. Both of these transitions pass
through territory sufficiently disowned by the larger society that the participants need to socially repossess it. In the absence of celebrations, the
pilgrims on these journeys are in need of healing rituals. Interestingly, the
rituals that have been invented for these states are recognized for their effectiveness as psychiatric treatments.

§

Alcoholics Anonymous (AA), for example, is regarded by most investigators as the most demonstrably effective "treatment" for a large
number of alcoholics. Certainly no other identifiable approach works as
well.[4] It originated in 1926 when two American drinkers, Bill Wilson
and Bob Smith, were attending meetings of the Oxford Group. This lay
religious movement involved making confessional speeches and telling
stories of personal failing, repentance, and regeneration through the
recognition of dependence on a Higher Power. The founders of AA at-
tribute their ideas to Bill's mentor in the Oxford Group, the Reverend
Dr. Samuel Shoemaker. Today, the slight flavor of ritual and religion that
still clings to AA makes it anathema to many "tough-minded" individualist alcoholics, since they regard themselves as too "realistic" to be
"taken in by it," and see it as a potential infringement on their independence of judgement.[5]

Not only is AA an effective treatment for alcoholism, but it has been
a model for other 12-step movements that deal in a similar way with
gambling, obesity, drug addiction, child abuse, chronic debt, and the
larger family repercussions of these problems (Adult Children of Alcoholics, for example). Members of the AA group are united in their intention
to achieve and help each other achieve the goal of sobriety. The beginning identification ("I am an alcoholic") indicates both membership in

---

[4] Recovery rates in AA vary widely, depending on how the study is done.
Better-designed outpatient studies show the most positive results, but even these are
of doubtful design. See Tonigan, Toscova, & Miller (1996).

[5] This antagonism is another example of where the beliefs of the "authentic"
self, the self of the romantic tradition, get in the way. Gregory Bateson discusses this
in a paper about alcoholism, romantic individualism, and AA, which is one of the
essential readings about these subjects and about Bateson's ideas of how therapy and
belief work together or against each other (Bateson, 1972a).

the group and acceptance of the path to the changed state that the members are traveling. The 12 steps are the way along the pilgrimage, a way that may have to be retraced many times as "slips" reverse the progress. Avoidance of the use of last names not only provides confidentiality but, more important, separates the group from the status categories of the outside world, a band of liminal brothers and sisters.

The group includes an audience — the other members of the meeting — and a sponsor, a member chosen by the novice as a mentor, but that sponsor is not an expert "therapist." He or she is an adept only a little further along the path. Wisdom and guidance come not from professional expertise, but from the accumulated experience of the congregation.

Members of AA celebrate important intervals of sobriety (90 days, a year) — stages in their pilgrimage — with public testimonials to the group and reflections on what new responsibilities they are able to assume, given the tentative success of their careful "one day at a time" approach. But cure, in the philosophy of AA, is never totally achieved. Even if the alcoholic succeeds in avoiding alcohol for the remainder of her life, she is always "an alcoholic," always in danger of relapse, and the local meeting will always be there to help. Alcoholics Anonymous and self-help groups for long-term illnesses contemplate the possibility of a lifetime of liminality and, indeed, make it their business to turn that status into a positive membership in *communitas*.

§

Another group of wayfarers on an especially slow route of pilgrimage is that of the families of patients with schizophrenia. Most such patients live with their families for many years, until they get a foothold in the community of halfway houses, sheltered work, and day programs that the state has prepared for them. During those years of living at home, the most effective treatment, as demonstrated by clinical trials, is the multifamily group, a group of families gathered together to apply the psychoeducational approach to the problem of schizophrenia in a family member (McGlashan, 1986; McFarlane, Lukens, Link, et al., 1995).

The evening meetings with families and patients that we developed at the Family Service at Bronx State Hospital were an early form of this therapy. By 1980, something like the multiple family group (MFG) had been invented in many different parts of the country. Both MFG and the practice of working supportively and educationally with one family at a time had acquired a name: the psychoeducational approach to schizophrenia. A number of research trials had demonstrated the method's superiority over other forms of psychotherapy in treating schizophrenia (Anderson, Hogarty, & Reiss, 1980; Falloon, Boyd, & McGill, 1984). Working with multifamily groups, in addition to being labor-saving, is, in some ways, more effective than working with one family at a time. The families' awareness of other families as pilgrims with the same quest mitigates the sense of isolation that is the main problem with this illness. It introduces them to the possibilities of an invisible village of people with like experiences.

In both its single- and multiple-family forms, psychoeducation has three distinct phases. The first is a series of interviews between the staff members and family members, usually while the patient is acutely ill in the hospital and not part of these introductory contacts. Here, the parents have a chance to pour out the story of their frustrations and disappointments with the experience. The key to this phase, and subsequent phases, is to provide the family with a sense of being joined, a sense that their feelings of frustration and loss are understood.

The second phase is an all-day workshop, conducted by the staff and a group of families (Anderson, Hogarty, & Reiss, 1981). This is the "educational" part. In the morning, the families hear lectures about the symptoms, medication, and medical models of the phenomena of the illness. In the afternoon, there are discussions of "family members' survival skills." And although the format is educational, it is not didactic. There is much discussion between family members and staff. It is an initiation into a group membership, as well.

The third phase of the treatment is the biweekly meetings themselves, joined at this point by the patients, who are sufficiently recovered from their acute illness to rely on the group solidarity that has been created by the work so far. The MFG project devises a ritual for these meetings that is really a distillation of *communitas*. The meeting begins with an obligatory period of "chat," in which each person, including the therapists, makes some mention of the part of their life that does not concern schizophrenia, some personal news or experience that establishes everyone's common humanity: trouble with travel arrangements, news of how a project is progressing, a visit to a friend, a trip to the movies. This is a ritual bridge from the outside world to the more private experience of the families with their special problems in coping with the consequences of schizophrenia.

Then the therapists invite the group to participate in the central ritual of the meeting; problem solving. The form, borrowed from behavioral psychology, goes like this: First, a definition of the problem is written down. Then all possible solutions (all that anyone present can think of) are listed without criticism or discussion. Pro's and cons are given for each solution, and finally, and only then, one solution is picked by the family, to be tried out as an experiment. Premature discussion and hasty dismissal of possibilities are strictly prevented by the therapists. Acceptance of a proposal is postponed until all the alternatives are spelled out.

Problem solving makes it possible to slow down the process and make communication so transparent that the confusion of schizophrenic information processing is penetrated by the clarity of written words. It is a ritual for summoning the powers of rationality and choice. Problem solving enacts one of the deeply held values of the group — that problems, broken into small pieces and externalized, can be solved, even at this most maddening and slowed-down pace. Looking at small increments of improvement over long periods of time, development is still possible. Problem solving is the method the group uses in order to arrive at the next day's experiment in the slow journey, the gallingly mundane difficulties of daily life that attend this illness. Schizophrenia is understood as an affliction, an objective complex of symptoms of brain dysfunction, communication difficulties, isolation, and social stigma, which makes life difficult for all members of the family, not just the patient.

At the end, there is another interval of chat as the group prepares to return to the outside world, which is unconcerned with the problems of living with schizophrenia. The group, including the leaders, is slowly growing in wisdom and experience, and the leaders claim any mistakes in judgment as their own failure to apply the method thoughtfully enough. Success, on the other hand, is attributed to the family members in their careful application of the problem-solving method.

Over time, the steps in the life pilgrimage become clear: First, there is the recognition of the reality of the illness and the possibility of becoming skillful at dealing with it. One or two years later, the patients' experiments in one of several areas of venturing into the outside world begin to succeed: making friends; living away from the family, perhaps alone; and work. It was demonstrated long ago that these are separate domains, in which adventures should be undertaken one at a time, with allowance for the differences between one person's abilities and another's (Strauss & Carpenter, 1974).

§

From studying these rituals, I finally understood how to conduct a family case conference. In the culture of the MFG, relapse is not a calamity. Admission of a patient to the hospital for an acute episode of psychosis is only a temporary interruption of the work — the necessary way to solve a problem that the group had attempted first to solve in other ways. Everyone expects that the patient will soon return to the group. The hospital admission is seen as a possibly valuable retreat for the contemplation of a new transition.

A directive in the regulations of New York State said that before a patient could be discharged from the ward, a discharge planning meeting should be held, one that includes the family and the outpatient therapist. I suggested to the Family Service that "discharge planning" was a better purpose for the meeting than the academic notion of revealing "family dynamics," and I wanted, in any case, to challenge the spotlight that the old form of this meeting had placed on the family as something that needed fixing. Accordingly, we designed a meeting that was a celebration of the joint accomplishments of the family, the ward staff, and especially the patient in getting ready to return to the world outside the hospital. It was a rite of passage, a graduation. To accomplish it, the staff members had to change their view of themselves as observers to contributors, which, as it turned out, they were delighted to do. The nurses, the family, and the patient, had all lived through a battle with the illness and had had some success. My job as the leader of the conference became easier as soon as the separate secret agendas of the old form dissolved into an open task: to find out from each other what useful new ideas we had learned from this painful passage, so that we could take them forward into life in the hazardous outside world. What supports did the family have? Were they members of an MFG that would be interested in what we had learned?

As the staff members participated in this ritual, they began to realize that it not only was more interesting than the old one, but was easier to do, and many people on the service began to conduct them. As it passed out of my hands, the ritual lost its professorial mystery and became the common property, part of the art and knowledge, of the service. Years later, I read that on the other side of the world in Australia, a group of family therapists — David Epston, Michael White, and Alan Rosen, all readers of Victor Turner — had made a similar invention (Rosen, 1994).

§

What is the greater import of these rituals? Diseases such as alcoholism and schizophrenia make a person a member of a community but with special limitations, special milestones in life, a separate pilgrimage, something like the lifelong liminality of the Franciscan brotherhood, but different because it is not self-imposed, not chosen. The ritual disciplines of AA and MFG have in common an emphasis on the pilgrimage as a long journey rather than as a life condemned by moral failure and ostracism. Above all, the importance of company, the accumulated wisdom of the group, balances and contains the intermittent failure of the individual.

The state of having an illness (subjectively, a dis-ease) especially a mental illness or distress, is formally — socially — similar to immaturity and ignorance. These ideas can all be used as metaphors for one another. That was Turner's point. Indeed, emotional distress in many ways may be indistinguishable from uncertainty about one's validity as a member of the group one was hoping to join, or the possibility of falling back from that achievement, or being ignorant, at a loss, about how to make the transition.

In our culture, the greatest transition — the one that is seen as the bridge from the immature first half of life to the mature second half — is marriage. And although our romantic tradition emphasizes the part of marriage that is a step from being single to being united with the perfect partner, becoming two against the world, it is also, in a larger sense, a change of audience. The change from the first family to the second family includes the partner's family and the children to come, as well as joining the vanguard of the married. Much can go wrong in this initiation, but one way it can go right is for it to be taken as the beginning of a process of gradually learning how to do it — a lifelong appenticeship of many stages.

CHAPTER SEVEN
Marriage and Its Therapy

Ah, love, let us be true
To one another! For the world, which seems
To lie before us like a land of dreams,
So various, so beautiful, so new,
Hath really neither joy, nor Love, nor light,
Nor certitude, nor peace, nor help for pain;
And we are here as on a darkling plain
Swept with confused alarms of struggle and flight,
Where ignorant armies clash by night.
— Matthew Arnold, from "Dover Beach," 1867

MATTHEW ARNOLD WAS 45, and had been married for 12 years, when he wrote "Dover Beach," surely one of the most touching expressions of antimodern disillusionment and longing. In it he calls to his wife:

"Come to the window, sweet is the night air!
Listen! You hear the grating roar
Of pebbles, which the waves draw back."

The moment of intimacy and shared reflection celebrates a special view of marriage, a secret, inviolate refuge, a place away from "struggle and flight," apart from a harsh world devoid of grace.[1] Marriage, like

---

[1] Christopher Lasch refers to family intimacy in just these terms in *Haven in a Heartless World.* Jackson Lears, in *No Place of Grace,* describes other places of refuge, retreat, and protest against the modern world developed in the nineteenth century: the Arts and Crafts movement, for example, as well as the development of psychotherapy.

psychotherapy, was becoming part of the new secular religion. Victorian romantic marriage was a place where two souls could find hope in communion, at least in the middle of the night. In such a marriage, "Let us be true to one another" meant not just sexual fidelity but being for each other the incarnation of truth in a false world.

More recently, sociologists of the family have been writing about changes in modern marriage that have made it an even more psychological refuge than it was in Arnold's day. The erosion of all other supports away from the family has left each couple standing alone. Today, without the family farm, or the cottage industry, or the yoking together of family fortunes, or the fear of God, or economic obligations down the generations, the function of marriage, apart from the rearing of children, is reduced to the psychological support of two individuals. Nock (2000) argues that the separation of marriage from childrearing gave rise to the family therapy profession.

As a union only of two spirits, minds, and bodies, a sentimental partnership without any other function, modern marriage is vulnerable to the shearing forces that begin when two individuals develop careers at different speeds or in different directions. It is still the refuge against the darkness that Arnold found, but a refuge could just as well be found with another partner. Thus, the institution of divorce has become a widespread alternative to the institution of marriage, each a different kind of career move. Family therapists see more and more couples about divorce, considering it, trying to avoid it, recovering from it, or remarrying after it. Certainly we consult more on this aspect of marriage than on the other classical problems, united parents trying to deal with children, with aging parents, or their own illnesses or fortunes.

The burden placed on marriage, since it was sentimentalized by these nineteenth-century changes, has made couples therapy the bread and butter of family practice. Couples and individuals now swarm into therapists' offices, searching for the relationship that will make their lives all right again. Bookstores and magazine stands too are overflowing with advice on how to find it.

Philip Rieff traces that ground in *The Triumph of the Therapeutic*. It seems that the way is now open for someone to write about the parallel development in the nineteenth century of modern marriage and modern psychotherapy as related institutions, sometimes in conflict because of the different prescriptions they offer for the career of the soul.

Some parts of the therapeutic culture sentimentalize marriage even further. The prominent cult of sex therapy, for example, offers one romantic solution. If the aging and drifting couple can find a way back to the sexual excitement that started the relationship, it might lead to a new beginning. This technical fix is heavily endorsed by our culture's delight in youth, and unquestionably, in my experience with sex therapy, when it works, it works. Its sheer popularity suggests that it must work a lot of the time (Gurman & Kniskern, 1991, pp. 492–504).

On the other hand, not everyone is talented in this area, and large parts of life take place between sexual encounters. Most people find that, for marriage to work in the sense of providing a home for the nurturing of the soul, more than sex is involved. Sex is one metaphor for the relationship, one enactment of it. Intimate conversation is another. Raising children, making a home, cooking meals: How can all this fit together to give a marriage stability when it seems to be coming apart?

Nineteenth-century psychology attempted to answer that question by simplifying marriage with a grand myth that imposed biological dimorphism on the temperaments of men and women. Thus, "science" endorsed a "natural" dominance and initiative for men and a submissiveness and weakness for women. Invoking nature to simplify the differences between husbands and wives solved some problems, mostly in the interests of men, but it has had consequences, especially for women, that the feminists have been pointing out for over a century. The nineteenth-century feminist campaign against this mythological reading of nature paralleled the abolitionist campaign against a similar mythological reading that "justified" the institution of slavery with an account of the "natural" inferiority and subservient destiny of African slaves.

The Southwest where I grew up had plenty of remnants of both myths, of the natural dominance of men and of whites. I am embarrassed now to read some of the stories I wrote in junior high school, reflecting my absorption of that culture. One of the effects of my coming east to school was to discover a different kind of woman from the yielding southern belle. I first discovered women of independent mind at Radcliffe College. Some of them were themselves escaped southern belles, making discoveries similar to mine. But most of those who fascinated me were independent, adventurous, and tough-minded women from northeastern cities with their minds more on career prospects than on the romance-and-marriage scenario that occupied mine.

Once again, anthropology opened up the alternative perspective.[2] Reading Margaret Mead's *Sex and Temperament* challenged the popular description of the differences between men and women.[3] Mead found societies where men were dominant, where women were dominant, where both were pacific, and where both were warlike. In my 20s, I was persuaded by her conclusion that cultural prescription and individual (as opposed to gender-based) temperament both decisively modified the biological influence of gender on a person's capacities.

The ultimate challenge to the problem of sex and temperament, however, awaited the more recent entrance of gay and lesbian scholars into the discussion. Now that the gay couple is out of the closet in family studies, and a variety of definitions of family life have opened up before us, old ideas about gender and marriage have to be reconsidered from still other starting points. As family therapists are dealing with the problems of gay couples, Margaret Mead's point is even more relevant: without gender assumptions about heterosexual marriage to go on, the influence of temperament and culture, especially local, personal culture, come to the fore.[4]

One piece of insight into sorting out relationships comes from one of the earliest and most influential anthropological studies on the subject.

---

[2] Two other pieces of anthropology, *All Our Kin* (Stack, 1983) and *Steet Corner Society* (Liebow, 1968), were books I used at Tremont to make the point that economic class and racial segregation have a profound effect on the way gender roles and marriage are seen in some parts of the African-American community. Case studies are used to understand a particular inflection of gender in marriage produced by caste and class. On the other hand, when it turns to grand themes, anthropology has contributed its share of myth-making to the debate about gender. From Bachofen (1967), *Das Mutterrecht,* to Eisler (1987), *The Chalice and the Blade,* both supposedly based on archeological findings, anthropology has generated myths about an ancient rule of mothers and worship of goddesses. Bamberger (1974), in her essay "Why Men Rule in Primitive Society," points out how very antifeminist this kind of myth-making is.

[3] Mead's research gets blamed these days for inspiring the sexual revolution of the 1960s (*Time,* March 29, 1999), and attacked for its methodology (Freeman, 1998). As to the first charge, it is important to remember that *Sex and Temperament* was first published in 1935. As to the second, the argument over her methods and findings mostly concerns her books on adolescence.

[4] Ann Hartman and Joan Laird, keynote address, Dulwich Centre Conference on Narrative and Community Therapy, Adelaide, Australia, February 1999.

In 1935, at the start of his career, Gregory Bateson (later Margaret Mead's husband and the inventor of the double-bind hypothesis and of family therapy's version of systems thinking; see Chapter 5) made a discovery.[5] It was a way of describing two different kinds of Difference. In *Naven*, Bateson's first book, he reported on his observations of the social and ritual life of the Iatmul in New Guinea. Like many other such societies, the Iatmul were preoccupied with ways in which men and women are different. They had exclusive men's and women's organizations and secret rituals in which only one gender could participate, but also other public rituals in which men sometimes enacted women's roles, and vice versa. As a step toward trying to understand all this, Bateson reached behind male-female differences to describe a more fundamental classification: Relationships, he said, could be either symmetrical or complementary.

A symmetrical relationship is one in which the participants are regarded as equal or as similar enough that their interaction is governed by symmetrical rules, such as taking turns, equal sharing, rule-governed competition, and so on. Symmetrical relationships are unstable and require much negotiation to keep them from breaking down into destructive competition, warfare, or total disengagement. Relations between siblings sometimes are supposed to be symmetrical, but rules are often imposed on them, such as older–younger, in order to settle disputes.

Complementary relationships are those in which inequality is built in, is an integral part of the relationship, such as parent–child, teacher–student, leader–follower. The emphasis is on the role difference, the mutual responsibility of each to play a complementary part so that the goal of the relationship — growing up, learning, or the success of the enterprise — can be achieved. Complementary relationships are problematic as well. They are in danger of becoming fixed, of outlasting their purpose, or worse. The master–slave relationship is an extreme form of complementarity. The madonna and child we worship in so many religions are the icon of a complementary relationship, where everything is just as it should be.

Social life, at least the life of couples, can be seen as a playing out of

---

[5] Bateson actually got these ideas not only from rethinking his field notes, but from discussing gender and the handling of difference with Margaret Mead and her then husband, Reo Fortune, while they were living together in New Guinea. See *Naven*, page 258.

these two kinds of differences between the members. The success of social life, in very practical terms, often depends on our agreement about our relationship: If we are symmetrical, are we playing by the rules we have agreed on? If we are complementary, do we agree on who is in charge, or who is taking care of whom?[6]

Family therapy that addresses parent–child problems is comparatively easy and rewarding, partly because all the relationships are complementary; you know how everyone should turn out, with the children growing up and the parents doing their part. Family therapy with adolescents is harder because the struggle is beginning to be about whether the adolescent is any longer in a complementary relationship with the parents, and if not, what equalities, symmetries, or independencies will prevail. Couples therapy is still harder. Marital therapy, like marriage, is a tangle of disputed symmetries, failed or misunderstood gestures of complementary caretaking. Marital therapy is hard in the way that marriage is hard; it epitomizes, on a daily basis and over the long run, the challenge and complexity of constantly redefining relationships as they change from moment to moment and place to place.

Bateson's way of looking at differences offers an improvement over generalizations about gender because it is dynamic. It focuses on the mutual influence of the participants on the moment-by-moment changes in the relationship, and that allows the construction of a complex narrative. It escapes from a fixed mythology and encourages us to make up our stories for ourselves, based on our immediate experience and our sense of how we are, in any situation, being invited, commanded, subdued, elevated, joined with, played with, partnered.

I also prefer this way of looking at difference because, rather than being derived from something supposedly comprehensive and profound like sex and aggression, it is relatively open to, and inviting of, a variety of descriptions. It makes the fewest possible assumptions about deep causes, and instead leaves the discovery of ideas about causes to the participants themselves.

To get an idea of how this system works in marriage therapy, let us look at an easy case, one where the issues of complementary caretaking are not made worse by the psychosis, major depression, illness, or addiction, that creates special burdens for the caretaking spouse. (And espe-

---

[6] Berne (1986) provides one of the practical-psychology versions of this.

cially, let us not consider a marriage where one or both are victims of traumatic abuse, as described in Chapter 3.[7] Here again, trauma complicates things.)

So, an easy case. Suppose I am consulted by a couple, John and Mary.[8] She is the former executive director of a charitable foundation who left her job to raise their first baby. He is a lawyer trying to make partner in a large, competitive firm. Their initial complaints sound as if they were taken from an advice column in *Cosmopolitan:* He is anxious, preoccupied with work, and uncommunicative. She longs for intimate talk, and feels ignored, devalued, lonely. A regular Mars and Venus problem.[9]

A look at their backgrounds adds information about another dimension of the microculture of the family. John's mother was intrusive, critical, and needy. She depended on him, as the oldest son, to fill the space in her life left by the emotional absence of his remote, achieving and hard-driving father. Mary, on the other hand, never got over the death of her gentle, understanding, and endlessly patient father. She and her mother agreed that no one in the world could take his place. A number of psychoanalytic and object-relations stories could clearly account for this marriage and its problems, in terms, for example, of trying to replicate, or avoid replicating, the marriage with which you grew up. But if I were to offer these stories at this point, they would be my inventions, not theirs.

Where to begin? I ask John and Mary what they want to change about their life together. They say they want to put an end to the terrible fights they have been having and get back to something like their life together when they first decided to get married. Seen in Bateson's frame-

---

[7] If both are victims (as is often the case, since trauma victims may seek each other out as partners), the therapy is even more difficult than the marriage. When one partner's search for a replacement for the bad parent fails in the marriage, the disappointment can be made even greater by repeated efforts to correct that failure in the therapy. It is hard for the two to work on these problems face to face, and couple sessions often degenerate into mutual attacks, where each tries to locate the enemy, the author of the abuse, in the other. I approach this situation with great caution and often see them separately for long stretches of time.

[8] These made-up composites are typical of couples in my New York City practice.

[9] Gray (1994) is the latest version of the biological dimorphism myth, and is, of course, a best-seller.

work, some of these quarrels are symmetrical contests about whose point of view will prevail in such matters as time, money, and childrearing; others are struggles over complementarity. I ask more about the second group, trying to get a chronological story of the changes in their feelings about the balance of caretaking.

When they first met, Mary as an officer in a charitable foundation, was surrounded by a group of women who had been working together for a long time. She hardly noticed how much these colleagues mattered in her life because she was searching for a "good man" — by which she meant someone with at least some of the attributes of her beloved father. Few of the self-centered young men she met even came close. John was a law student, doing well in his studies, and one thing Mary noticed about him was that he listened. He found her problems with the foundation and her relations with her mother's family interesting. He appreciated that she filled their time together with talk about these people. Especially, when they began having sex, he was grateful for her active initiative, her pleasure in talking about it. She was completely different from the more anxious women he was used to, and thus a great relief. And so, each having discovered someone who would take care of them in a way that seemed unique, they fell in love.

Marriage brought changes. John entered a firm, where the competition was very different from law school, and for the first time he faced the specter of failure. This was something he did not want to talk about, especially in view of Mary's increasingly anxious inquiries, which reminded him of his mother's way of poking into his life.

Mary dropped out of work to take care of their baby boy, and then discovered how lonely she was without her old office companions. Her cheerful initiative in sex disappeared with pregnancy and the baby, as did the flow of news from work that had made up so much of her conversation with John. For the first time, he did not resemble her sympathetic father at all.

As their apartment turned into a nursery for raising an alarmingly active toddler, something almost totally unexpected happened. John became severely critical of the way Mary took care of the house, the baby, and all the other things that fell to her now that he was working the long hours of a law associate. This was unexpected because, while living together before the baby arrived, they had both taken pleasure in having everything in the apartment look just right. John was a little alarmed to hear the tones of his distant, critical father now coming out of his own mouth — but not enough to be able to keep them to himself, when he came home late to find the place a mess, Mary exhausted on the couch, the baby waiting for a good-night story amid a ruin of toys, and supper an uncertain prospect. Mary was worried but immobilized about what she had learned, from John, to call "letting herself go," a kind of giving up in the face of all these overwhelming demands. They had terrible fights over this situation, and these fights were the immediate reason they found a marriage therapist.

Let's examine the possible causal explanations that fit some of these facts. John, by becoming the father of a boy, and at the same time, feeling isolated in the threatening world of work, has unconsciously entered the constellation of his own family of origin, and is turning his wife into his mother, opposite whom he plays his angry, critical father. Mary, her mourning for her father unfinished, responds to the stress and isolation of her new life as a mother with a depression, perhaps one that could be helped by medication. The couple, having entered marriage after a courtship that included no practice in sharing work, is overwhelmed by the sudden demands of childrearing, and by John's work, which exploits the family by assuming it has first call on his energies and loyalty. These psychodynamic, psychiatric, and sociological formulas might be useful at some point, but they are inert unless they are activated by being encountered in the process of other work.

I ask for details of these fights, since the fights are what they want to change. Mary has a psychologically sophisticated description: "My husband is just so full of anger, but he holds it in until he explodes at me over something completely trivial." I am wary of this last formulation — the hydraulic reservoir theory of anger — because I sense that I am being invited on an internal expedition. She is suggesting that if we take a journey upstream to the source of his anger, we will find a way in which he can "let it out." I know that if I accept her invitation, and her metaphor, I will be making him and his anger the problem. I file this away as an idea that might be useful later in another context, but for now I want to see if they can collaborate on the construction of something positive for both.

I tell them I assume that fighting, especially if it is under control, can be a beneficial part of marriage. What kind of fights would they like? Has it always been difficult for them to have good fights, or is this a recent development? Can they remember a conflict they thought was well done, one that resulted in something like a decision or a compromise?

The form of the questions makes fighting into a fact *external* to the individuals involved, and allows for seeing it as a skillful performance of a scene. It helps, in this work, to think of life as theater, as being performed in a series of scenes. If the scene is going badly, you can go out and come in again. Rehearsal often helps, and a discussion among the actors of presentation and choreography is often essential to the end result. The question about fights that resulted in something beneficial emphasizes the *effect* of the enactment of such scenes rather than the upstream *cause* ("He's so full of anger").

Fights, relationships, differences, and rituals are externalizations with consequences rather than motivational causes. Their consequences can be guessed at, even tried out in a practical way. The causes of trouble, on the other hand, are many, often unsearchable, and when couples debate causes or motives in an atmosphere of tension, the cause each prefers will be one that blames the other for the problem.

Getting away from blame is not a matter of accusing oneself instead of the other. Although the art of apology can provide a good turning point, it is possible to get away from blame on either side and think of the problem as one of stagecraft, of choreography. There are ways to construct a ritual of reconciliation and construction from the ashes of a fight. A start would be to regard the occurrence of anger as a valuable signal that identifies something important in the relationship that needs repair. It is a red flag and has no other meaning than "pay attention." Then, instead of the competitiveness of the fight, over the outcome of which no one has any control, we can organize a different kind of discussion, which will lead to a different result.[10]

I have two purposes in mind with these proposals. One, I want to help them increase their sense of flexible control over their fights. And two, I am interested in what other issues remain after that control is established.

Since John and Mary are interested in this way of looking at fights

---

[10] Harriet Goldhor Lerner describes a process like this in *The Dance of Anger* (Lerner, 1985), which I strongly recommend as a practical guide.

(not everybody is, but that's a different story[11]) our work continues with:

1.   An anthropological investigation of the natural history of fights. How and where do you prefer to have them? What happens if one of you goes out of the room? In the argument, what is the effect of an interruption or change of subject? How do you feel about threats, insults, and mindreading? Mary is especially good at mindreading, which infuriates John. How do you know when a fight is over, or at least is at a stage where it can be turned into something more useful? Do you prefer a period of disengagement before ending a fight? John sometimes needed a whole day.

2.   A look at possible endings for fights. Would you like to appeal to an authority for a decision? Your mother? The rabbi? How does that work in practice? I make it clear that my services as an authority are not available. I say I think they have the resources with which to reach decisions, but they may have to reinvent the form of their conflicts.

3.   A consideration of ritual. John and Mary agree that they are in favor of equality and rationality rather than authority, but don't know how to achieve it. I ask: What would be the effect of having a ritual, a celebration of equality, that would put them in a position to observe an outcome rather than enforce it? Suppose they ritually agree that he is right on Mondays, Wednesdays, and Fridays; she is right on Tuesdays, Thursdays, and Saturdays; and Sunday is a day of rest, in which they can share the interesting observations that they have made. On their off-days, they might notice that, even when the other is in charge of being right, nothing disastrous happens.

As the couple tries this out, some interesting reservations arise. They agree intellectually that fighting is necessary to delineate problems that

---

[11] People who have an intense commitment to their own version of "authenticity" in all their dealings dislike this way of thinking, especially when they have had an experience with psychoanalysis that has taught them that the only route to resolution is through strenuous introspection. For them, life as theater is not a way to go.

would otherwise remain hidden, but John begins to realize how afraid he is to go into conflicts with his eyes open. The anger in the household he grew up in was very toxic, and he felt safe from it only when he had enough blind righteousness to silence his opponent. Mary realizes how ill equipped she is for conflict because in her "ideal" growing up, conflict was completely invisible. These ideas appear in the midst of efforts at constructive change, and each partner begins to think of improving on the model of his or her parents as a personal goal.

This practice of ritual transmutation of a fight into a crisis of progress for the marriage can take years of work to achieve, and it is always in danger of being neglected. But like the rediscovery of sexual excitement, it is one of the great ritual artworks of the middle stages of marriage, the stages after the small children and the sustained romance have gone, when the children are at school and romance is limited to Sunday morning.

In the midst of some of these efforts to change the fights, it becomes obvious that some parts of the relationship do not fit the symmetrical model. They cannot be fitted into what Don Jackson famously called "the marital quid pro quo," which is a symmetrical notion, an idea of fair exchange. So as John and Mary make some progress with the elaboration of fights into problem-solving experiences, they encounter discoveries in the other area, the area of complementary imbalance.

They find that they are not similar in their need for care from each other. Mary needs much more listening than John does. In fact, she needs more listening and responsiveness than he finds it easy to provide. At some point in these heartfelt personal conversations, he feels too close and needs to come up for air — take a walk, sort the mail. Mary can tolerate more disorder and delay than John can, and is willing to neglect plants, laundry, and unbalanced checkbooks to an extent that outrages him. Mary needs time on the phone with her mother, which can only be evenings and weekends because her mother works.

John, for his part, wants Mary to participate in the social activities of his law firm, including big weekend parties, which she finds utterly stupid. They are not the same, she says, as his spending time with her friends and family, which he actually enjoys. John admits that it's not the same, it's not a matter of enjoyment — it's a *contribution* he is asking for. John is asking Mary to make a contribution to his career, which would ultimately benefit the family because he would be making more money. But they both recognize that it is impossible to balance contributions of this sort from Mary with a symmetrical quid pro quo from John. Certainly, Mary feels that she is already making a major contribution to the marriage by taking so much responsibility for the social side of it, the connections with family and friends.

One way of thinking about these impasses is to look for a new image of the marriage, different from the symmetrical image of trade, bargain, negotiation, or deal. There is another kind of economy, little discussed in our culture, that has been called the gift economy (Hyde, 1979). Philanthropists and artists often look at their work as rewarding when they do it in order to make a contribution rather than to secure payment in kind. Artists, in particular, think of their work as the exercise of a gift (in the sense of talent) and the bestowal of a gift (in the sense of a present), and the fulfillment of that side of themselves may remove their work from the trade economy. Indeed, in some cultures, art is ritual ornament and religious expression, in the realm of the sacred rather than the profane. To make a contribution, you do not have to be rich like a philanthropist or talented like an artist — all you need is someone to receive the contribution.

As John and Mary try thinking of their marriage as an art form rather than as a trading pit, they take an interest in the unresolvable differences of contribution. John tries to shield their life at home from the worst of the damage his work can inflict on it. He encourages Mary to go back to work part-time, and helps her get the apartment back in shape once a week instead of attacking her for letting it get into a mess. Mary learns to let John escape and then return to their conversations about the things that are on her mind, training herself not to feel abandoned, and to believe his assurances that he will come back with his full attention, which, with practice, he does.

Then comes the ultimate asymmetry. A few years after stopping therapy because they have made enough gains to go on, Mary has an affair with an older, married man at work, and the aftermath of this brings them back to me. I don't suggest that an affair is a fortunate way for these changes to occur. Indeed, it often has a fatally destructive effect. But somehow in this case, it clears away all the clutter and brought forward the question, "What are you able to give to the marriage, and what do you want it to give you?" (Lusterman, 1998)

After the initial shock, withdrawal, and recriminations, John finds he wants to listen to Mary in a way he has not before, because he wants to understand what she had been going through. John realizes, listening to the details of her disappointment in him, that she is expressing a desire for things that he wants as well. Some of these may be expressed sexually, but as he begins to look beyond the obvious sexual challenge of the affair, he discovers other opportunities for paying attention to her. Mary discovers, in the course of these long talks about disappointment, that she is disenchanted not only with John, but also with the man of the affair, and realizes that she has feelings locked up in her ideal memory of her father that she wants to reexamine in the light of experience. She talks to me about this in individual sessions. John begins to think of his marriage and his family as a resource he has taken for granted. He starts to look for other contributions he can make to it.

Together, they decide to make their marriage something external about which both of them are concerned, the way they are about their children. This is the spirit in which David Epston asks couples, "Now that we've heard from each of you, let's ask, 'What would love's point of view be?'" I know a couple with a little calligraphy on the wall that reads, "Be of Love a little more Careful than of Everything."[12] When Virginia Satir says, "Treat all differences as opportunities for growth," these are the issues she is talking about. "Difference" is an externalization of something that is separate from "you" and "me" but depends on the relationship between the two. So are "love" and "marriage." In that sense, what new things can you think of to do with the differences in your life besides fighting over them? The work of recovering from an affair is an ultimate example of one-sided forgiveness, in which something very different is required from each partner. But for both it can be, as Satir says, an opportunity for growth, because it shows the way to the next stage of growing up, of relinquishing and claiming.

§

The marriage of Fausto and Maria Vargas was not an easy case. It was different from that of John and Mary because it suffered from a marked imbalance in caretaking. Like John, Fausto indulged in the traditional men's preoccupation with work and its anxieties, but he was anxious about other things as well, and required considerable soothing and

---

[12] Sister Corita Kent, 1969, calligraphy reproduction.

attention when he brought these worries home. Maria worked overtime as the conservator of the relationship and the family. This could be seen in many ways, including the way in which she and I fell into a partnership in the couple sessions: I often felt I was helping her to help Fausto to change, to be less alert to danger, less dogmatic about how to avoid it. I asked if there had ever been a different kind of balance in the relationship. Maria said, "Yes, when we were first married, I learned assertiveness from him. I wish now he could learn sympathy from me." Fausto agreed in principle to practice sympathy and acceptance, but as soon as they left the office, he was back to his old preoccupations: his work, his struggles with the family in Argentina, his employees, all the things that were not exactly as they should be.

Fausto expected intense loyalty from himself and from others. If someone fell short in that department, he talked about "firing" that person. A business or personal misunderstanding, a slight, even another's indignation over Fausto's behavior, would prompt him to say that he never wanted to see that person again — and mean it. He told with some pride the story of discovering that a girl he liked in grade school had gone on an excursion with someone else. He told her with tense self-control that he would never speak to her again. This mastery of what Murray Bowen calls "the cutoff" was one of his greatest consolations. It had helped him to protect himself against the emotional storms of growing up: his father's tirades; his mother's dark, guilt-inducing depressions; and his crazily checkered pattern of failure and accomplishment at school. Like a bad business deal, he tried to write these things off simply as a loss and forget about them, clear them out of his sight.

In looking over my notes on working with the Vargas family, I am struck by how hard they worked on changing the climate of their family for Mercedes. Their conscientiousness and good humor, and their determination to make it work, had a real effect on her progress, and it inspired me to keep working on new strategies with them. But somehow, Fausto and Maria could not focus this attention to their own relationship. As Mercedes' life improved, we were increasingly aware of something malign that stood between Fausto and the world, as if he lived in a different house, a different neighborhood, from the others. He suspected conspiracies and collected evidence about them. He watched the comings and goings of neighbors. He wanted to control, punish, or avoid all traces of evil in the world. Maria patiently talked him through plans of getting even with business partners, of closing charge accounts. And then one day, at the end of a terrible exchange of calls from Argentina, his uncle, the head of the family, told him they had decided to reorganize the business without him. They would buy him out.

Fausto was badly shaken. He called Maria and the children together and told them they must promise never to speak to anyone in the rest of the family again, including his own brother and the cousins who lived in New York. They were outraged: this was their family! What about Christmas? Birthdays? Maria was very close to her sister-in-law, with whom she would prepare a feast for the whole family every Three Kings Day.

Fausto was depressed, and haunted, slept badly, lost weight, and finally consented at least to negotiations with the New York relatives, some of which took place in my office as the one place where everyone felt safe. A limited peace was worked out. Fausto had to think about a new a job in this country, unconnected with his home and family, something he had never imagined he would have to do. Thus, at the moment when Mercedes was becoming independent and getting ready to move out of the home, leaving him and Maria together as a couple for the first time in 30 years, Fausto became a casualty.

I had tried, over the years, to work on the marriage relationship, but this had always been a fitful effort between crises, and now here was another crisis. Exhausted, Maria agreed that we must once again postpone the marriage therapy that she had imagined would help them to get into this phase of their lives. They were stuck in a complementarity that did not yield to negotiation, and Fausto was unable to see his need for care as susceptible to anything but greater caution and alertness. He and I met from time to time, but I could not find a way of describing his problem so that he could work on it. Instead of psychotherapy, he prescribed for himself vigorous exercise and diet, and concentrated on the challenge of finding a job. I was content that he seemed to be succceeding in that.

§

Writing about these marriages leads me to reflect on my own experience and the ways in which marriage has been more therapeutic for me than the three analyses that I have had. Compared with the work I did with Mendelson when I was a resident, for example, marriage went a step further. Jerry Lewis (1997, 2000) draws on the vast data from the

Timberlawn Research Foundation and creates a persuasive description of marriage as therapy.

Mendelson described the problem as getting me out of hiding in the corner of my room where I had closed the door. That part of our work was successful. I got out. I went from retreat in my corner to vigorous involvement in a career at NIMH, Tremont, and the Family Service. What I didn't notice was that the cure for retreat was an opposite response, an obsession with work. The surrounding culture supported this, because no one criticizes a young psychiatrist for being seriously and intensely involved with his work or his patients.

No one, that is, except his wife. His young children and his other family learn to do without him. Actually, my mother did complain; she was part of our lives during the first 10 or 15 years of our marriage. But like my father, in spite of her complaints, I managed to hide out from her by finding her impossible to talk to. And at home, like John and Fausto, I used the cultural institution of career success for my own concealment.

Whenever I emerged from that preoccupation, it seemed to me that married life with Margaret abounded with intense engagement and diversion. In particular, to make our marriage as different as possible from that of my parents, there was plenty of serious talk in ours. But the strength of that determination to have a different marriage in that way blinded me to other dimensions of it. I didn't notice, although Margaret tried to point it out, that there was more to sharing life than serious and high-minded talk. That was another compulsively opposite response to the defined problem of my parents. In fact, what Margaret wanted from me beyond serious talk was rather similar to what my mother wanted, companionship, paying attention.

The work of being a therapist, too, was a specially camouflaged escape, a closed room of intense professional concentration where my role as the serious listener would be correct, not challenged. I little suspected the arrogance, or the shyness, of talking to people only about what is of the greatest importance. Therapy was a sort of narrow, ritual sociability where my work role was clear, and I didn't have to give away anything out of my private supply. Both public psychiatry and psychotherapy were a kind of structured sociability behind which I concealed and preserved my childhood privacy. Doing psychotherapy, I was "hiding in plain sight" — hiding from people in the midst of an intensely personal involvement with them, and being paid in money and praise.

Realization of the narrowness of this strategy came slowly, partly because Margaret challenged it, and partly because I learned another way from watching her. We are both shy people, for different reasons, but she is a generous, tireless adventurer in the construction of friendship. Slowly, I learned from watching her make friends and keep relationships going over the years. I also learned to watch the fights and crises we had with each other for evidence of my initiative, or the lack of it. I learned slowly to go back into the dangerous passages, looking for instruction.

It helped that at the same time, both Margaret and I — in our private practices — were guiding other couples through these dangerous straits. We were in a kind of invisible couples group, from which everyone benefited. And most important of all, it helped to look at marriage as unfinished work-in-progress, what Victor Turner would have called a lifelong liminality. The marriage contract is never finished or settled, is constantly renegotiated, one of the meanings of " 'til death do us part." And from time to time, I relaxed into some nonserious companionship, always surprised to find that that was the missing ingredient.

CHAPTER EIGHT
Thinking About Therapy
in a New Place

IN 1975, I LEFT THE BRONX STATE HOSPITAL to work at the New York State Psychiatric Institute. It was the end of a journey and the beginning of a new project, understanding the nature of psychotherapy, that I took up as I became responsible for teaching family therapy there.

I was 45 years old. What I left behind in the Bronx was the scene of our youthful adventures in social and community psychiatry, the Tremont Crisis Center, the Family Service, and all those perilous experiments that had been possible at Bronx State Hospital because Israel Zwerling sheltered us from the state bureaucracy and channeled resources in our direction. Now the money for social experiments was drying up (not only in New York, but everywhere), and Zwerling was not to become chairman of the psychiatry department. As he left for the chairmanship at Hahnemann University in Philadelphia, we who stayed behind, his merry band of outlaws, realized we had to look elsewhere for work. For me, it was a good time to look around and see what had been happening in the world.

I found a half-time teaching job at the Washington Heights Community Service, a part of the New York State Psychiatric Institute. The institute, one of the towers of Columbia-Presbyterian Hospital, was perched on a cliff above the Hudson River, with the George Washington Bridge leading to New Jersey on one side and the tenements of Harlem stretching away on the other. As a research center, the Psychiatric Institute was second in prestige only to the NIMH itself. From its beginning in 1896, it was funded by the state legislature as the first truly interdisciplinary psychiatric research institution in the world, with a range of divisions from anthropology to cell biology. Adolf Meyer, its second director for a short, but crucial, time in the early 1900s, had secured permanent state support by adding a training and record-keeping mission. Thus, in addition to research, the institute was to train psychiatrists and others in the treatment of the severe illnesses whose victims filled the state hospitals. It was also to keep useful statistics on the type and course of illnesses from which they suffered. This unique combination of functions was the beginning, in the United States, of government support for training and epidemiology to help the severely mentally ill.

When I got there in 1975, the Washington Heights Community Service was the only part of the Psychiatric Institute that was still carrying out the training part of Meyer's charter. The larger institute's program of biological research had succeeded splendidly over the 80 years, with illustrious discoveries in biochemistry, pharmacology, and genetics. But the training in treatment, apart from medication, had become, and remained, psychoanalytic. The building even housed the Columbia Psychoanalytic Institute on one of its main floors. The Psychiatric Institute had moved to Washington Heights in 1929, to become the psychiatry department of Columbia University, which meant that the state paid most of the salaries of the residents and faculty, but the only part of the institute that, in return, studied and taught the treatment of the state's patients was our service. We were responsible for the citizens suffering from severe mental illness, mostly black and Hispanic, who lived in west Harlem, Washington Heights, and Inwood at the northern tip of Manhattan.

My main job on the service was to train yet another generation of psychiatric residents, psychologists, and social workers in discharge planning, family therapy, and community support. I took heart at the thought that Adolf Meyer and his wife, Mary Brooks, the Chicago social worker who had gone forth from Manhattan State Hospital to visit the families of the inmates, might look down upon my sometimes discouraging struggles and smile. They might have appreciated the irony that the great public institution they had started on its course at the turn of the century could recruit candidates for training only by offering them the prospect of private psychoanalytic practice.

I was impressed as never before by the separation between public and private practice, as two different worlds, deeply divided — two different communities of membership and accountability. The Psychiatric Institute was a kind of twin peak, having a commanding promontory in each world: the Psychoanalytic Institute in private practice and the

Psychiatric Institute as the research and training headquarters of the public state hospital system. Being a half-time employee of the state institute, I had time left over for many hours of private practice in my own office. I shuttled every day between public work in the daytime and private work in the late afternoon and evening.

The two worlds have different regimes of accountability. As public practitioners, we are paid by the state or the city to be responsible for the people assigned to us. This responsibility to a population is an important part of our sense of who we are. When I worked in the Bronx at the state hospital, I was involved not only with families, but with churches and politicians, and with the lives of people working on the service under the state bureaucracy. All of us worked together for common purposes that defined us and made us proud.

In private practice, on the other hand, patients choose and hire their own therapist from the variety of soloists in the open marketplace. Private practice is ultimately based on a contract between two people, a patient and a professional hired by the hour. Even family therapy in private practice requires the backing of whoever controls the money. These simple and obvious facts generate two different worlds of responsibility.

The world of public practice is pragmatic and atheoretical because its conscience, its accountability, is ultimately anchored in public support. Sooner or later the people responsible for the program want to know how it is working. They want to hear about the success of this program as compared with that of the next city or state or country. Public systems that are not working are exposed in the press. Abusive scandals such as the one at Willowbrook Hospital for the mentally disabled, are the most famous (Rothman, 1984), but reporters cover public psychiatry meetings as well. Programs that are working have records supported by research, such as that which demonstrated that the Day Hospital, where I went in my first year of residency, worked as well as the locked ward for most patients. Public practice is ultimately accountable, through evaluation research, to the government agencies that pay for it.

I don't mean to suggest that, as a result, public practice works with scientific precision. Looking back on my experience with the bureaucracy, the politics, and the underfunded, neglected people who labor in the public system, I would be the last to suggest that public programs work well, even most of the time. But some are clearly working, and when they do, it is easy to see why.

One program that works is the community mental health service network in a residential part of Sydney, Australia, under the direction of Alan Rosen (Rosen, Miller, & Parker, 1989). Rosen, a psychiatrist, is the medical director and his wife, Vivienne Miller, directs both occupational therapy and the program's outcome research. The service provides emergency home visiting, sheltered work and job training, day programs, family therapy, group therapy — the whole gamut of social procedures that have been found to be effective in research studies worldwide. But what is special here is the level of accountability in the communication between this work and the world around it. The records kept by these teams of workers are designed to measure progress, document the need for funding from the government, evaluate changes and improvements, focus skills, and also produce statistics for reports in professional journals.

The journals where these reports appear are full of program descriptions and tables of numbers describing results. What little theorizing accompanies these results mainly serves to connect the descriptions. The administration of the service is eclectic. Rosen hires consultants, ranging from psychiatric and behavioral experts to narrative innovators, such as Michael White and David Epston. Public work is accountable to the population being served, and the theories or beliefs of the practitioners are of secondary importance.

The world of private practice in psychotherapy is accountable to a different membership. Its efficacy is largely unsubstantiated by research or public opinion. Instead of being assigned by the community, patients are referred by colleagues. As a private practitioner, I recommend and receive recommendations from a group of philosophical allies, old friends, people with whom I have worked as a teacher or student. This *referral system*, rarely written about and never systematically studied, is the lifeblood of the supporting culture of private practice. To get referrals, you have to be known in a network as a teacher or a fellow student, and to be so known, you generally have to be part of a *school*.

Psychoanalysis provides the most extreme example of school development. From the days of Freud's small circle in Vienna, the supporting culture for private psychotherapy has been the school, the group of founders and their disciples whose distinction is the brilliance or elegance of their theory — a theory they share in common. No one knows whether their cases do comparatively well or not. There was, and is, hardly any public accountability, and certainly no outcome research, nor can there be under the circumstances.[1] The school and its teachings flourish until a heretical group forms a counterschool, with a more philosophically current theory and practice. Private psychotherapy from Freud onward has been a succession of heresies marked off from the preceding school by schisms of philosophy, rifts large in rhetoric but of unknown practical consequences.

Within each school, the supply of students and patients is governed by connections between teachers and students. Most journals of private psychotherapy practice, and certainly of psychoanalysis, contain, in addition to the case studies you would expect to find, articles about philosophical and literary theory that not only strengthen the bonds between the writer and readers of the essay, also members of the school, but also raise the respectability of the school by connecting it to "higher" culture. Statistical studies of outcome are rare.[2]

§

I was the only family therapist at the Psychiatric Institute, so I began to get a trickle of referrals to my private practice, mostly for marital therapy, because no one knew anyone else to whom to send them. I had

---

[1] Outcome research requires what private practice doesn't have: access to the records of large numbers of patients, settled standards of treatment and outcome, influence on what happens in the treatment room, and an untreated or differently treated comparison group. The intrusion of managed care on private practice could have the benefit of producing a little research, but neither the practitioners nor the insurance companies have so far been interested.

[2] There is no way of knowing whether treatment of comparable cases is more effective in one system than in another. People who can afford to hire a private therapist often get better long-term individual therapy, if that is what they need, since a careful investigation of the referral system by a professional informant, with knowledge of the training provided by several schools, will sometimes produce a talented therapist. On the other hand, even the rich, who are in a position to pay and choose where they will, can be badly served in the treatment of some illnesses, since the school they are referred to may not be informed by relevant research or training. Sometimes the public system manages schizophrenia better, for example, because it has access to more of the necessary supports. But since the public system makes the class demotion that usually attends that illness too painfully obvious, rich families may prefer to keep their schizophrenic relatives in elegant, but ineffective, institutions rather than face that issue.

a school, in a sense, simply by virtue of being a teacher. But I had learned from my experience in the public sector that school formation, even though it is good for business, can be bad for the development of new ideas, so I tried to stay uncommitted.

It was awkward sometimes. I was honored one day by being asked to present some videotapes of my work with a family to Otto Kernberg, one of the leading experts on borderline personality disorder, and his group. They watched with polite interest, it seemed to me, and then Kernberg asked me what the theoretical ideas were upon which the work was based. I said honestly that I couldn't think of any worth mentioning, and the discussion ended shortly. I was not asked back.

Compared with the camaraderie of the Bronx, the atmosphere of the Psychiatric Institute had a chilliness that reminded me of some of the draughty corners of Harvard. I snuggled down in the Community Service and recruited Bronx people, building up a family therapy faculty slowly by filling places as they were vacated by Columbia people leaving for what they regarded as better jobs. While waiting for reinforcements, I had to think about how to present what in the Bronx had been self-evident — the social therapies of severe mental illness and the general practice of family therapy — to students and faculty at the institute whose practices had other priorities, either biological or psychoanalytic. The debates that resulted were sharp and searching: I had to back up my position.

When I was invited to give a course on social factors in psychiatry, I took some courses myself at the School of Public Health (another near-by peak in the public sector) and eventually got a master's degree in psychiatric epidemiology there.[3] I studied the statistical evidence that long-term family and community support is more important for improving the course of schizophrenia than the treatment of acute episodes with hospitalization and medication (Beels, 1981; Beels, Gutwirth, Berkely, & Struening, 1984).

Since my second job, apart from the Community Service, was teaching the general practice of family therapy to residents, I also had to think that through from a more critical standpoint. What is the intellectual

---

[3] I had met my public health mentor, Elmer Struening, when we were both in the Bronx. He and his welcoming staff in the Epidemiology of Mental Disorders Research Division gave me not only an education, but a home with a desk and a place to make a cup of tea. Another rescue from the hazards of migration.

ground on which family and couples work can be based, especially in private practice? If not analysis, what? How would a practice of a social therapy be integrated with medical psychiatry? For this project, what the Institute had to teach me was more important than my research in social support.

It was impossible for anyone at the Psychiatric Institute not to learn about diagnosis and treatment in modern biological psychiatry; that was the air we breathed. The Psychiatric Institute was the cradle of the third edition of the *Diagnostic and Statistical Manual*, or DSM-III, and it was also one of the many places where the medication of these more sharply defined diagnostic entities was being refined and tested.

As skeptical as many in the profession were about the validity of DSM-III, there was no denying the fact that medical psychiatry had changed in the years I had been in the Bronx. It was no longer a cloak for the narrowness of the psychoanalytic theorizing I had known in Rochester and at the Bronx residency. It was well on its way to becoming a scientifically responsible medical specialty. In the decade 1965–1975, it began to test its ideas more rigorously, both in scientifically controlled trials of treatment and in epidemiological-statistical surveys of the general population. The DSM-III itself was a provisional research document, designed to be tested and revised in subsequent editions. During the following decade, while I was at the Institute, the question of what is mental and emotional illness and what is treatment was constantly debated and confronted with new evidence.

This medical environment encouraged eclecticism. Doctors are accustomed to gathering methods of treatment together from different disciplines. If a patient has a stroke, the neurologist who makes the diagnosis and does the anticoagulation to prevent further blocking of the arteries of the brain doesn't hesitate to recommend, in addition, rehabilitation exercises, even though rehabilitation is taught by a different department that is interested in the brain's learning and retraining capacity rather than in its nerve-functioning aspect. Surgeons and internists, in spite of different interests, are supposed to know the advantages and disadvantages of each other's methods. They are, or should be, interested only in effectiveness: careful technique, and demonstrable results.

This medical model of eclectic treatment effectiveness was part of my own collection. Family therapy and community psychiatry were already the foundation. The other two pieces — hypnotherapy and the narrative art I had learned from White and Epston — were acquired at conferences and workshops far from the classrooms of the Psychiatric Institute. Since the Institute, like most official departments of psychiatry, had little to say about treatment that was not warmed-over psychoanalysis, the other family therapists and I looked for training elsewhere, in the invisible university of workshops and conferences.

The meetings where we learned the most were small week-long retreats. On the East Coast, Cape Cod in the summer is a favorite place for these courses in the invisible university. A collection of students — perhaps 20, from many different places — check into a hotel among the dunes or in Provincetown and spend most of each day watching videotapes and practicing exercises with each other under the tutelage of a few teachers, often only one. There is time to ask: What is really going on here? It is possible to concentrate, to ask questions, to carry uncertainty from day to day and perhaps resolve it in an unexpected conversation. The teaching goes on for only half a day, leaving plenty of time to talk and reflect. Back in my office in the city, I realize what a world of possibilities for my work I have found in those rooms by the sea. It is as if a blue Atlantic horizon runs through the places of these summer pilgrimages, to which my winter clients and I can somehow find a way out, no matter how trapped we seem to be. Cape Cod was where I first began to study the work of Michael White and David Epston.

Of all the teachers at these meetings, White and Epston brought the clearest picture of a new way of working. I don't mean to suggest that I chose them for my collection after surveying all the alternatives offered. Too many teachers, hundreds of them, were crying their wares in every corner of the therapy fair. In fact, I met these two partly by happy accident. But I do have a sense of why they worked out as models for me, what the nature of the attraction was. Although they distanced themselves in many ways from the "medical model" of psychiatry, in one important sense their ethic was the same as that of medicine. They devoted their ingenuity to the requirements of the specific clinical problem that was in front of them with the least possible concern about unified theory and, more important, with the greatest willingness to put whatever resources were available into solving the problem. And to keep the way clear for seeking out those resources, they do what they can to avoid becoming a school.

CHAPTER NINE
White and Epston:
The Background

MICHAEL WHITE AND DAVID EPSTON are both social workers, family therapists from Australia and New Zealand, frontiers almost completely untouched by the Freudian revolution. Perhaps for that reason, among many others, they were free to invent their own pragmatic approach to psychotherapy. Family therapy was, for them, not a reaction to another tradition, but a starting point. Having no analytic theory to discard, they did not replicate it unawares, as the American family therapists did. Instead, they were able to construct their work straight out of social work and anthropology.

David Epston majored in anthropology as an undergraduate at the University of Auckland. There he did an investigation of the kinship network of a Pakeha logger and his family, an effort to understand how features of their culture help these men manage the ups and downs of their lives.[1] He was later a lecturer in anthropology at Victoria University of Wellington, and then went to Australia, where he worked for the Department of Aboriginal Welfare in the Northern Territory. The beginning of his partnership with Michael White had something to do with this common interest. When they met at the First Australian Family Therapy Conference in Melbourne in 1980, White attended Epston's workshop and they began to discuss a collaboration. Hearing White's remarks at the final session of the conference, in which, among other

---

[1] *Pakeha* is the Maori word for "white" or "European." New Zealanders, in addition to acknowledging that the original people have their own language, actually try to use it for such distinctions as this one.

things, he recommended that anthropology be considered as a fundamental discipline of training for family therapists, Epston recalls, "It was one of those experiences in which you think someone is reading your mind."

Their interest in anthropology as a framework for thinking about therapy provides an answer to the question that traditionally trained therapists frequently ask: What is their model of the mind? The question presupposes something corresponding to the Freudian or Jungian, or even Jamesian, mind, with separate faculties or compartments, like the Freudian id, ego, and superego, or the conscious and unconscious. Certainly, if you asked them, White and Epston would say that they believe in the unconscious, but I think what would impress them, as it does the modern hypnotists, is how full the unconscious is of unstoried material, hidden resources and strengths, powers that have not been mobilized.

But in a sense, it is beside the point to ask about their model of the mind, since their method does not look to mental structure as the center of complexity and interest. Social structure is their guide. They are on an anthropological search in which the client explains to them the special culture of his life, kinship, language (Chamberlain, 1990). They take each person as a competent teller of his story, and having made that assumption, they say, "Tell me this story, let us see what we can make of it together." This is what is meant by collaborative, narrative therapy. The telling and hearing of the story are a collaboration on one of many versions, one of many ways that consultant and client can travel across the landscape of experience together, perhaps retracing their path again and again, ultimately looking for a preferred path to a preferred place.

Another parallel between anthropology and this work is the ethics of the collaboration: the sense, for the therapist, of being a guest, camping out in the other person's world, receiving what the person has to tell you as a gift that is very precious for your work and, particularly in modern ethnography, regarding the informant as the ultimate authority on the meaning of his or her culture and experience. From this standpoint, as an ethnographer or as a therapist-consultant (consultant is the word White and Epston prefer[2]), the worst mistakes you can make may arise from a preconceived set of meanings you have ready to impose on the narrative. It is hard to avoid these mistakes, but you can try. You can

---

[2] Lyman Wynne (Wynne, McDaniel, & Weber, 1986) has developed this idea into a philosophy of therapy.

constantly ask such questions as: What would you prefer? What are you hoping to accomplish here? Does this suit your sort of person? Is this what you intend for your future? If you were to tell this story to someone else, who would you especially want to hear it? Who would you like to catch up on these developments in your life?

These last two questions suggest a different audience for the story besides the therapist, a chosen membership for the storytelling as a group ritual. They assume that, even if the audience is imaginary, the teller will be strengthened by the inclusion of others. Like the *espiritista*, everyone can summon *protecciones*, figures from their tutelary past, as well as the present. This is the most fundamentally anthropological assumption of this work: that the meaning of the story is strengthened by the embeddedness of experience in local and historical culture. One reason the storytelling can be therapeutic is that the audience can be chosen for the strength for which one is searching.

As social workers, White and Epston are part of a group that makes up the majority of the world's family therapists. But a closer look at their particular time and place, their culture, tells more about their contribution to this story. They were both educated in a 1960s world of social activism similar to the one I knew in the Bronx of Israel Zwerling. That is one reason I feel connected to them. Michael White has spent most of his life in his home city of Adelaide, South Australia. He didn't start out to be a social worker. When he was in high school, he was given an aptitude test that showed, according to his adviser, that he ought to do something with his hands, so he became a draftsperson for an electrical engineering company. He soon realized that this work was completely wrong for him, that he was interested in people rather than machines, and so in 1967 he went to work as a clerk in the Department of Welfare, one of the few jobs that would allow him to earn a living and get a degree in social work at the same time. His clinical work at the beginning of his training was with long-term patients, both in and out of the hospital. His school was founded by Amy Wheaton, a community organizer from the time before psychotherapy became the main ambition of social workers. The first model of psychotherapy that he learned was the positive reflection approach of Carl Rogers (1995).

After he received his social-work degree, White moved to a psychiatry department in a children's hospital. Working with children led him to an early interest in family therapy, and without any formal training, he started to write about it. Publications in international family therapy journals encouraged him and a group of colleagues to found the *Australian and New Zealand Journal of Family Therapy*, of which he was the first editor. He joined with others, including his wife, Cheryl, in founding the Dulwich Center in Adelaide as a family therapy institute for teaching and treatment. Cheryl started the *Dulwich Centre Newsletter*, which has, over the years, become an international publication. It disseminates readings, not only about narrative and family therapy, but also about a great variety of intellectual and community concerns: ethnography, high school education, and prison reform, for example. The center's work ranges from family therapy practice to consulting with Aboriginal people's councils and helping them influence what they receive from the government in the way of health care, counseling, and treatment by the police. Finding that services in Adelaide for former mental hospital patients was inadequate, the center organized its own team of home-visit workers and financed it out of the income from teaching programs.

The social work profession of Australia and New Zealand was much more focused on community organizing and less on psychotherapy than in the United States (Lubove, 1965). Brian Stagoll, a cofounder, with White, of the *Australian and New Zealand Journal of Family Therapy*, said, "By 1908, both countries were a worker's paradise — especially New Zealand" (personal communication). He recalled that the first Labour prime minister of New Zealand in 1935 was an Australian radical, Michael Savage, whose government introduced systems of medical care and public pensions that were far in advance of the changes Roosevelt was bringing to the United States, and even more socialistic than most of the European experiments of that time. Thus social work in the two countries developed in an activist political environment. And in spite of devastating reversals for the welfare state, the tradition continues today in the determination of the rank and file of many health professions to keep up the coordination of social agencies with political action.

David Epston traveled a longer route through the social movements of the 1960s to family therapy. After graduating from college in Auckland in 1966, he returned to his native Canada to do a year of sociology at University of British Columbia. After anthropological work in New Zealand and Australia, he went to Scotland to do community development in Edinburgh, arriving just too late to work, as he had hoped, with the freelance community organizer, Saul Alinsky. He then went back to British Columbia to drop out into the hippie world of Vancouver. In 1973 he returned to New Zealand to work as a medical social worker, and then returned to the United Kingdom to earn a master's degree in social work at Warwick University. During a year's study in family therapy at the Family Institute at Cardiff, Wales, he and his wife, Ann, also a trainee at the Institute, watched videotapes of American family therapists and decided, as Epston recalls, "That's what we want to do when we grow up." It was also at Cardiff that Epston got his first training in hypnosis from a surgeon who consulted at the Institute.

Upon returning to New Zealand in 1977, Epston had his first experience in working with children and families. He found that the traditional methods taught in official schools and hospitals were alien to his spirit, and that, more important, they alienated families and patients. The procedures of admitting patients to clinics, and, in particular, to psychiatric hospitals, reminded Epston of what one anthropologist would call "rituals of degradation" (Garfinkel, 1984). Epston searched his experience for other, more welcoming types of rituals on which patienthood could be modeled, and Turner's ideas of liminality and *communitas* came to mind. As his reputation has spread, many of Epston's consultations are in child psychiatry and hospital settings dealing with life-threatening conditions such as childhood diabetes, asthma, and anorexia.

§

In reviewing these careers, I am reminded that one thing that all of us in the psychotherapy professions have in common is our training in the public sector. The public system of hospitals, clinics, and other agencies of care for patients the government defines as most in need is the training ground where we all begin.

Family therapy and narrative therapy both show signs of the influence of the public training ground. They import into private practice, on a small scale, at the level of the family, some of the ethic of "public" accountability — the public in this case being the family and its environment — and some of the social support that can exist in public practice. Family therapists pay attention to the larger social and economic environment of the family, and even try actively to do something about it, working with schools and employers. They tend to be more open to the world around the patient, and to take into account class, ethnicity, and gender as factors in the problem and its solution. The conferences and journals of family therapy are full of discussions of those social factors. There are research reports and statistical evaluations of programs designed to treat particular problems.[3] Narrative therapy, the kind I am talking about,[4] which is derived largely from the family therapy movement, is based on "accountability" and "collaboration" as basic guides in the construction of the client's narrative.

But as it comes into contact with the private practice system, whether through the marketing of books and conferences or the marketing of one's self as a teacher and therapist, narrative therapy proves to be susceptible to school formation. I found myself in the middle of it a few years ago at a meeting where White and Epston, together with a large group of American colleagues, were giving demonstrations of their work. It was the 1993 Second Therapeutic Conversations Conference in Reston, Virginia. Our name tags simply listed our names and cities of residence; mine said, "New York, N.Y." under my name. These egalitarian therapists were looking for another way to organize themselves aside from university appointments or professorships, or titles like M.D., Ph.D., or M.S.W. Part of the stir at the conference was about other definitions and labels: we were still calling what we were doing "conversation" because we didn't know what else to call it. I studied the program. We were to have a talk by Kenneth Gergen about the connection between our kind of therapy and the literary and philosophical movements of postmodernism, definitely a sign of school forming.

§

This conference was a sequel to the First Therapeutic Conversations Conference, held two years earlier in Tulsa. That first conference had been quickly transcribed into a book entitled *Therapeutic Conversations,* which contained dialogues among American, Canadian, and other teachers of family therapy, brief therapy, solution-focused therapy, and

---

[3] Family therapy has developed its own kind of research, called qualitative research, which looks very like detailed anthropological analysis of social interaction.

[4] There is another whole narrative therapy movement within psychoanalysis that sees itself as deriving more from literary theory than from social pragmatism (Spence, 1982; see also Chapter 12).

hypnotherapy. These were all "our" kind of therapists, but we were still feeling insufficiently defined. Who were we? What label should we use for our approach? Here at this second meeting, the search for identity continued in several workshops and informal discussions.

The word "conversation" helped to distinguish us from the "treatment" people. We wanted to emphasize that we were not "modernist" therapists, coming on as if we knew something the customers didn't, but rather postmodernist, deferential, open to discussion. But if therapy was not to be "treatment" by an "expert," a relationship we felt had too much imbalance of power, then what kind of an exchange was it?

The name *conversational therapy* suggested an approach more level than the tilted playing field of conventional therapy, but, on the other hand, it also suggested something casual, not serious. Why pay someone for something that is only a conversation?

What about *collaborative therapy*? That did suggest that something is being worked on, constructed, and it emphasized the essential contribution of both parties. But it didn't say much about what was going on. Constructionist therapy? That certainly sounded like an academic distinction, and indeed many papers had been devoted to the difference between deconstruction, construct*iv*ism, and social construc*tion*ism, each a different way of constructing narratives. But *construction* might suggest that we are making up the client's world out of whole cloth.

Narrative therapy? This name answered the question of what was being constructed. It had a satisfyingly literary connotation, connecting the work with deconstruction and postmodernism in art criticism. But perhaps too much so: Was one narrative as good as another?

What about *consultation therapy*? This term came from the medical vocabulary, but had less of a disinfectant odor about it than *treatment*. A consultation can go two ways, like a conversation. As White has pointed out, we can "consult with our consultants" to check with them on how we are helping them.

I overheard a discussion among a group of journal editors who sounded as though they were beginning to favor *collaborative*. Sure enough, a month after the Reston conference, I got a letter asking me if I wanted to contribute to a new journal called *Collaborative Therapy*.

This proliferation of labels and debates about "what to call it" may be more pronounced in the United States, like the proliferation of brand names in merchandising. If we respond to the uncertainty of our work by founding a school, giving it a name, and starting a journal, it may be an effort to attach ourselves to a less uncertain and less lonely way of making a living in the private sector.

White and Epston described their attitude toward school formation in 1992.[5]

> So far, at least, our work seems to have defied any consistent classification. Although others have presented us with many simple and apparently conclusive descriptions of it, most of these descriptions have been widely disparate, and none of them have been wholly satisfying to us.
>
> We have been steadfast in our refusal to name our work in any consistent manner. We do not identify with any particular "school" of family therapy, and are strongly opposed to the idea of our own contribution being named as a school. We believe that such a naming would only subtract from our freedom to further explore various ideas and practices, and that it would make it difficult for others to recognize their own unique contributions to developments in this work, which we regard to be an "open book" We are drawing attention to the fact that one of the aspects associated with this work that is of central importance to us is the spirit of adventure. Most of the "discoveries" that have played a significant part in the development of our practices have been made after the fact (in response to unique outcomes in our work with families) with theoretical considerations assisting us to explore and to extend the limits of these practices.[6]

Seven years later, after most of the writers and reviewers had agreed to call the new movement narrative therapy, the Dulwich Centre put on its first international conference, titled "Adelaide '99, Narrative Therapy and Community Work Conference," reminding us that work in the community was part of its definition of this field.

By turning away from schools and their theories, and by constantly returning to the alliance with the families and their experience, White

---

[5] In the introduction to *Experience, Contradiction, Narrative, Imagination* (1992).
[6] See footnote 5, pp. 8–9.

and Epston have fashioned a kind of narrative therapy that is concerned not only with the telling of stories, the *language* of the narrative,[7] but also with the purposes of whatever group is available to underwrite the stories' future development — the family, other sufferers, the "re-membering" of alliance with figures from the past — and any other experiences of solidarity with others that might provide support for their struggle. One of the things you will notice in the examples of their work in the next chapter is their consistent curiosity about how memberships and partnerships have affected the people who consult them.

The other point that comes out of White and Epston's quotation is the voice of the partnership, the "we." Especially in the early years of White and Epston's work together, the essential membership was their partnership with each other. This made it possible to keep from forming a school and to lower their profile, hand over initiative to others, and avoid the claim of invention.There is, for me, something very Australian about this avoidance of the limelight. Its negative sense is expressed in the aphorism that "tall poppies are the first to be cut down." But I am attracted to the positive side, the impulse toward the equality of workmates who are just getting on with the job, and it seems familiar after spending time in Australia.

Stagoll writes about this atmosphere in a summary of the history of the Australian family and its connection to family therapy (Stagoll, 1995, pp. 8–10):

> It was a male dominated frontier society with few women around. In the lonely bush, against overpowering elements, a character style developed: skeptical, practical, fatalistic yet somehow optimistic. Ideas of democracy, egalitarianism and "the fair go" were shaped (at least for White men) in the shadow of British Imperialism.
>
> Then from the 1840s a "typical" Australian family emerged, as the "civilising" element of women, "God's police," started to arrive. The Colonial family was described as "born modern." It was nuclear from the start, a breakaway from the large family networks of the Old World. Husband and wife shared alone the

---

[7] Language is the theoretical focus of some of the American schools of narrative therapy; for example, Anderson & Goolishian (1988).

tasks of building family life, basing this on a rigid separation of roles. Women controlled the private, domestic spaces within, while outside the family the texture of public life remained very strongly masculine. Nineteenth century observers commented on the solidarity and inclusiveness of the Australian family unit, invested in home ownership, child focus, and intense domestic engagement by women.

But by the 1970s the "naturalness" of the "typical" Australian family was under question. More women were working outside the home, families were smaller, divorces were increasing, and the culture was much less homogeneous. The fiction of "normal" could no longer be maintained. The rise of Family Therapy coincides with these changes. A new set of professional definitions and solutions for the problems of family life was called for. Family therapy did not come out of nothing, but was both a symptom of and answer to new doubts and demands, surfacing in Australian family life in the 1970s. Family therapy with its emphasis on outer space, optimism and newness, and its techniques for rapid engagement and problem-solving, found fertile ground in Australia. It fitted in only too well. The risk was that by offering quick relief and readjustments to families, the sociocultural bases of family life in Australia were not questioned, and gender stereotypes and rigid roles were maintained.

The women whose role had been to preserve the family found the social work profession a natural place to labor for fairness and justice, and one of them, Margaret Topham, went to study with Don Jackson at the Mental Research Institute in Palo Alto in the early 1960s. She was the real grandmother of family therapy in Australia.

David Epston (personal communication) says[8]:

Family therapy in Australia and New Zealand was really developed by social workers. The social work profession was

---

[8] As in America, the psychiatrists who were part of the organization of family therapy in its early days in Australia were influential and tenacious, but they did not reproduce. They did not train enough of their discipline to influence the profession in the present.

different from the others. The psychologists and the doctors don't look any different to me from the way they are in the States, except that psychoanalysis had no impact in New Zealand and very little in Australia. But the family therapists were social workers and social work was dominated by women. The feminist critique of therapeutic practices came into our work early and it hit very hard. I still remember Kerrie James giving the plenary address at the 1985 National Australian Family Therapy Conference in Canberra. It was entitled, "Breaking the Bonds of Gender". That was a watershed event in the history of family therapy in our two countries. The feminist critique was taken seriously and has shaped much of the family therapy for the next decade. And if you add that to the working assumptions that come from delivering services in a welfare state, you can see how, for us, fairness and justice would be a natural basis for doing therapy as a social worker.

Following some of the developments in the feminist critique of family therapy, we can hear also the voice of Michel Foucault (see Chapter 4 for my debt to him). The Foucault of White and Epston is a much more constructive critic than the bad boy of modern philosophy described by Richard Rorty. In particular, narrative therapists respond to the attention Foucault pays to the "least heard voices" in the social discussion.

For a long time in the United States, the least heard voices in the development of family therapy were those of the women social workers who were doing it. American social workers have justly resented the tendency, in American histories of family therapy, to ignore the fact that they were doing the work of seeing families together long before it acquired its status as a school. But since the early school founders of American family therapy were mostly male psychiatrists,[9] they brought with them a number of the assumptions of midcentury social science about the "natural" relations between the sexes (see Chapter 7). Some of these assumptions were very conservative, however revolutionary the practice of family therapy was by comparison with what went before.

---

[9] Of course, the great exception to patriarchy among the founders of American family therapy was Virginia Satir, the only woman and the only social worker in that first rank.

A number of sexist assumptions about the role of wives and mothers in the family tended to show up in the early work. The women in the family therapy profession, by far the majority of those on the front line, could see the damaging effect of ideas such as those of Talcott Parsons: that men are naturally "executive" whereas women are just as naturally "expressive," and that those two role divisions are essential to the smooth functioning of both families and organizations. Such ideas did not help to solve the problems women actually faced in their lives, where the realities of divorce, single parenthood, low pay, and home management presented grave challenges to their executive resourcefulness.

In the hands of the male school founders of family therapy, even the apparently progressive idea of "equality" between the sexes led to a curious blindness to the power consequences of gender. As Virginia Goldner (1985) wrote, observable differences in power atributable to gender were covered over by the founders' greater interest in the power of the older generation over the younger. Thus, a way of treating the mother and father as similar because they were equal in the exercise of that power ignored the way in which the *culture* reinforced very real power differences between men and women, husbands and wives.

The first American book that put this critique together was written by Maryanne Walters, Betty Carter, Peggy Papp, and Olga Silverstein (1988), students of three men who were the founders of different contending schools (Ackerman, Minuchin, and Bowen). They got together and studied the growing literature of feminism in psychotherapy. Looking at their experience with families from the point of view of the women and from their own experiences as women, they worked out a coherent group of questions to ask and approaches to try in the construction of a feminist family therapy. Putting aside their school differences, they found, like White and Epston, that paying attention to the productivity of their collaboration, rather than the ownership of the ideas, produced something new. As Foucault would say, they gave expression to what up to then had been an official taboo, a subjugated knowledge.

One of the most direct effects of the feminist critique was on the approach to family violence. Here the systems thinking of conventional family intervention had led, at best, to a muddle and, at worst, to the iatrogenic perpetuation of the violence. Assuming that the system of interaction that ended in a husband's hitting a wife was a runaway in a Batesonian system, a failure of mutual regulation, conventional family therapy tried to readjust the mutual regulation forces by doing couples therapy. This meant that both husband and wife had equal responsibility for the outcome. Feminist clinicians who were running programs for battered wives pointed out that because of real differences between men and women, this approach just didn't work. Couples therapy prolonged the violence. The responsibility for hitting lies not with the system, it lies with the hitter, from whom the wife may have to be protected if she cannot protect herself.

The Foucauldian analysis does not stop there, however. Now that the least heard voices of the women in the battered-wife scene have been attended to, and the power imbalance rectified by bringing their point of view forward, it is time to look again for marginalized bits of experience. Virginia Goldner and Gillian Walker have succeeded in identifying a subgroup of couples with whom, once violence is interdicted in this way, it is helpful to explore an unnoticed side of the man's experience (Goldner, Penn, Sheinberg, & Walker, 1990). In addition to the impulse for power and control, he may also experience, just in the moment of her challenging him, something in his own experience of trauma. A look at his inner thoughts at that point may reveal the boy in the man, a boy who suffered something like what he is about to inflict. In some cases, he may have an impossibly ideal image of the husband's responsibility for this family that comes out of his experience of having been solely — and impossibly — responsible for the one in which he grew up. Examining this problem in couples therapy can be the basis for his responsible reintegration into this family on nonviolent terms. So in a carefully discriminated subgroup, listening to the marginalized voice of the perpetrator of the violence, especially to a neglected aspect of his experience, gives this clinical adventure in couples therapy a unique outcome.

Another turning of the Foucauldian gaze into an unexpected corner of this scene is Michael White's (1992) work on men's culture. He has developed a group of self-examination exercises for violent men, whose purpose is to help these men think about the aspects of men's behavior and experience that lead to the subjugation of women, and in the worst cases, to violence. The exercises help them actively to search their experience for the unrecognized "taken-for-granted thinking" about the nature of masculinity that leads to gender injustice, and to actively imagine alternatives or exceptions to these experiences.

Sometimes, for example, White suggests to such a man, "Imagine that we have just taken a prisoner or a hostage. What are the techniques we might employ to make it clear that our prisoner had better give in to our control? How would we act?" The parallel between subduing prisoners and keeping women in line begins to dawn on the man, who never thought of himself as having such an effect, except as a consequence of what he regards as the "natural" ways in which men and women are different.

White then asks the man to try to recall times in his life when he was not under the influence of these ideas about men's "natural" behavior — times when he was aware that men did not always behave in "manly" ways. Does he remember feeling a little uncomfortable or out of sorts with that experience? A series of questions leads from these exceptional experiences to others, such as memories of having known other men whose behavior went against the grain of men's culture, or times when taking an unconventional stand might have given him an inkling of a different way of defining himself as a man. Questions like these, in an atmosphere of shared reminiscence, lead to a breakdown in the conventional, dominant narrative of the man's life, and thence to a picture of how, as the banished perpetrator of violence, he might seek to reenter the family on different terms in his own eyes.

But what about the others' view of him? How could his wife, for example, believe that in such a reentry she could be safe from further violence? Here the question of membership in the narrative becomes crucial. Together, White and the husband have discovered that an essential social condition for the violence was secrecy, the violence not being known outside the family. They invite the other members of the family to organize "escape from secrecy" meetings (White, 1992). A committee of family members, friends, and neighbors recruited by the wife and children agrees to meet periodically to review the family's success in overcoming the threat of violence. This committee and its meetings are the audience support, the membership, necessary for such a reentry to be successful. It is the recruitment of a small society to which the man can be accountable. This kind of attention, not only to the changed narrative, but also to the membership needed to support it, appears again when we look at White and Epston's recruitment of support for the struggle with encopresis, anorexia, and schizophrenia.

CHAPTER TEN
White and Epston: The Work

THIS CHAPTER IS A PICTURE — a snapshot of a moving vehicle — that shows the work of White and Epston at the time I was learning the most from them, in some cases years ago. They have moved on. Indeed, their most distinguishing characteristic is that they are always moving, escaping characterization and definition.

When Michael White was a social worker beginning to see families in a clinic for children's problems, he encountered a number of cases of encopresis. Encopresis is a child's loss of control over his (usually his, not her) bowel movements, long after toilet-training age, usually in the grade-school years. White conscientiously explored the literature on the subject and learned that behavioral psychologists often succeeded in helping children to gain control over encopresis by using a behavioral program of rewarding success, but that ultimately these programs had to be continued and carried out by parents, especially mothers. Relapse was frequent because the mothers and children often found it difficult to keep up the treatment regimen that the psychologist had established. This relapse was called "noncooperation and noncompliance" in the behavioral literature. The psychodynamic literature took a darker view, as White (1989) wrote:

> tracing the problem to inadequacy and negative intent on behalf of mothers. Over-controlling, intrusive and ambivalent mothers are believed to be the predominant "root cause" of the problem, the "encopretic symptom often reflects the child's rebellion against the mother's nagging and excessive preoccupation with his bowel function." This sort of explanation leads to specific clinical practices that usually include attempts to give such

mothers insight into their own feelings and behavior that are so destructive to their children. (p. 116)

Describing his attempts to apply these ideas to his own work, White wrote:

The psychodynamic explanation of encopresis left me rather puzzled. The encopretic children and their families who were coming for treatment did not seem to fit this explanation. I was unable to find a single case that was caused by an ambivalent or intrusive mother. I naturally assumed that the children I was seeing could not be diagnosed encopretic. This led to the development of a new diagnosis of "pseudo-encopresis." Pseudo-encopresis can be diagnosed if the child presents as a chronic soiler and where this soiling has persisted despite various attempted solutions, but is not caused by ambivalent or intrusive mothers. For years now, I have tirelessly but unsuccessfully searched for cases of "real" encopresis to compare with the sample I have treated. Therefore, the approach outlined in this paper has only been applied to a biased sample. This sample is one in which the parents of the encopretic children were experiencing defeat, helplessness, impotence, hopelessness, despair and frustration. They were becoming increasingly distant from their child [and the children] were experiencing increasing domination by their symptoms. They felt out of control, impotent, despairing, and cut off from their parents.

The starting point of White's approach to encopresis was to rewrite the story, so that it is not about mother blaming and guilt inducing, but about helping the family to find its story of domination, frustration, and alienation caused by the problem.

In all the examples to follow, there are three different stages of work. First, the *problem narrative* is recast. The pathological narrative is told and heard, and then recast as an *affliction* of the person/group/family, by reviewing the *effects* of the problem on them rather than the *causes* of the problem. Second, *alternatives* are discovered: experience is re-searched to find *exceptional* instances of partial triumph over the affliction. Using these instances, a different story of effective action, with techniques, alliances,

opportunities, and plans, can be built. And finally, *support* is recruited —
the plan of action is consolidated by convening or imagining a group.
This group could be the family, or the family plus the community, or
members of the community without the family, if that is preferred, to
carry the life journey forward. The psychology of pragmatism, and the
ideas of G. H. Mead about the dependence of psychology on intentions,
and on the organization of the immediately surrounding society, rever-
berate deeply in this plan (Chapter 4).

In White's work with encopresis, the first step, recasting the problem
narrative, is not always easy. Family members often come in with theories already prepared, which suggest a psychodynamic or interpersonal
purpose behind the symptom, such as an expression of family conflict.
These members have to be invited into a more externalizing story, so
that all the family members are on the same side fighting against their ad-
versary. White (1959) gives an example:

> Mr. and Mrs. Smith believed that their son Jason, since he
> never soiled at school but always did on the way home, in-
> tended to distress them with his symptoms. In order to chal-
> lenge this idea, I suggested that it made sense that Jason's soiling
> occurred when he reached the relative security of his home.
> There was evidence that Jason spent his energy by fighting
> against the soiling all day at school, and only let his guard down
> and relaxed in the vicinity of his home. Under the circum-
> stances that he was not wholly in charge of his soiling, it would
> not be reasonable to think that he could have successfully main-
> tained his guard after his energy was spent. (p. 118)

But the essential moves in the approach do not depend on the therapist's bringing out his or her own interpretation. They begin with an exploration of the family's experience with the symptom or the problem.
The externalizing question is, "What has been the effect of the problem
on your lives and on your relationships?" The story of its dominating
their lives and alienating their sense of ease with one another emerges as
they respond to the questions. The soiling becomes something external.
It acquires a character, a presence, as the family members tell their stories
of how it has made them feel, how it has altered their lives.

The second phase, discovering alternatives, begins with the therapist's asking a series of questions designed to bring out the fact that the

domination of the problem has not been total, that at times the child has successfully resisted the soiling, made it to the toilet on time. "What made that possible?" the therapist wants to know. "What is the effect of those successful occasions on your opinion of how strong the problem is, on its ability to get the better of you?" White calls this phase of the work "picking out the sparkling exceptions to the dominant story, the problem-saturated account."

To further externalize the enemy, it is given a name. Consultation with one family, for example, came up with the name of "sneaky poo." Its character as a devious opponent is developed: we discover that it is full of guile and nasty surprises. Finally, in the third stage, allies in the fight are recruited. The child is asked to nominate some helpers with whom he can discuss his struggles. (Parents are usually the first choice.) Some imaginary supporters, such as an internal tiger, are recruited, and a plan is made to organize these resources against the attack of the sneaky poo. Time trials are held for running between frequent places of attack and the toilet. The bathroom is explored for design features that might make a difference: light, decoration, a step for the feet, pictures of tigers, tiger costumes. Parents and child work together on these ways of highlighting the possibility of victory over the family's common enemy. The therapist is available by phone to cheer the first successes, as well as to hear about any failures that show the sneaky poo to be a stronger and trickier opponent than anyone suspected. Renewed efforts may require the recruitment of an additional tiger, or consultation with a small colleague of White's named Rupert Bear, who is able to make home visits and is on call at any time if needed. The enterprise is not only a welcome relief for the family but more than a little amusing and sometimes "outrageous clean fun."

§

Encopresis is a distressing, but often manageable, problem of childhood. At the other end of the spectrum, anorexia can be a life-threatening problem in adult life. The following transcript is of Epston talking to Marian, a woman near death from the starvation of anorexia.[1]

---

[1] Provided, with the patient's permission, by David Epston. The names have been changed.

Notice that the three stages of the approach (externalization, alternative, and support) appear in many ways throughout this interview. The condition, anorexia, is externalized as a personal enemy, Anorexia. In dealing with this enemy, a sense of critical danger is carefully balanced by an awareness of adequate response. As in any good war, the enemy is deprived of all moral standing: it is a trickster, a murderer, a taker of unfair advantage, a violator of the rules. The struggle is undertaken with a band of veterans as companion fighters, and is on behalf not only of the self, but also of other future fellow sufferers who will learn from the protagonist as she has learned from her comrades.

Epston is careful to work from Marian's own experience and judgment, and from that of the other veterans, and avoids her dependent search for his authority. When she says, "Is that right?" he says, "I don't know, what do you think?" He continually urges her to search her experience for contradictions and exceptions to the simplifications that her enemy is proposing to her.

Marian's cousin, Beth, who has also suffered from anorexia, and Beth's partner, Richard, with whom she is living, are also present at the interview.

RICHARD: She's just been to the doctor, the GP.

EPSTON: Do you want to fill me in on that? Did anything come out of that?

RICHARD: Significant for our conversation, yeah. Just about her physical condition, and how close she is to dying and all that. But she still, like, still feels that she feels fine and Dr. Jones was trying to explain to her —

MARIAN: But I do feel fine.

EPSTON: Yeah.

RICHARD: But what I'm saying is that —

EPSTON: Yeah, but can I just ask you why you think it is that Anorexia tricks people into going to their death thinking that they're feeling fine? Why do you think that is? What purpose would it have in getting you to go to your death smiling? Most people go to their death upset or opposing it, especially when they're being murdered, right?

MARIAN: Yeah.

EPSTON: I've wondered about this, and you've probably wondered about it. Probably it confuses all of us right now how anyone could be on death row, and — How is anorexia telling you that you're feeling good, when in fact, it could kill you at any moment?

MARIAN: Well, I've got energy. I just —

EPSTON: No, no — no, no. How's Anorexia fooling you into that? That you're on death row, right? Everyone knows it except you, okay? Although you know it sometimes when you take our word for it.

MARIAN: Well, if I take your word for it, then I'm there, yeah.

EPSTON: So, if you didn't take our word for it, then it would kill you. It would have killed you. It would have murdered you by now, if you didn't take our word for it. You'd be dead by now.

MARIAN: Yeah.

BETH: Yeah. We should actually tape this.

EPSTON: It is being taped.

BETH: Yeah, good. Because this is something that she constantly says.

EPSTON: This is actually very important, to undo the ruse. This is a lethal trick. How do you trick a person into their murder?

§

EPSTON: If it weren't for these people [referring to Richard and Beth], you'd be dead. I don't know how you'd imagine that, whether you'd be cremated or under the ground. Can you explain to us, and I'd want to ask you to remember that you're not only speaking to us, you're speaking to other generations of women who will come after you, and whose lives you may save. It may sound like a trivial thing to you, but you could save not only your own life but many other people's lives. One purpose of this tape is that it may be for you, but at some time you may allow other people to see it so they don't have to die, okay? I think you have to understand its motives, its purposes, why it would hurt a person to

make them think they were happy to die with an ano-
rexic smile on their face.

§

MARIAN:	I've got energy, I'm —
BETH:	You don't have energy, though.
EPSTON:	How does it do this?
BETH:	Because you can't walk to the letterbox, and you tried to play bowls last night, and you couldn't move your body to play bowls. You don't have energy.
MARIAN:	I couldn't move freely.
BETH:	You couldn't move really at all.
MARIAN:	But I feel really energetic.

§

Epston asks her to remember that some months earlier she would
have asked for help and gone to the hospital, and he again asks how
Anorexia is tricking her.

MARIAN:	By telling you you're fat when you are thin.
EPSTON:	Okay, okay.
MARIAN:	Is that right?
EPSTON:	I don't know. What do you think? Tell me; tell us. What is it telling you? It's telling you you are fat when you are thin?
MARIAN:	Yeah.
EPSTON:	Yeah, is it telling you that right now?
MARIAN:	No. I do — No, I am too thin.
EPSTON:	You know that?
MARIAN:	Yeah, because that's what everyone tells me.
EPSTON:	Yeah, okay. So that's Anorexia telling you you're too fat, and other people telling you you're too thin?
MARIAN:	Yeah.
EPSTON:	Right. Who are you believing? Who cares about you most?
MARIAN:	Them [nodding toward Beth and Richard].

EPSTON:	Do you think Anorexia loves you?
MARIAN:	No, it's killing me now.
EPSTON:	When did you realize it was killing you? (Marian says she began to realize it when she went into the hospital the last time in order to stop exercising.)
EPSTON:	How were you able, how did you have the courage to play that trick on Anorexia, to go into the hospital?
MARIAN:	Because I, Marian, knew what was best for me.
EPSTON:	I see. And how did Marian, the Marian that I know and talk to at times, how did that Marian know what was good for her? How did you know it? Because Anorexia tells you that death is good for you, I guess.
MARIAN:	I fought back.

Marian then got very involved in a description of a number of ways in which she had fought anorexia, what the enemy's countermoves were, how she had borrowed tactics from audiotapes of the experiences of other women's struggles with anorexia. She and Epston made up a list of things that were on the side of anorexia: fear and hate, feebleness, weakness, murder, and obsessive and compelling rituals; and on the side of anti-anorexia, fun, creation, vitality, acceptance of self and others, and strength, both moral and physical.

Marian then got into a discussion of whether people blame her or are angry at her because "I did this to myself — it is my fault." Epston said, "Now if you're going to blame yourself, I want you to blame Beth that she's caused her problem." A discussion of the problem of blame led Beth and Marian to talking about mistaken approaches they thought other counselors and therapists had made in talking to them about anorexia: putting blame on them, making them feel bad or responsible for the way they had upset other people, getting angry, telling them, "You got yourself into this, now you have to get yourself out." By contrast, they recalled the ways in which members of the Anti-Anorexia League, the group of women veterans of the condition, had spoken to them, either directly or on tape. Marian said, "They just reminded me of all the things that I could do for myself and the things that I was missing by being this way, and the sooner I got there, the better. They reinforced Marian as a person, whereas I had been going to the counselors who put the blame on me."

They went on to talk about ways of using signs of being tempted back into anorexia as signs that something was happening in Marian's life that she needed to pay attention to, such as the beginning of an exploitative or otherwise unacceptable relationship. Epston and Beth recalled times when they had helped others locate the thing in their lives that really upset them, and helped them to deal with it directly instead of giving in to the temptations and incitements of anorexia again.

Beth, reviewing her history of anti-anorexia, said toward the end: "Yeah, I'm still vulnerable to it. It still doesn't — you know — it would have taken at least seven years until I got to the stage where it doesn't matter. To go without being conscious of eating a doughnut and thinking, 'Well, I've eaten a doughnut, so now I've got to skip dinner,' you know?" Then she laughed.

Epston ended by saying, "Can I tell both of you, we have these anniversary days, one year after the start of your anti-anorexic. That's why we make these tapes, and then we just circulate the tapes about one year after freedom day. Your freedom day will come. I don't know when it will be, but you'll know when it comes. I can't tell you. One woman, Terri, said 'I have a present for you.' And she just gave me this calorie counter and said, 'Here, I don't need this anymore.' So you'll know. You'll know when you're out. And we're all here to keep helping you struggle, and when you get driven back, to pick you up and remind you what's ahead of you — to remind you of your hopes and dreams. I think that's what Anorexia does. What shall we say, it blinds you to your hopes and dreams and then there's only hell, like you talked about, there's only down, hell, the grave, you know, that sort of stuff. Well, look, I think we should stop here. Don't you think?"

§

I have presented this transcript to show two things: (1) the questions that externalize the problem of the anorexia, and (2) the audience of others that provides support in the struggle. Epston is the archivist and chronicler of the Anti-Anorexia League (he is now writing a book in collaboration with many of his former clients), circulating tapes and transcripts, answering long-distance calls from all points, and referring them to archives and transcripts that his clients have made. And here the two others, Richard and Beth, bear witness and support in the interview. Clearly, the problem and its solution have been situated in a social environment.

The next transcript is from White's work with what some outsiders would call a group of chronic mental patients but which they themselves call the Power to Our Journeys group.[2] The group meets every few weeks to discuss the problems they encounter in their lives, and White acts as the secretary of the group, helping them to draw up "documents," summaries of their discussions, that they can carry with them and read at times of difficulty. The tone in this meeting is different from that of Epston's battle with anorexia. White says (personal communication):

> "I have for many years done what I can to dissuade therapists from reproducing battle/competition metaphors ... [Since 1983] I have proposed alternative metaphors that are not about vanquishing anything, and have emphasized notions like relative influence, revising one's relationship with the problem, re-claiming one's life, and so on. An understanding of the potential hazards of these [battle metaphors] is particularly important to work with people who have psychiatric diagnoses ... I have drawn attention to the dangers of encouraging people with a diagnosis of schizophrenia to enter into a battle or contest with their 'voices.'"

The group at this meeting consists of Sue, Chris, Veronika, Mem, Julie, and Brigitte. White takes notes and afterward prepares the final document that summarizes the group's work. Sue has just been saying that, in addition to the voices of her auditory hallucinations, she also has a "good voice."

WHITE:	How did you discover that?
SUE:	The good voice?
WHITE:	Yes.
SUE:	It was just sort of realizing that I had thoughts that were the opposite of what the voices said, and I discovered I had a voice, and I named it Flea. That's named after my grandma — Florence, Lillian, Emily, Alexandra.

---

[2] Provided, with the group's permission, by Michael White.

WHITE:	Florence, Lillian, Emily, Alexandra. My mother's middle name is Lillian.
SUE:	Oh, right. I just think it's a fabulous name.
WHITE:	Flea?
SUE:	Yes, so Flea, she helps me. You know, if I am getting a bit confused and I don't know what to do, then she will say, "Now, first of all, you have got to do this. Do this, because that will be good for you." And she sort of talks to me. She doesn't boss me around, but she sort of helps me structure my life or get me activated to do things. If I'm spending too much time on my own and not enough contact with people, then she says, "How about making some phone calls and catching up with people?" So she's just like a pal, and she's wise about what the voices are doing. So when the voices are being active, she will say, "It's just the voices are doing that because —." And she knows that I have a political campaign against them, because originally I used to do just the opposite of what the voices said, and the chances were that it was usually something good for me.
WHITE:	So Flea has been very helpful in helping to challenge the authority of the voices?
SUE:	Yes.
WHITE:	It's a pretty significant achievement, because these voices speak in very powerful ways, you know, like their own —
JULIE:	They make you feel guilty.
CHRIS:	They'll feed on insecurity and fear.
VERONIKA:	Yes, that's right.
SUE:	Something might happen if you don't obey them.
WHITE:	So they make you feel guilty, and they feed on insecurity and fear?
CHRIS:	They like to control you and threaten. They threaten.
WHITE:	I might write some of these things down, if that's okay. They feed on your guilt, you said?
JULIE:	Yes. They just make you feel guilty.
WHITE:	Right, and they feed on insecurity?
CHRIS:	And fear.
WHITE:	What did you say, Mem?

MEM: They scare you — that something will happen.

CHRIS: Basically they go on your weaknesses. Whatever is weak in you, they can somehow come in.

Later in the meeting, the group talked about the effect of having the group's documents to refer to.

MEM: The respect that you give me as a person is not like — you go to doctors outside the good doctors and they make you feel like you are somehow crazy or you're sick, and they take all the power. But now I've come to sessions with you, and we've worked on documents and things, I've felt empowered and walked out to conquer the world.

WHITE: Right — so they give you power, they have that effect?

MEM: Yes.

WHITE: Yes. Okay. That makes a bit of a difference in terms of your — how does that work for you, feeling more powerful, I mean, what —

MEM: More prepared to love myself, and to acknowledge my failures and say that you did the very best that you could, and that's okay. And that when I hear voices — I still hear voices now and again — and I think, "Oh, it's a voice." And I say to myself, "It's okay, just love yourself." Being able to feel loving toward other people and sense love as a movement through my life, I feel a sense of action rather than inaction, or expansion rather than contraction. These are feelings I've had since I've been better.

WHITE: Okay — wow! I am just thinking about what you are saying about love as a movement through your life, and how getting in touch with that has been a really important thing. And in some ways the documents help you get in touch with that, making you prepared to love yourself?

CHRIS: Yes.

WHITE: How about for you, Sue? What's been helpful about the documents for you, or what have the documents been like for you?

SUE: I guess they are like a mirror to who I am without the voices. Or even with the voices, I am still me, and I'd agree with what Mem is saying, it makes me feel — When I read them, I think, "Yes, I'm okay." The voices are telling me to hate myself, and trying to get me to kill myself, and go into panics, and not eat, and I just go off the air. And then when I read the documents, I think, "Oh, so and so said that I'm okay." Well, they don't say I'm okay, but this is what I can do, this is what I do, well, this is how I am with people. It helps me redefine my story about who I am and not about what the voices think I am.

WHITE: Redefine who I am, not what the voices think.

SUE: Yes.

WHITE: What about for you, Chris?

CHRIS: I could say a lot, but it just basically empowers me against the negative things I've experienced. And also, when I'm reading a document, I think in my subconscious, it plays it back like the situation where it was made up without me actually viewing it or whatever, the last session or whatever.

WHITE: So it brings back the last session in a way?

CHRIS: Yes, it just played back without me interpreting or whatever.

WHITE: Well, that's interesting. So the last session plays back in a way?

CHRIS: In a way. But I'm not aware of it. But I know it does. Maybe with some people, it's the spirit of the last session or something.

WHITE: And for you, Julie?

JULIE: It mainly just helps me to see reality and the truth, because the voices tell lies, and it helps me to see things in a clear way. It kind of puts it in my subconscious. I don't know how to explain it. It reinforces it, put it that way.

To give an example of a document, I have selected one, a summary of a discussion at another meeting. It gives an idea of the range of experience the group covers. In addition to the sense of pilgrimage, of *communitas*, it also has something more assertive: protest or defiance against the order of the outside world, an important source of resolution for people on the margins, or indeed for any group.

Our Determination

1. *Mentioning the unmentionable.* We are committed to mentioning the unmentionable, and acknowledge the courage and strength that this requires of us. Our achievements in mentioning the unmentionable undermine guilt, fear, panic, and self-doubt. It also is a service to others in that it brings relief to them. It helps others to break out of restricting stereotypes.

2. *Doing things at our own pace.* We are determined to proceed in life at a pace that suits us, and not at a pace that suits the voices. The voices can be counted on to push us into doing things before we are ready, and if they succeed in this, then our minds get clogged and we lose sight of how we want to be in life. The voices at times rely upon outside support in their attempts to push us into things, and at times this support is unwittingly given by people like rehabilitation officers.

3. *Acknowledging our teamwork.* We are determined to keep in sight the fact that we are members of a team that is the size of and as strong as the ocean, and as intelligent as dolphins. Regardless of the exertions that some others engage in over their attempts to elevate their authority over our lives, we will stay in touch with the strength, the intelligence, and the beauty of our teamwork. Staying in touch with this is effective in shutting the voices up.

4. *Honoring the little steps.* We are committed to the honoring of the so-called "little steps" that we take in life. These are the sort of steps that so many people in this world overlook and include getting out of bed, having a shower, and caring for our lives in general. We will not allow this culture's overriding concern with control to take away our appreciation of these little sacraments of daily life. Instead, we will take pride in these and, in the process, take note of our specialness.

The group has, in a sense, constituted itself a dedicated support system that has some aspects of being a family. The members have clearly taken the position that, as a group of people with a special affliction, they are not the problem, but their *teamwork,* their membership in a team, is a big part of the solution. It is striking, comparing this work with that of most other

therapists, including family therapists, how much more willing White and
Epston are to go into the ritual possibilities of this kind of work.

In addition to documents and videotapes, they hand out other
papers. To young anxiety disorder patients, they give diplomas (in their
capacities as co-secretaries of the Fear-Busting League). They visit the
outpatient clinics where their patients were enrolled and organize "discharge parties." At a meeting of the Power to Our Journeys group, one
of the members had written a song about the group's work, which, with
a friend, they had set to music. White said he was going to present the
work of the group to an American therapy conference, and asked if he
could take a recording of the song to the conference. Of course. He then
got the members of the American conference to make a videotape recording of the conference singing the song, which he then took back to
the group in Australia.

White would say, borrowing a phrase from anthropologist Clifford
Geertz (1973) and psychologist Jerome Bruner (1990), that he helps the
patients or families to organize a "performance of meaning" with respect
to the problem. The family or group develops a planned group of actions
that express the fact that they have chosen one meaning of their experience over another. The choice is made emphatic because it is expressed
as a public enactment rather than as the insightful private reflections of
an individual.

How do these practices of White and Epston change the way I think
about therapy? As much as their work is derived from family therapy, it
provides a new way of doing individual therapy as well. What is that
impact on individual work, and how does it replace the model of psychoanalysis?

White and Epston's work is an example of narrative therapy that is
not simply an exchange of stories or a change and elaboration of meanings, but it also involves an audience of witnesses who are sought out or
constructed. The work of the Anti-Anorexia League, the Power to Our
Journeys group, the planned family attacks on encopresis, and the consultations with Rupert Bear are recruitments of a supporting membership.

This interest, not just in the suitability of the narrative that is arrived
at, but in the social practices that will be entered into by the participants
to actually work these changes into their lives, is the place where the idea
of ritual begins to be useful to us.

CHAPTER ELEVEN

Reflecting Team:
The Development of a Ritual

THE PROBLEM I WAS TRYING to solve in developing the case conference into the discharge planning meeting was this: how to combine the training of the staff and the consultation with the family into the general sense that all of us were learning something together, that the training and the consultation were the same thing, or at least moving in the same direction. Natural as this sounds, it is not an easy thing to bring about. Psychiatry and medicine have struggled from the beginning of their history with the relationship between professional learning and the relief of suffering, a history often marked by the focus of the oracular knowledge of the doctor on the painful endurance of the patient.

I stepped into this history in medical school, where the most gruesome part of our training was the unwilling involvement of patients in the process. Medical students were at the bottom of the physicians' hierarchy, wearing the short white coats that distinguished us from the interns and residents (all-white tops and bottoms) and the attending staff (long white coats). Knotted in our buttonholes was the rubber tourniquet, the insignia of our lowly function as blood letters. Our job was to do the extra physical exam, the one the patients knew was not necessary, including the rectal exploration without which our preceptor would not accept our work as complete. Ours was the performance of the laboriously complete interview, repeating the questions they had already answered. And finally, ours was the task of inserting the needle for bloodwork, reminding both them and us that we must bear each other's part in our debt to scientific medicine. The patients were rarely given an opportunity to refuse to play their part in our education, or to ask what was in it for them.

And then there were ward rounds, in which the professor and the house staff and students all visited the patients in bed, the professor demonstrating fine points of physical examination or questioning, and then, as if the patient were no longer participating in the discussion of his care, holding a murmured discussion at the door of the room, sometimes not quite out of earshot. The patient sensed that the medical oracle was revealing his fate, not to him, but to us.

As a teacher in the Family Studies Section, I thought of ward rounds often, congratulating myself that the exposure of families to the process of training family therapists was somewhat better negotiated: the student asked the family members if they would be willing to have a group of colleagues and a teacher observe the work from behind the one-way screen, and promised explicitly that the consultation would be a help to the therapy. This practice is as old as the field of family therapy, and it continues as the principal way of training in institutes and study groups everywhere. The essential literature of the field is a collection of videotapes of these consultations.

The one-way observation room, the inner sanctum of family therapy training, was at first an obviously practical arrangement. The audience of trainees was there to learn by observation, and the one-way window, between the room where they sat and the room where the interview took place, was a device to shield the student audience from the interviewer and family, making the group in each room more comfortable.

Late in the development of family therapy, training institutes began to think about what in this situation could be a form of therapy in itself. Here was a meeting of three traditions: the scientific education of ward rounds, the artistic master class, and the healing ritual of the congregation of witnesses. The shift among these points of view was what I had been working on as I turned the case conference into a discharge planning meeting (Chapter 6). The further development of this ritual in family therapy is the story of the reflecting team (described briefly in Epston's work with Marian in the last chapter). It is a story about the ways in which the metaphors of science, art, and religion all combine, and sometimes clash.

§

Early in the history of medicine, we can see in medieval woodcut prints the professor of anatomy in academic robes sitting above the cadaver with a long pointer, indicating the mysteries to the students, who are making notes as they crowd around the table. The students are the receivers of magisterial knowledge, in this and all the other depictions of anatomy demonstrations, from Rembrandt's to Eakins'. Even the body on the table is seen as a contributor to science, offering itself up. The wall of the morgue in pathology class at Rochester bore the motto: *Hic locus est ubi mors gaudet vitam succurrere* — "This is the place where death rejoices to rescue life" — almost as if these corpses might be happy to be there, giving their bodies to science. I pondered this idea over and over again as I sat in the autopsy reviews. Even in death, a story of collaboration had to be imagined to give meaning to the hideous but necessary pursuit of science.

Later in the history of medicine, the rejoicing body is alive: in the surgical amphitheater the professor performs the operation as the students peer down from the steep ranks of seats above him. Anesthesia, like the one-way screen, mercifully separates the patient from the painful art that the professor is performing. In its beginnings psychiatry was magisterially unconcerned with the feelings of the patient as a participant in the demonstration. Modern psychiatric education began in a lecture hall in Munich in 1890 where Emil Kraepelin had patients brought out by their keepers to face an audience of students so that he could question them, demonstrating to the students the characteristic delusions of dementia praecox, of mania and melancholia, symptoms that foretold the patient's fate (Laing, 1960, pp. 29–30). Ward rounds in Bedlam: the professor and the students, having no story to cover this situation, pretend that the patient is too crazy to understand.

From the beginning, family therapy training tried to establish a different atmosphere. When Virginia Satir started teaching couples therapy by gathering together therapists who happened to be couples, then treating each couple in turn while the others watched, this was more than just training: it was an initiation into a mystery. It was a weeklong retreat, involving the participants in the new culture of family therapy in a way that affected both their own lives and their view of therapy and relationships in general. And it had two parts. One was the experience of Satir's mastery of her craft — she was certainly the magus, the magister. The other was the powerful experience of learning together, and of learning with one's partner, becoming at once giver and receiver of the art, an experience of *communitas* that the participants described as profound.

The earliest uses of the one-way screen room had something of a surgical atmosphere about them. The window provided partial anesthesia, insulating the emotions of the interviewed family from the responses of the audience. Still today, sometimes, the consultant interviews the family, demonstrates the technique, and then has a separate conference later with the group of students. This is like the postoperative conference in which the surgeon takes off his gloves and addresses the amphitheater as the patient is wheeled out of the room, still asleep.

In a more advanced family therapy class, the student audience sits behind the screen with the teacher–consultant, while on the other side an apprentice does the best he or she can to provide an exemplary interview. Sometimes instruction comes from the teacher by telephone, and sometimes it is saved for a "halftime break," during which the instruction of the apprentice takes place decently out of sight on the other side of the mirror while the family waits to see what new approach he or she will bring back.

Many teachers, like Salvador Minuchin, come out from behind the mirror to take over the interview and, in a flash of surgical brilliance, demonstrate how it should go. For the family this is a little like being awake for your operation and knowing that it is being done by the assistant. Since it sometimes takes him only five minutes of watching the student's efforts to decide on his master-class move, Minuchin's demonstrations are relatively benign, from the family's point of view. The greater distress is that of the student, with his double role.

The most surgical and most oracular of all these rituals was invented by a group of Italian analysts from Milan, who developed a system of therapy under the direction of Maria Selvini Palazzoli. In this system, the observing audience really became the oracle. The Milan group had a theory (derived from a psychoanalytic reading of Bateson) that the family members who consulted them were unconsciously but subversively out to do each other in, in the interest of resisting change, and so much so that they would defeat all constructive advice. In this view, the family "system" of mutually regulating responses is determined to keep everything the same, troubles and all.

The group's first book was *Paradox and Counter-Paradox*. The best way to get the system to change, they believed, would be to give the family paradoxical advice to do more of the same, on purpose, only more so, so that the forces of resistance to change will be enlisted in making changes in spite of themselves. The family members will either follow the advice, and as a result become conscious (and critical) of their intentions, or they will resist the instructions and thus move in the direction of change in spite of themselves. Such moves have been compared to judo tactics, in which the opponent's force is used to defeat him by going with it to produce his fall. A medical comparison would be to the old practice of setting a dislocated shoulder by pulling it farther out and letting it snap itself back.

Intrusive parents, for example, were told to be more careful and explicit in their efforts to guide their children, and so on. The emphasis here was on getting the technique exactly right. These messages had to be crafted very carefully, with just the right amount of positive connotation, in order to keep the basic cynicism of the approach decently out of awareness. Soon it was evident that the interventions should be written down in order to get them exactly right.

The most truly surgical form of the ritual was this: One member of the team interviewed the family while the others watched and made notes. The family was told that an instruction, a recommendation, would be forthcoming at the end of the interview, and that it would come from the team members who were watching from behind the window. After about an hour of carefully neutral questioning of the family, the interviewer would retire to the observation room and shortly reappear with a written prescription from "the team," which he or she would read to the family. At the end of this reading, the messenger would give the family its copy of the instructions and leave, staying neither for comments nor for questions, and the family would go away, with an appointment for a month later.

The paradoxical instructions and the "drop dead" delivery, as well as the utter invisibility, not only of the team behind the window but also the team members' attitudes toward the family, raised all sorts of ethical and technical questions. The instructions seemed to be ingenious, and often subtly appreciative of the feelings of the family members, but many Americans who tried this method found that as often as not the families were baffled, pained, or insulted by the experience, or just didn't come back. Maybe it was something that only worked consistently in Italy. In the United States, there was great debate about which families it was "appropriate" for.

The American teachers principally responsible for bringing the Milan group to the United States were Peggy Papp and Olga Silverstein of the Ackerman Institute in New York. They continued to experiment with the format in study groups there. They began to think that the reason paradoxical instructions are effective is not that they throw the system off its self-regulatory steady state, but because such suggestions allow the family members to embrace their ambivalent feelings about change rather than being stymied by them. A paradoxical instruction allows them to think about their mixed feelings for and against change, from the outside, as if they had some choice about it. Papp and Silverstein emphasized the supportive, as well as gently restraining, aspect of their paradoxical advice.

A group working with Papp did something different with the "team"audience behind the mirror. Instead of bringing the oracular prescription forth with a single voice, the messenger reported several different opinions from behind the screen — different, sometimes conflicting ones. Papp's group had noticed that, in fact, the team members behind the window did have several opinions, and they decided not only to reflect this in the instructions, but also to use the different voices to respond to the different points of view of the family members, or the different horns of the ambivalence dilemma.

Papp's (1980) paper on this subject is "The Greek Chorus and Other Techniques of Paradoxical Therapy." Like a Greek chorus, she noted, the team responds to the action of the drama with antiphonal voices. Listening to these voices, the family makes a *selection* of possible meanings, all positive, all possible. In Turner's vocabulary, the consultant, the family, and the team, over the weeks of meeting together, have become a liminal group journeying together toward an end stage, relying on the process of their conversation to get them there. As the meetings go on, they look forward to each other's contributions. The continual dialogue avoids the intrusion of authority and promotes an atmosphere of *communitas*.

This richness of response resembles another exercise of Papp's that she calls "family sculpture." She asks the members of the family to arrange themselves in a living tableau that dramatizes their present relationships, then to take turns choreographing the moves, the changes they want to make. It is a sort of wordless psychodrama, and it has a powerful impact on everyone's experience, perhaps because each person can observe, suggest, and enact, without consequence or penalty. It is only a play, a pantomime. It feels creative and surprising, and since expression and discovery are its purposes, and the family members take turns being the choreographers, the therapist is a consultant to their invention, rather than their oracle. If divination is going on here, the oracle is the *process* of play and creativity of the family members, not the magisterial *knowledge* of the therapist. Many voices are speaking, and several versions of the dance are tried out. The therapist and the family are choosing, selecting, weaving together, editing. We have moved from science to art.

The one-way mirror has become an optional prop. In the discharge planning meetings I conducted on the Family Service, I actually preferred not to have a mirror-window, since the audience was expected to make an active contribution to the discussion as it went along, rather like a visible Greek chorus. By contrast, in the Milan method, the mirror was used to enhance the oracular power of the team, like the Wizard of Oz behind his green and red puffs of smoke.

The rituals described so far are special events, since they require the presence of a teacher-consultant to bring the team and the family together. At first glance, this method appears to be a difficult — almost impossibly labor-intensive — way to conduct an ordinary psychotherapy practice.

§

In fact, there is a very labor-efficient type of team consultation with families, one that grew out of the wide-open spaces of Texas. Multiple Impact Therapy (MIT) was developed by a group in Galveston in the early 1960s (MacGregor, Ritchie, Serrano, et al., 1961). Robert MacGregor and Kay Ritchie wanted to do a research evaluation of the effectiveness of family therapy with different kinds of child and adolescent problems. In order to get a large research sample of several different types of problems, they had to offer service to families throughout the southern part of the state. Some people think nothing of driving a hundred miles to dinner in Texas, but for most of these families, the distances they would have to go for repeated sessions were too great, so the clinic team devised a modification of the usual once-a-week-for-an-hour meeting. They decided to do the entire treatment in two days of uninterrupted concentrated activity. The family would drive to Galveston, check into a motel, and spend two days with the team.

Once MacGregor and Ritchie began to think in terms of this kind of marathon undertaking, other inventions followed. They realized that a two-day effort could be exhausting but it would be less so if everyone on the team felt supported by larger numbers, so they made sure that the team outnumbered the family. Each family member had someone to whom he or she could talk individually, and, in addition, there were team members who could work with couples, groups of siblings, or the whole group together.

The morning of the first day would begin with a meeting of every-body together, to outline the problem. Then, while the senior team members met with the parents individually, the psychologist might shoot some baskets with the boy who was supposed to be the problem, and a medical student could take the other kids for a walk to see what they thought was the reason everybody had come all this way. If Kay Ritchie, the senior social worker, was talking with the mother and came upon something she thought was useful, she might ask if they could take it up with Robert MacGregor, who was talking with the father. If the mother agreed, Ritchie would phone MacGregor to suggest a joint meeting. In this way, the family and the team pieced together the structure of the consultation through a series of discussions, until, at the end of the day, everyone reconvened in a large group, where they summarized the day's work and thought up a topic or an exercise that the family members might work on by themselves after dinner, before they went to bed in the motel.

The second day was a shorter version of the first, but more concen-trated. Individuals and subgroups worked out specific plans and responsi-bilities for the coming months; and then, in a final meeting at the end of the second day before the family drove home, they summarized them. Goals and objectives were written down, with ways of achieving them. The family was promised that in six months a two-member follow-up team would visit them at home and interview them about their progress, in order to find out how things had worked out.

I understand that MIT is still practiced in parts of Texas and the South, where graduates of the original program have taken it. It is effi-cient; the team members finish two therapies a week. It is instructive and exciting; they know what they are doing because their ideas have to be explicit for maximum clarity at the end of the day. They are buoyed up by the discussion of the group; they learn and teach as they go, activities inseparable from the therapy itself. They have only two private planning meetings, one on each day: most of their thinking is done aloud with the participation of the family and the apprentices. Their thinking is transpar-ent to the family: there is no time to be cagey.

The families, for their part, like the way the two days of intense attention are followed by many months of responsibility left to them. Resistance has no time to develop; the therapists do not have time to become part of the problem.

§

The most striking thing about MIT as a process is that the treatment, the training, and the research — the follow-up interview — have all been combined into a ritual that suits the lifestyle and convenience of the family and is transparently an effort to be helpful to them. Recently, family therapists in many different centers have become interested in transforming their meetings behind the one-way screen into collaborative rituals similar to those of Papp and Silverstein, but with some differences. Tom Andersen of Norway, for example, invites the family into the team's discussions. The group of students has been renamed the "reflecting team" to clarify their active role in the conversation.

Michael White, describing his way of working with such a team of students, notes that Andersen's approach has been "enthusiastically embraced by many therapists who appreciated the possibilities associated with working with therapeutic teams, but who had found the ethical issues raised by the autonomous and anonymous team increasingly difficult to ignore."[1] White likes the openness of this method, but he has other concerns: What negative effects might patients feel when exposed to a "ward rounds" kind of experience? How could the family/patient be protected from the team's falling into an objectifying, pathologizing discourse? What to do about the expert "truth" claims of the principal therapist/consultant, or about the theories that the team members were interested in learning? How could the whole process be protected from the tendency of "official" therapy movements to reproduce the unspoken assumptions of the dominant culture? Would that be especially likely to happen if the members of a *group* of therapists participated openly and spontaneously in the process?

In his version of the reflecting team practice, to deal with these concerns, White gives a very clear orientation to groups who are about to participate:

[1] White describes this method in *Re-Authoring Lives* (1995).

I tell visiting therapists that they will be discouraged from theorizing about the 'truth' of the problems people bring to therapy.
Instead, it will be their task to attend carefully to the discussion
that is taking place during the interview. I also inform them
that I will be discouraging them from the idea that it is their
role to prepare and to deliver some intervention into people's
lives or into the "system." It is not the task of team members
to "strategize," to "problem-solve," to "teach," to "role-
model," to "perturb," or to advise.

Students new to this version of teamwork often feel that these pro-
hibitions take away all their best moves, so White gives them very clear
models for what they *will* be asked to do. First, their attitude toward the
family should be an awareness of the rare privilege "granted to team
members by those people who open up their lives to others in the course
of this work — an act of inclusion that reflects an extraordinary act of
faith and of trust in the therapeutic team." Therapists are privileged
people in another sense, he says, the sense of having options in their own
lives that the people seeking their help often do not have. And specifically in the interview, a balance of power that is strongly in favor of the
therapist and team members, arising out of what remains of the ancient
supplicant-oracle relationship, persists no matter what steps are taken to
make it egalitarian in the modern world. The client is vulnerable simply
by virtue of being a client.

To counteract these natural inequalities, the meeting must have a
strong structure. It is divided into four parts: (1) consultation with therapist and family; (2) reflection by the team on item 1; (3) reflection by the
first group on item 2; (4) meeting of everyone together.

In the first part, the family (or the individual) and the therapist who
is presenting them for consultation meet with White, who introduces
them to the people on the team. The team is often sitting behind a one-
way window, but a video monitor in an adjoining room will do just as
well, or the entire meeting can be carried on with the team in the same
room but sitting apart. So the team is not anonymous from the beginning, and it becomes less so as the meeting goes on.

The first part of the meeting is an interview with White, with the
therapist sitting in and the team observing, for about half an hour. This
interview might follow a format such as those described previously: exploring experiences and actions that are exceptions to the problem-

saturated narrative, for example. In addition, the therapist and client(s) are asked about successful developments in therapy and how they would account for them.

While watching this consultation, the team is in a very special state of mind. They are searching for ways of joining and empathizing with the experiences of the family members, which they will be reflecting upon in the next part, when they are on the other side of the window. They are watching for "developments that have been judged by the people to be preferred developments — that is, those sparkling moments, exceptions, unique outcomes, or contradictions. Team members respond to those preferred developments as one might respond to a mystery — one that an outsider can be curious about, but one that only those people (the family) with the inside knowledge can satisfactorily unravel."

Now, this state of mind is quite the opposite of that of most groups behind the window in the history of family therapy. In particular, it is the opposite of the Milan group's experts in paradoxical advice, who tried to come up with an intervention so clever that it would trick the family members into changing in spite of themselves. There the wizardry was all on the dark side of the mirror, and the family was seen as too hopelessly involved in systemic defensiveness to be able to think of a way out.

One effect of the respectful attitude recommended by White, and of the fact that the team is getting ready in a few minutes to demonstrate that respect by having an unrehearsed discussion while the family and therapist watch, is a profound search for the basis of admiration and empathy, which encourages comparing team members' personal experience with those of the clients. Once the team abandons the expert objectifying role, it is left with curiosity, wonderment, sympathy, and introspection.

So as the second meeting begins, with the family and therapist as audience, the team members begin their discussion of what they were curious about or appreciated in the previous discussion. The family members get to watch 5 or 10 people talking about their lives and struggles while they sit, as in a theater, and ponder what is said from a safe distance. This experience is usually extraordinarily memorable and luxurious, rather like the two-day intensive encounter of MIT, and it opens up the field of possibilities and comparisons even more than the first interview did.

By the time the third meeting has begun, with the team back in the observation room, and the family and consultant commenting on the team's comments, the possibilities for what Clifford Geertz would call "thick description" are building up. The family members and the consultant are asking each other, "What did you find particularly helpful or interesting in what the team had to say?" An editing process begins, drawing on previously unnoticed possibilities. And finally, when the group reconvenes at the fourth meeting, attention turns to the consultant and the *process* of the discussion so far. The group asks White, "What led you in that particular direction?" "What suggested that possibility to you?" Then at the end, the client or the family members have the final say. They are asked, "What would you like to take forward from this experience?" They are the final editors and selectors from the rich field of the different discussions.

As for the members of the team, in addition to their understanding of "the case" and learning about interviewing by watching the consultant at work, they get something more. White describes this so well that I will again quote him at length. Under the heading of instructions for making comments within the context of one's personal experience, he says:

> The sharing of personal experience . . . is clearly not in the tradition of the "bare-it-all" approaches; it is not about team members expressing all their distressing and difficult experiences with people who seek consultation. This sharing of personal experiences is not done with the goal of smuggling in "Here, take a leaf out of my book." It is not undertaken to give people the sense that the team member has arrived somewhere in life.
>
> Team members do not meet together before the second interview to prepare their comments and questions. And as their interaction evolves across the second interview, they often find themselves talking about what they would not have imagined they would be talking about ahead of their reflections. At times, team members find themselves contemplating previously forgotten or half-forgotten memories, and filling in gaps in the primary narrative of their own lives. At times, team members find themselves talking about or thinking about their own lives in different ways, ways that contribute to an entirely new appreciation of some of the events of their lives. And at times, team members have vivid experiences of some of the alternative stories of their lives, ones that bring new options for action.

By submitting to a discipline of self-denial, in particular, abjuring the temptation to give expert advice, the team member enters into an unexpected communion with his or her own life and its possibilities. The sense of *communitas* here can be quite profound, since, as in the spiritist *reunión,* the AA group, and the psychoeducational multifamily group, the leaders provide a discipline that channels the process of the group in such a way that that process, more than the secret knowledge of the leader, can be trusted.

On the other hand, the expertise of the leader-consultant in the reflecting team is very specific and necessary, and is publicly displayed: it manifests knowing how to conduct an interview, how to instruct a team of observers, in such a way that the result is helpful for the family members. This not only is "clinical" knowledge, the experience that comes from long practice with many people and situations, but it is also the knowledge of the dramaturg, the priest who knows how to make a ritual work.

These rituals are about life in transition. And although there are many of the images of childhood here — the presence of spiritual parents, the acceptance of not-knowing, of being unfinished — it is not the same as the psychoanalytic image of childhood's predicaments and conflicts. What it does present to its members is the experience of being part of a tradition of others who have done this before, who have succeeded in coping with the inherently unfinished nature of life's business, the constant moving from uncertainty to the next stage. In this sense, the metaphor is not childhood, but every phase of personal development.

Another feature that the spiritist *reunión,* the multifamily group, the AA group and the reflecting team have in common is the opportunity for members to shift repeatedly from the role of spectator to the role of actor and speaker, then back to part of the audience again. Such frequent shifts of perspective have something hypnotic about them, and hypnosis provides access (as I describe in the next chapter) to unsuspected corners of the imaginations of all the participants, not just those who present themselves to be healed.

But having traveled all this way to the *communitas* of these rituals of healing, we seem to have strayed far away from those other practices of science, the medical arts with which we began. Actually, we have come to a point where we can look back at the divide between science on the one hand, and ritual and narrative, on the other, between those "two cultures," as C. P. Snow denoted science and literature. The next chapters each describe a central part of those different cultures.

CHAPTER TWELVE
Hypnosis:
Narrative and Science

AT FIRST, I THOUGHT THAT THE THREE TOOLS that I had assembled to work with in this latter part of my career — narrative, hypnosis, and medical psychiatry — all had as little to do with each other as the blood pressure cuff, ophthalmoscope, and reflex hammer I carried in my black bag as an intern. Each was designed to do a job, and since I knew how to use each of them, I didn't have to explain how they were related to each other. In fact, as a teacher at the Psychiatric Institute, I rarely told anyone about White and Epston or hypnosis. My job in that busy medical workhouse was to teach family therapy and community psychiatry, and I used the simplest means I had to get those subjects across.

At the same time, I was also a reviewing editor for family therapy journals and a member of the American Family Therapy Academy. In that world, a discussion was under way between modernist systems scientists and postmodernist narrative philosophers over how to think and talk about psychotherapy in general. Margaret and I wrote a paper for one of the journals urging caution in the appropriation of models from science into this enterprise, and warning that talking about psychotherapy in general was like talking about medicine in general (Newmark & Beels, 1994). Or cooking in general, as a friend of ours said.[1]

Having taken that position against generalization, I am cautious now about taking the last two instruments — hypnosis and medical psychiatry — out of the black bag in these last chapters. But now, as I lay them at opposite ends of the table, I realize that between them they frame the

---

[1] Henry Grunebaum.

problem of understanding the mind and its treatment. They represent the opposite instrumentalities of consciousness, hypnosis the most inward narrative and scientific psychiatry the most outward observation. I also realize that untangling them from each other, and integrating them into therapy, has been the main study of the last part of my career.

The contrast between these two opposite ways of using the mind was not always recognized. In fact, during much of European history, what we now think of as hypnosis had a very ambiguous position, first as part of religious healing, then as part of medical science. After allegiance shifted from religion to medicine, the proponents of hypnosis tried, not very successfully, to appropriate the look of science. Many of them were doctors. In other parts of the world, hypnotic processes — yoga, meditation, shamanic healing — were content to remain part of religion.

But in the West, hypnosis had to choose between being a recognized part of science, or being condemned as superstition and humbug, and this choice until recently has interfered with our understanding of it. In my own education, for example, the 1950s were a low point in the fluctuating scientific respectability of hypnosis. The only mention of hypnotism in my eight years of psychiatric training, in medical school and residency, was a half-hour film in my second year of medical school.

It was one of those grainy black-and-white classroom films, the sort I remembered from high school biology class. A middle-aged professor in a cardigan sweater sat at a table with a young man and woman, probably students in his college psychology course. He put them into a trance by suggesting in a soothing voice that they relax and let their hands float up off the table. Then he told them they would each have a dream — a dream about pennies — and that they would not remember his instruction when they woke up. After he brought them out of the trance, they could remember only the sound of his voice, not anything he had said. But they did tell each other their dreams, and there were the pennies in disguise: copper dinner plates, red poker chips, checkers.

I was fascinated. It was the first and only piece of experimental behavioral science I had encountered in all my psychiatric education. I wanted to know more about the phenomena demonstrated by the film — posthypnotic suggestion and amnesia. Were these phenomena similar to other forms of knowing and forgetting? What did they have to do with the kind of poetic remembering that made use of the imaginative powers of the mind? In college I had read a book called *The Road to*

Xanadu that traced all the elements in Coleridge's great poem, written in a trance of inspiration, to the books in his library. Did he *know* that he remembered those sources of his rapture? Did these hypnotic subjects in the film really *not* know that their dreams of pennies had been suggested? Do people really remember or really know the *truth* of the stories they tell their analysts, and how are they different from the stories or the dreams that their analysts "suggest" that they should tell? I was immediately caught up in the questions about truth, memory, suggestion, and scientific objectivity that hypnosis has presented to the Western scientific mind.

That contrast between the "real" experiences of the subject and those other, perhaps deceptive, fantasies that were *made up* by the hypnotist and suggested to, or "put over" on, the subject is a by-product of our Cartesian psychology. Since we believe, following Descartes, that the mind is an observing, recording, and reasoning machine enclosed in the individual's braincase, we think of phenomena such as one person "putting" another into trance as a contest of wills, a contest of influence between two individual centers of power. In this psychology, information taken in by the brain recorder is either true or false, and false information comes about because one individual mind can be deceived by a more clever, more powerful individual mind. The hypnotist does something to the subject's usual independence so that the subject, for some reason, submits and believes that what is "really" a fantasy, is true.

In medicine, this scene appears as the problem of distinguishing the charlatan from the true healer. In our scientific tradition, the charlatan is a deceiver who cynically exploits the wish to be cured, whereas the true healer makes benign use of science and objectivity — the magisterial tradition in medicine again (Chapter 11). The Cartesian (scientific) interest is in the "real" outside world that we can see clearly, or otherwise we are deceived.

Before the arrival of scientific medicine and Cartesian psychology, the same scene was played out in religious healing and divining. The puzzle was how to distinguish between the deception of evil witchcraft and the true working of the Holy Spirit, evidenced through the miraculous intervention of the saints. But here again, the distinction required by theory was not so easy in fact. Saint Joan of Arc experienced both sides. The politicians encouraged popular enthusiasm for the voices she heard in her trance, then persecuted her when her fortunes changed. She was burned at the stake as a witch for insisting that the voices were of God when the Church said they came from the devil.

The scene took its scientific turn in the eighteenth century with the founding of what later came to be called hypnosis by Anton Mesmer (1734–1815), a physician who practiced in Vienna.[2] The inventor of mesmerism was the first European to suggest that being in an altered state of mind was not a religious phenomenon, a state of possession by either God or demons, but rather a natural capacity of human beings. But what he meant by "natural" was that it followed the recently discovered laws of magnetic and gravitational fields. He also pointed out the *interpersonal* nature of the trance state, that it was something one person could induce in another. He himself, he noticed, was particularly able to produce it in others, an ability that he attributed to his possession of an unusual amount of "magnetism." He actually carried some magnets under his clothes to boost his powers. There was the key to both his popular appeal and his scientific error: his misappropriation of "science" because of his need for a theory.

Magnetism was a glamorous subject, rather like nuclear physics is today. No longer considered magical stones, magnets were a topic of study in the new physical science of magnetism. Naturalist philosophers, such as Benjamin Franklin, were experimenting with electricity to define the laws by which static electrical attractors and magnets acted on other bodies at a distance. Thus, when Mesmer discovered his ability to act on other people at a distance, he called it "animal magnetism." He also borrowed from Newton and called it "animal gravity," another force that acted at a distance. When two humans came near each other, he observed, the power of their influence on each other increased, and as with the gravity of planets, the more bodies in proximity, the more influence. This was his explanation for the phenomenon of group suggestion that accompanied hypnotic practices. Many scientists thought that the forces of magnetism and gravity acted through a medium, a subtle fluid "ether" that connected everything in nature, and this image also found its way into mesmerism, a science of the "ethereal."

Mesmer became famous when he lent himself to an Enlightenment attack on religion. In 1775, a village priest, Father Johann Joseph Gassner,

---

[2] I first read this story in Ellenberger (1981) and followed it up more recently in Gauld (1992), Miller (1995), and Lopez (2000).

became renowned in his Catholic part of Bavaria as an exorcist. Crowds gathered on the church steps of towns where he demonstrated the casting out of devils. He had cured some highborn people and enjoyed the protection of the prince of Regensburg, as well as a number of bishops. Some Enlightenment thinkers, on the other hand, including some Protestant theologians, wanted to prove that this Catholic healing did not come from God. They persuaded the prince-elector Max Joseph of Bavaria to appoint a commission to investigate Gassner's claims to divine healing. The commission secured the consultation of Mesmer, who demonstrated that he could control seizures, even those suffered by a priest who was a member of the commission, with the touch of his finger, an effect that, he assured them, had nothing to do with divinity but was the result of animal magnetism. The effects that Gassner produced, Mesmer said, were attributable to the same material agency, however sincerely he believed that he was casting out devils in the name of Christ. Following this demonstration, the imperial court prevailed on the prince bishop of Regensburg to dismiss Gassner, who, with the intervention of the pope and a few cardinals, was allowed to retire to a small religious community.

As Mesmer's notoriety spread, he calmed people's fears — and perhaps his own — about the state of trance by making it part of contemporary science and clearly separating it from the world of spirits and powers. But in claiming trance for natural science, Mesmer only defined the terms for the next round of ambivalence. Before long, the fear, and role, of the charlatan was thrust upon him, and he became, in turn, the object of a "scientific" investigation.

Mesmer's large following in Vienna had benefited in many ways from being mesmerized and cures of various illnesses were reported. But conventional medical circles in Austria were suspicious at best, and hostile at worst. In 1778, Mesmer took his growing international reputation to Paris, where, through the offices of Marie Antoinette, he secured a pension as well as a large estate with extensive gardens outside the city, where people came to be healed. A cult formed around him that included many aristocratic families. Mozart and Haydn visited him. King Louis' ministers became alarmed that some of his disciples were voicing republican sentiments in their lectures. This cult, they feared, might constitute a new center of power, or, at the very least, a public scandal.

A Royal Commission was formed to investigate. It included Lavoisier, the founder of modern chemistry; Guillotin (the physician who invented the beheading machine used in the coming revolution); and

Benjamin Franklin, who happened to be in Paris on a diplomatic mission. They inspected Mesmer's operation thoroughly, including a large copper vessel with wires running from it by which an entire group of people could be magnetized at once. The commission gave Mesmer a qualified stamp of therapeutic effectiveness. They found no cures other than of conditions outside the scope of medicine. But they were quite clear that these phenomena operated through the imagination of the participants, not through any physical agency, and performed experiments to prove this. Although he was free to practice, Mesmer left France in disgrace to seek a better reception in other countries.

Much as this verdict was a blow to Mesmer, it hardly affected the popular enthusiasm for his many disciples. On the eve of the revolution, France had two marvels to contemplate: hot air balloon flights and mesmerism. They were the rage. "Mesmerism offered a serious explanation of Nature, of her wonderful invisible forces, and even, in some cases, of the forces governing society and politics" (Darnton, 1968, p. vii). Compared with contemporary medicine, which was still bleeding, cupping, blistering, and purging the wretched patients, mesmerism was a very compassionate regimen, and its treatment of the conditions that affected the average man and woman — then, as now, depression, anxiety, and psychosomatic malaise — was, at least in the short term, observably effective.

§

In the nineteenth century, a second incursion of science began when the British medical establishment, represented by such sober practitioners as the surgeon James Braid (Miller, 1995), began to study the phenomena of trance as evidence of the existence of newly recognized "unconscious processes." It was Braid who, in 1840, named the medical-model induction of trance "hypnosis," from the Greek *hypnos*, "sleep." These medical men were interested in similarities between the imaginative and unconscious ideas produced by hypnosis, and the "automatic" internal functions of the nervous system, such as the reflex arc, which they had recently discovered. This marked the start of systematic medical interest in dissociative phenomena. In France, Charcot and Janet drew the parallel between hypnosis and hysterical symptoms (Chapter 3). But like Freud, these medical researchers were so preoccupied with fitting the new phenomenon into their theoretical categories that its true place in therapeutic work continued to elude them.

"Scientific" hypnosis and popular "magnetic" mesmerism went on side-by-side for over a century. In the face of the competing medical metaphor, the popularity of animal magnetism as a mysterious action at a distance did not go away; on the contrary, it flourished. It was alive not only in France, but even more so in Victorian England (Winter, 1998). Elizabeth Barrett and Robert Browning were only the most famous of its devotees, discussing the powers of trance as they wrote poems to each other. They saw in the relationship of magnetizer and subject the type of relationship that existed between man and woman, or between pursuer and pursued. The influence or power of one individual over another, whether based on intellect or social class or gender, was the theme of the Victorians' discussions. In their changing society, mesmerism was a metaphor for the conflict between power and sympathy.

In 1836, a disciple of Mesmer, Charles Poyen, brought magnetism to the United States, where it became the basis of an enthusiastic and evangelistic blend of folk-healing practices. The leading American exponent, Phineas P. Quimby, wrote many books on the inner forces of health, wisdom, and religious enlightenment whose liberation was made possible through mesmerism and other powers of the mind over the body. He called it "developing the daguerrotype of the Soul," borrowing a scientific image of his own time. Two of Quimby's students, Julius and Anetta Dresser, became leaders in New Thought, and promoted an extensive lay ministry of neighborhood practitioners of "mind cures," for which anyone could qualify by paying a fee and taking a training course. A number of educated and enterprising people, mostly women, set up practice. William James engaged one of them to treat his depression. These movements were flourishing at the end of the century when Freud arrived (Chapter 4). The American version of mesmerism welcomed spiritism and clairvoyance of the kind that so preoccupied James (Fuller, 1982). If all this suggests merely a quaint rehearsal for what we now call New Age philosophy, it is important to remember the steady ascendance of Quimby's most famous and successful student, Mary Baker Eddy, the founder of Christian Science.[3]

---

[3] Although Eddy began with the version of mesmerism as a cure for bodily ills that she learned from Quimby, like many other such students, she shaped its extraordinarily plastic and adaptable ideas to her own ends. In fact, at the end of her life, she had come to see "malignant animal magnetism" as the very type of material evil, from which her vision of "the All that is Spirit" was the deliverance. See Fraser (2000).

Another mesmerist, a French physician named Allan Kardec, writing in the middle of the nineteenth century, produced a volume that became the bible of spiritism in the French and Spanish Caribbean islands and in Brazil (Kardec, 1953). There mesmerist theory combined with African and other belief systems to produce another system of lay practitioners, the *espiritismo* that Vivian Garrison found in the Bronx, preserved intact for over a century (Chapter 6).

Thus, each culture to which mesmerism spread gave it a unique popular inflection, and turned it into a variety of local folk-healing cults. The American ones had their special blend of hypnosis, spiritism, uplift, an inner power as a special connection to the Infinite (transcendentalism), and revival-tent ecstatic conversion. And each in its own way pretended to have the blessing of science. The scientific claims of Christian Science were particularly dangerous when taken literally: my paternal grandmother was a Christian Scientist, and, some time before they were married, my mother got my father out of her care just before his appendix burst on the operating table.

From its beginning, mesmerism offered a rich pseudoscientific imagery of "fluids," "powers," and "influences," easily translatable into spiritual terms. This was the odor of sanctity that so offended the scientist in Freud that it contributed to his rift with Jung, whom he correctly saw as having occult leanings even as a young psychiatrist.[4] But openness to the occult was precisely what made the disciples of Mesmer attractive. They could use these rich allusions to incorporate vividly imagined powers of the mind and spirit, collating into one coherent whole what appeared at first to be contradictory categories of experience.

Several students of this history have noted that although the procedures for inducing trance, and the effects of being in trance, vary widely, they all have one thing in common.[5] They begin with a particular kind of endorsement by a public group — a teacher with a following, a group that has assembled to learn, to witness, to participate. Consider the role of the group, the audience, in these scenes.

---

[4] See Bateson (1972b) on Jung's experience with the occult at a crucial point in his life and its contribution to the resolution of his career crisis. McGinn (1999) describes perceptively the opposite consolations of Freud's world view: the feeling of being urbane, wised-up — disillusioned, but canny.

[5] See Gauld (1992, pp. 596–608) for a review of this "social psychological" view of hypnosis. Jaynes (1990) makes a similar observation (pp. 383–387).

As people sit in tubs of magnetized water (separate tubs for the aristocracy), Mesmer in his purple robe walks among them, producing "crises" of convulsions with a penetrating glance. Charcot, surrounded by visiting students and other patients in the fashionable lecture hall of the Salpêtrière, touches the patient on the "sensitive point" of her abdomen about which she has heard him lecture, producing a hysterical swoon or outcry. The hysterical patients have lived at the hospital for months or years, developing backstage intrigues and jealousies. And in a scene that made a great impression on Sigmund Freud when he visited Nancy on his second trip to France, Ambroise Auguste Liébault, a country doctor of peasant stock, would cure the patients who visited his free clinic of a wide variety of complaints. As they assembled in the single room of his sunlit garden cottage, he would interview them about their aches and pains, feel and stroke the afflicted parts of their bodies, and calm them into a trance with his voice and his hands, inquiring, explaining, soothing, suggesting, while the others watched, awaiting their turn. And in other parts of France, as in England and the United States, stage hypnotists would call up volunteers from the audience. Whatever means of induction they used — the touch, the pass of the hands, the candle flame, the "look into my eyes," the watch swinging on the end of its chain — they were able to get both groups and individuals to pantomime whatever hilarious or touching scenes they pleased. The phenomena were whatever they were supposed to be.

Supposed by whom? Around every hypnotic practice exists a microsociety whose culture defines what hypnosis is. This collaborative effort of the group is one of the things that the different methods have in common. Attempts to define and evaluate hypnosis in scientific detail have obscured what these groups share, and what they might share with others. Father Gassner stands on the church steps casting out demons from the convulsing bodies of the penitents who kneel before him, praying for a miracle. The crowd around him is like an American congregation in the revival tent. At the spiritist *reunión*, the mediums are in a trance on behalf of their clients, but in that room scented with orange water and ritual cigar smoke, who in the group murmuring prayers is in a trance and who is not? As I sit in the dark watching Michael White on the other side of a mirror interviewing a young woman, waiting my turn to speak as a member of a reflecting team, thoughts about my own life and work come to me in new forms that I would never have expected. And years ago, in the 1980s, as I sat on the bright porches of Cape Cod learning hypnosis, taking turns with the other students in putting each other in trance, similar doors kept opening in my mind, no matter whether I was the entrancer, the entranced, or the audience.[6]

§

The approach to hypnosis I was learning was the hypnotherapy of Milton Erickson. He was the man who plucked from the American jumble of folk-healing practices and hypnotic techniques a practice of modest assumptions and real use in psychotherapy. His point was simply that hypnosis is a matter of collaboration rather than influence. Although he was a psychiatrist, in fact, for many years the president of the Society of Medical Hypnotists, Erickson's great contribution to this history was to take hypnosis out of medicine and locate it in that part of the life of the mind that includes storytelling, conversation, ritual, and psychotherapy. He saw that the hypnotist and subject are a pair of collaborators working on a story. The hypnotist's contribution to the work is not the subjugation of the other's mind, or the connection to Mesmeric fluids, or the mastery of a medical technique, but it is, rather, the skillful offering of a particular kind of assistance. It is a tuning in to the body, the awareness of breathing and the little variations of posture and sensation that are the common experience of any two people in a safe and intimate conversation. From this soothing talk about the body's awareness, it is possible to go easily into other parts of experience and imagination, trusting the hypnotist as a companion who has proved to be reliable on the journey so far. Ericksonian hypnosis is a skillful way of bringing together into collaboration a mind connected to a story, an unconscious, a memory, and a body, all at the same time. As in theater, orchestral performance, or religious ceremony, that experience takes on special power with the larger collaboration of certain kinds of audience.[7]

---

[6] My teachers on Cape Cod were Anne Linden, Steve Goldstone, and Paul Carter. But before and after them, I worked for years with Nina and Richard Evans in a group that still meets to work on difficult problems. Nina Evans cured my swimming phobia in one of the many demonstrations to our group that reminded me of the power of the audience.

[7] I think this helps to explain the variable effectiveness of hypnosis as an office treatment. Freud, for example, learned it as a method of "suggestion" and abandoned it in favor of free association when he found that it did not always work.

Erickson had been interested in the phenomenon of trance ever since, as a young man, he had become paralyzed by polio, and lay day after day in his family's farmhouse, exploring the power of his mind to make the paralysis retreat. Later, as a psychiatrist, he realized that the kind of mutual hypnosis that occurs in psychotherapy is one of the most common facts of human experience. Far from being a specialized professional technique, it is something we all use every day to connect with the resources of our imagination. Thus, he returned trance to its pre-Enlightenment status as a way of connecting with powers, but the powers were not supernatural, not only of God. As in Turner's *communitas,* they could appear when a group met for a ritual purpose, even a group of two.

A further point made by Erickson and others, and more systematically by his student Michele Ritterman, is that the hypnotic phenomena of selective and imaginative remembering and forgetting are just as important in understanding the causes of psychiatric symptoms as in producing their cure (Ritterman, 1983). The induction of trance can be part of the creation of symptoms.

If the trance is taking place in a family bedroom, and if going into that altered state is the way a child protects himself or herself from the recurring experience of physical or sexual abuse, serious symptoms can follow. These experiences of childlike helplessness and exploitation by a powerful, once-trusted older person are part of the genesis of the dissociative disorders (Chapter 3).

The symptoms created out of the victim's desperation are different from the therapeutic use of hypnosis in surgery in only one important degree: the relationship involved. I remember a surgeon in the emergency room suturing a scalp wound that a small boy had suffered in a fall. Local anesthesia was difficult to achieve in this situation, so the surgeon used hypnosis as an adjunct. Before he began, he found out that one of the activities the boy loved most was hunting. He talked the boy through an imaginary experience of hunting quail. As he sewed, the boy squeezed

---

Some hypnosis fails because there is no supporting group, no help for the subject to change "beliefs" about it on the basis of experience. And some subjects, with or without group support, are not good hypnotic subjects because they are not ready to venture into an area where they may encounter reverberations of their own experience of trauma. This must have been a frequent problem for patients in Freud's office. Here again, traumatic experience provides an exception.

his father's fingers like triggers whenever the surgeon raised an imaginary quail in the bush. Fifteen stitches — 15 quail shot. The boy was hunting in one part of his mind, while in another *dissociated* part, the pain of the surgeon's needle was barely perceptible. This scene of undergoing pain and its dissociation at the hands of a trusted adult is different from child abuse in many ways: in the abuse scene, the child has to hypnotize himself or herself. But the mechanism is the same.[8]

Hypnotic trance is a special state of concentration, in which the subject is able to focus without distraction on remembered experiences and fantasies. It is the ideal narrative space. It is separate from the more wakeful and alert state, keyed to the environment, which includes thinking critically, looking for comparisons and contradictions, and searching for and recording facts. That is the space of scientific observation. The person in trance is not unconscious of the environment; rather, trance is handled in a separate compartment of attention. Whether deep attention is paid to trance, as in hypnosis, or to the outside, as in a scientific laboratory where new information is being uncovered, access to the other side is always possible.

A common example of such a trance is driving a car while thinking about a problem that is very absorbing. You arrive at your destination and realize you have no memory of having driven the car, and yet obviously, you did drive it safely, observe traffic signals, and so on. You were driving the car with an outward focus, a different part of your attention from the one that was paying attention to the problem.

An example of the opposite, the outward focus, is this: Scientists in their laboratories often find that while they are searching their meters and computer screens for facts, their unconscious minds are sifting the data for new patterns seen only by an inner eye. The split between com-

---

[8] There is an interesting scientific debate about this propositon, spelled out in Putnam and Carlson's chapter in Bremner and Marmar (1997). Among a number of other comparisons, they look at the evidence that trauma victims are highly hypnotizable, and find evidence to the contrary. I think a similarity of mechanisms in hypnosis and traumatic dissociation would not require that trauma victims be easily hypnotized. Many traumatized people have good reason not to want to be so trusting as to be hypnotized, so that clinically the two phenomena are different. This is an interesting example of puzzles arising at the overlap between clinical narratives and scientific investigations, an area that is elegantly explored in two books, one by Bremner & Marmar (1997) and the other by Spiegel (1994).

partments of the mind is not the conscious on top and the unconscious below, buried or repressed. They are side-by-side. The unconscious is simply another room in the mind where different rules of thought apply, and we all visit it all the time, with or without the help of a hypnotist.

As the example of child abuse shows, people can, and often do, hypnotize themselves, especially in situations where they have feelings that they want to avoid — where they want very much to be in one room of consciousness in order to shield themselves and remain unaware of what is going on in another. My out-of-body experience in the school chapel was a dissociation from the experience of finishing my life at school, of which I was trying not to be conscious.

§

Does this model help us to understand how psychotherapy works? Let us try the experience out and see if there are parallels, first, between hypnosis and classical analysis, and then between hypnosis and family therapy.

An Ericksonian hypnotist starts with some talk for the purpose of establishing rapport, an exchange of assurances of comfort and trust that is the basis for any collaborative conversation. The hypnotist then invites the subject to relax her natural waking vigilance by considering a physical sensation, sometimes offered as a subjunctive kind of question: "I don't know whether you will prefer to keep your eyes open or let them close," or "You might begin to notice that your breathing is getting deeper, or that for the first time, you notice the difference between the cool air coming in with your breath and the warm air going out." This is the beginning of hypnotic induction, paying attention to a nonthreatening physical experience associated with relaxation. Breathing, or having your eyes open or closed, is inevitable, and by going along with what the hypnotist is saying, the subject enters into a completely safe collaboration, grounded in a comfortable awareness of the body going about its business.

Free association, the first instruction in classical analysis, is a similar induction technique, a suggestion to pay attention to something that happens by itself.[9] It is similar to automatic hand levitation; both are instructions to let something happen "spontaneously." Whether saying every-

---

[9] These ideas were first proposed by Jay Haley (1968).

thing that comes to mind, or feeling small differences in the weight of the hand, the subject wearies of trying to tell the difference between spontaneity and control and goes into a state where the easiest thing to do is follow events and thoughts wherever they lead.

In hypnotic inductions, as in analysis, the subject is aware of being in a special situation, supported by a history and an implied group of witnesses. Both situations are so fraught with self-conscious membership that the participants in the beginning are saying to themselves, "So *this* is what it's like!" There is a sense of initiation, part of the group phenomenon described above. Sometimes this experience is negative. Part of my problem with Dr. W. was that I was not sure I wanted to become a member of his group, the cloud of witnesses that included some of the senior members of the psychiatry department.

Once embarked on the journey into trance, the subject supplies all the details of the reverie, so that when the hypnotist says something like, "If you wish, you could take a journey in your mind to a place where you remember feeling calm and relaxed," the fantasy is completely under the subject's control. Similarly, the analyst's abstention from all but the process of the conversation gives the patient a feeling of freedom to discover and explore a safe space.

The next step in hypnosis, the change in orientation, may begin with an invitation to take a walk in that place the subject has created as the destination of the journey, to explore it, to find something new. Or the hypnotist may weave into the flow of talk a story, a fable, a fairy tale, a reminiscence of exploration. Elements of the problem for which the subject seeks consultation begin to appear in the story, in a disguised or amusing form, or a fantasy may be suggested in which the subject looks at the problem from a different standpoint, such as a later stage in life. The subject's waking standpoint, a preoccupation with a limited, difficulty-focused version of the problem, is gently broken up, opened, transformed. When the subject's facial expression suggests that she has entered into a trance, the hypnotist weaves in language and references leading back to memories of confidence and resourcefulness, lets the subject dream a dream or tell herself a story of how it works out. Sometimes, if the problem is specific, such as a childhood experience that the subject wants to look at in a different way, the hypnotist suggests a conversation between the remembered child and the adult doing the remembering: "Go back, if you like, and talk to the little girl you once were. You can tell her what you understand about it, now that you are older — things she was too small to know at the time."

The similarity to analysis here is obvious. Questions or hints from the analyst lead to alternative stories, some based on a reinterpretation of childhood events, some on stories from current life that can be reinterpreted. The reinterpretation is in the interest, it is hoped, of the patient's agenda, but it sometimes has to be done by way of the analyst's theory, which may be the long way around. Patients I see who are well trained in analysis often have to take extra time to rethink their problems in terms of the drama of their childhood, and I have learned to join them on that journey, even though it is a long detour for me.

In the course of the long work, all therapies need a source of news — something to shake up their formalism and let in a little random irrationality. Novelty provides something unexpected with which to work, like challenging suggestions from the audience at improvisational theater. In psychoanalysis, one such fermenting ingredient is the interpretation of dreams.[10] Freud thought that this was one of the more scientific parts of the analytic art, but we can think of it as a sort of mutual storytelling between analyst and patient. There are so many narrative leaps between the experience of the dream, whatever that is by the time the patient remembers it the next morning, and the telling of it, the patient's associations to the elements of it, the analyst's associations to the patient's associations, that the appearance of scrupulous care that this process wears in the literature of interpretive technique has always seemed dubious to me.

Hypnotists, on the other hand, are quite open about the narrative chances they take by introducing fanciful elements into their patter. They tell stories and make poetic leaps, but they trust the subject to reject the ones that don't fit. They can do this because Ericksonian suggestions are made in such flimsy subjunctive language that no one needs to take responsibility for them if they are discarded, and the subject takes them

---

[10] There was a great argument a number of years ago between some sleep researchers and analysts about whether the actual content of dreams meant anything, or whether dreams were just the brain's way of clearing the disks, emptying files at night that had been filled up during the day. The answer to this question is not crucial, but it does raise further questions about whether the exact details of dreams are important, or even knowable, given the enormous reinterpretation that apparently goes on between the dreaming and the remembering of the dream (Wade, 1998; Goode, 1999).

over if they are accepted.[11] The hypnotist avoids being specific about details because it is the subject's reverie, and if the hypnotist supplies details that are not there, the subject will notice the discrepancy and start to wake up. The emphasis is on helping the subject to discover, and continue to explore, what she knows already.

This aim is clearly similar to the overall strategy of White and Epston's narrative therapy, as well as to that of a number of other "resource-based" schools. It is beginning to be the goal of some analysts. One group, led by Roy Schafer, has shed the scientism of classical analysis and embraced a narrative philosophy (Schafer, 1994). My favorite writer in this regard is Stephen Mitchell (1993), not only because he writes so elegantly, and uses extensive case examples to get his point across, but also because he underscores his debt to the English Object relations writers and to Sullivan (Mitchell, 1999). These analysts regard themselves as in the Freudian tradition because they are interested in conflicts, both internal and interpersonal, and because they use the transference relationship as a key to understanding what conflicts are about. But apart from that, as far as I can see, they are openly collaborating with their patients in the construction of new narratives on whatever terms will move the work along. The tone of these conversations suggests that the engagement with the patient is very much the same here as in other conversational narrative work. Mitchell even discusses with his patients alternative scenes they might try out at home.

§

The hypnotic model of psychotherapy we have been developing could be summarized as involving three steps: (1) developing a hypnotic rapport or trust, and, within its protective embrace, supported by a sometimes invisible audience; (2) allowing the loosening or breaking up of old fixed beliefs and behaviors, with their supporting narratives; so that (3) safe experiments with new and different stories can be tried out, and perhaps new actions with an audience redefined.

Now to apply this model to family therapy: Consider, for example, one of the classic problems in child psychotherapy, school phobia, more

---

[11] The art of burying or embedding suggestions in hypnotic patter is covered by Lankton & Lankton (1983).

accurately called "school refusal." At first sight, this symptom is baffling. The child cannot say what is frightening about going to school, or seems to be "making up" reasons, such as pretended illnesses or attacks of anxiety. Although young children may refuse to go to school for a variety of reasons, school refusal often occurs in a particular family situation: the mother is facing a degree of emotional unemployment in an empty house, or fears being alone with an abusive man, against whom the child's presence has been some protection.

The actors in this drama have several areas of awareness. Looking at it from the point of view of the child, he[12] knows that the culture says that it is important for him to go to school, but it also provides a tradition that children may be anxious about leaving home. At the family level, the mother and others agree that the child should go to school. In the child's best interests, and in the mother's own image of herself as a good parent, she is *not* attending to her fears of being alone, or of being alone with this man. But on the individual level, in a part of her mind, her fear is still there. From this conflict, the mother and child select the child's anxiety about school as the more acceptable story that explains the tension in the household. Questions and answers exchanged between the mother and child highlight this possibility, rather than the more unacceptable stories of the mother's fears for herself. The child finds himself with a mysterious symptom for which he has no explanation, and the family is stuck in one compartment of experience: a family dilemma with school refusal. They find themselves worrying about the problem or despairingly accepting the stubbornness of the child.

Following Ritterman, I call this group induction of a state of mind a type of hypnosis, because even though the resulting state is anxious rather than somnolent or calm, and group rather than individual, the family experiences a limited state of concentration on only one story, and other possible interpretations, other stories, are kept out of awareness. Like the patient facing surgery, the child and mother are hypnotized — they hypnotize each other — so that everyone can stay in a space where this conflict between pain and waking can be resolved. The child's "fear" is ratified by the family members as the place where they need to be, the problem for which they need a solution. It has the advantage of

---

[12] This child is a boy so that he can have a different pronoun from his mother.

acknowledging both the demands of society and the child's development, and, at the same time, taking no risks with other agendas.

I also see this state as similar to the effect of group membership described above. There is an extensive literature on the effect of group membership on perception. The Asch "brainwashing" experiments, the most famous example, showed that even if a group of people is assembled to perform an apparently objective task (comparing the length of lines on a chart), the concerted influence of the group affects the outcome (Asch, 1951). Jury deliberations and the experiences of cult members are other examples. The singular contribution of family therapy is facing the power of membership directly and offering to do something with it.

Family therapy's way of treating a problem such as school refusal follows the hypnotic paradigm. I think of the way trance works in family therapy as similar to the way it works in the theater: both involve the experience of being an actor in company with others, as well as the entranced experience of the spectator. It also borrows from the theater the experience of rehearsal, of experimental "play," a performance that is not final and that, therefore, affords the possibility of imagining action with diminished risk. Openness to invention is encouraged; the players can always go out and come in again. If they blow their lines, the script can always be rewritten, many possible scenes tried out, and the actors can say which they prefer and why.

In treating a case of school refusal, the therapist invites the family to enter the scene on another stage, where she is dramaturg and improvisation coach. The family tries out (imagines, rehearses) a scene in which the mother takes the child to school, firmly reassuring him that she has lots of plans for the day and that when he comes home, they will tell each other about their adventures. The mother talks with the therapist about what adventures she can imagine for herself; this is an important conversation for the child to overhear as audience. Or in the case of the mother's fear of an abusive relationship with her husband, the therapist may arrange to work with the couple on this problem, substituting herself for the child as the mother's guardian. In either case, the key is the change in the mother's view of herself and her powers, rehearsed in the presence of the rest of the family and then enacted at home, with collaboration.

The change that family therapy has introduced is the opportunity for the family members to move from being spectators to being actors. What makes these performances now safe, if once they were dangerous? The family therapist creates a stage setting where positive interactions are preferred and where attacks and other dangers are headed off. The therapist models inquiry and curiosity rather than projection and blame. She asks what would mitigate the child's fear of school, rather than accepting it. She searches for counterexamples to negative perceptions (the mother can take care of herself, and has plenty to do), and so on.

Individual therapies depend on beliefs shared among the patient, the therapist, and an implicit, unseen audience of others (Chapter 6). The essence of the hypnotic device operating in family therapy is the simple fact that, for the purpose of changing the scene at home, all the actors are present. They themselves embody that culture of the home scene and its beliefs, and they are able, by themselves, to decide to make changes in it. The family becomes a determined small group with an interest in defining itself and its future. Sometimes, an examination of the genogram may indicate that, in addition to those family members present, some ancestors who might have had an interest in the performance and its outcome can be acknowledged, as well as some absent characters whose witness would support these changes. But often it is enough that the family group intends to take this performance home and try it out.

If these arts are not enough to get the family to carry the scene home and play it on that stage, therapists introduce other devices: schedules, contracts of agreement, and documents that get carried home with the actors to study, to read to one another, to post on the refrigerator. Acting aids, such as note cards, make the home exchanges more predictable and less emotionally charged. Family therapy is a method of transferring elements of the office culture to the home.

This problem of transfer is well known in individual therapy. Therapist and patient meet in a special atmosphere where mutual encouragement and support make it possible to create an imaginary world of heightened possibility. But this world can vanish into amnesia as the client leaves the office. Especially when therapy becomes a routine of life once or twice a week, it is common to experience therapy sessions and life as going on in separate compartments.

White and Epston have made a particular contribution to this problem of office-to-life transfer: the art of writing letters. Letter writing was the central focus of their first book together, *Literate Means to Therapeutic Ends*, which I would also recommend as a first reader on their general approach to treatment. In almost every therapy they do, White and Epston write letters, usually immediately after a session is over. Because they live in countries with efficient postal systems, the letter usually arrives the day after the session, and it says something like this: "I had some further thoughts and questions that occurred to me after you left, and I wanted to write them to you in this letter. Perhaps you could think them over between now and our next meeting, and we could talk then about the items that you think are important." The letter then goes on to ask questions about the implications of what came up in the meeting. It may also tell a story about another family or person who had a similar problem. Most important, it is carefully phrased in the language the client used in the interview: it is a transcript of the resources and ideas that the client produced during the interview, and that the therapist carefully wrote down.

Getting a letter from your therapist, which you then use as the basis for planning the next session, is a novel experience and can lead to novel expectations. It opens a door: We can work on this at home, as well as in the office. We can keep the letters as documents after the therapy stops. The difference between writing/reading and talking/listening can be an important change of state. I sometimes suggest to family members that instead of talking about a difficult topic, they write letters to each other, since writing can be a less challenging or threatening modality. If you are reading a letter from someone, you can supply your preferred tone of voice, reflect on it, think about various possible replies, make it part of your own story in ways that suit your expectations.

§

In this chapter, I have been using Ericksonian hypnosis as the simplest model of therapeutic narrative. Next I move across the table toward that other mental instrumentality, science, taking up what is, for us the most relevant case, scientific psychiatry. I will be steering toward what I regard as real science, having left to the side the claims of Mesmer, Freud, Bowen and some of the followers of Bateson, who have tried in various ways to dress their narrative practices in scientific clothing.

CHAPTER THIRTEEN
Psychiatry:
Science and Narrative

THERE ARE TWO KINDS OF REAL SCIENCE in medicine: experimental medicine and epidemiology. In psychiatry, experimental medicine includes brain imaging, pharmacology, genetics, and all the other exciting technology that gets into the newspapers. It has produced such drugs as Prozac and Ritalin, which have profoundly changed psychiatric treatment. Epidemiology, however, is the medical science that has had the most impact on our thinking about psychiatric illness and treatment. It is a science whose laboratory is the community.

Epidemiology is the science of counting cases. It was founded by John Snow, an English physician, who counted cases in the London cholera epidemic of 1849, and showed that most of the victims were users of a single water source. Thus, he was able to define the cause of the disease without seeing anything but the numbers. This is the genius of epidemiology: it produces scientific information without a complete picture, or even a theory, of the phenomenon under study. All it needs is a large enough number of cases (the larger the better) and some good questions, such as: "Is it something in the water?"

One of the most famous studies in psychiatric epidemiology counted cases of depression among a carefully defined group of people — women living in a London suburb in the 1970s (Brown & Harris, 1978). This study departed from the usual findings that depression is related to gender (more women are depressed than men) or heredity (depression runs in families) to examine the social influences on its occurrence. By going from door to door and interviewing a large enough sample of women, the researchers were able to find out not only how many had had an episode of serious depression in the previous year, but also how that experience was associated with social class, marriage, employment, close family support, and other environmental features. It was clear from the study that "life events" — especially such losses as the death or departure of an important person in the family — have a prompting effect on the occurrence of depression. Also, having small children at home and the absence of a male confidant independently contributed to vulnerability to depression, regardless of class. But among the working class, the pressures of child care and loneliness were more conducive to depression. We have always known that psychiatric illness is related to class, but from studies such as this, we learn what it is that increases the risk of illness: working class women have fewer resources to counter the effects of isolation and the burden of caring for children. This knowledge is valuable, but we learn it at a certain cost. We have to decide what constitutes a typical case of depression, so that we will know how to count, and as we shall see, thinking about typical cases restricts our vision.

A second use of epidemiology is in evaluating treatment. If we have enough control over a treatment situation, we can do outcome research: comparing the effectiveness of different methods with similar cases. A good summary of outcome research in family therapy is offered in Carr (2000). Two of the treatments I have described in this book have been proved effective by outcome research: psychoeducational family therapy for schizophrenia (Chapter 5) and dialectical behavioral therapy for borderline personality disorder (Chapter 3). But in these experiments, again, we have to define a case of schizophrenia, or, more difficult, of BPD.

The heart of epidemiology lies in the precision of the comparison of cases. To corroborate his findings, John Snow needed to find people who used other water supplies and did not get cholera. In this respect, psychiatric epidemiology is the opposite of narrative. It depends, not on finding good examples that illustrate the story you are trying to tell, but on searching carefully for contrary examples and not finding them — or finding few enough that they don't disprove your main story. I will leave aside here the definition of few enough and enough cases, since that belongs in the noble, but abstract, edifice of statistics. The point is that by finding and comparing cases and noncases, epidemiology turns the great jungle of nature into a laboratory, a place where "experiments of nature" can be performed. In order to perform an experiment, you need a "control," a sector of experience where the "null hypothesis," the description of the noncase, prevails. To do outcome research on the effectiveness of a particular treatment, for example, you need untreated cases, or differently treated cases, to compare with ones that are receiving the treatment in which you are interested. Instead of pushing the narrative of the treatment's success, you attempt to "falsify" it by proving that it is *not* successful. A scientific proof is one that withstands the effort at falsification. This is the process in which the definition of a case needs to be very specific.

§

So far I have used the abstract language of science. For psychiatrists to use the knowledge that this science provides to help the people who come to us, we need to reexamine the process of becoming a case — accepting and entering into a diagnosis — from the inside, from the point of view of the individual. To consider what it means to become a case, especially a psychiatric case, I will move back from science into narrative and tell the stories of some people who entered, or refused to enter, medical diagnosis and treatment. This is where narrative and science meet.[1]

A family came to consult me because the mother, Agnes, was suffering from a variety of symptoms, the most distressing of which was intense anxiety. Her husband and three married sons were concerned about her care. They had just persuaded her to see another psychiatrist, a medication specialist, who had recommended an antianxiety drug, but she hesitated to take it because she had negative reactions to most drugs.

An internal struggle within the family about the nature of her distress may have played a part in the decision to consult me as family therapist, as well as psychiatrist. Here is the way Agnes' story appeared to the men in the family, especially to her husband, George. In their view, she suffered from hypochondria, that is, a variety of physical complaints that especially occupied her attention whenever independent action was required of her. Over years of struggling about planning trips and activities, Agnes had acquired an invalid status in the family, a reputation as the one who could not, or would not, participate, the one for whom special arrangements had to be made because of her health.

Throughout the rearing of her sons, Agnes had been a devoted, vigorous, and perfectionistic mother and homemaker. Her main com-

---

[1] My thinking in this chapter owes a lot to Arthur Kleinman's *The Illness Narratives* (Kleinman, 1988) and to Susan Sontag (1977).

plaint had been a sometimes debilitating back pain after the birth of the youngest child. As the boys grew up, married, and moved away, however, she acquired more and more physical complaints. She had not cooked for many years, depended on the services of a housekeeper, and blocked the resolution of family conflicts by asserting her pain, fatigue, dietary requirements, and so on.

§

On the other hand, until a year and a half ago, she drove regularly to her job as a technical expert on costume design for a major film and television company. She met friends, shopped, and organized the family's social schedule. But with less and less energy for getting to work, she had, with great regret, resigned from her job.

During the months before consulting me, she had become anxious and depressed, suffered a sleep disturbance, lost weight, and became unable to leave the house unaccompanied. This condition progressed to an inability to spend any time alone without anxiety, so that by the time we met, she had begun to employ a companion for the days of the week when the housekeeper was not there.

Agnes resented her family's diagnosis of hypochondria. She resisted its moral implication that she could pull herself together simply by changing her attitude. Her illness was real and had been diagnosed by the specialist in whom she had the most confidence, her nutritionist. This woman had, for many years, provided detailed diagnoses of Agnes' allergies to various foods, of hypoglycemia (which required careful attention to the timing and content of meals), and of muscular and nervous problems (which required massage and manipulation). These diagnoses were confirmed by the internist who had referred her to the nutritionist, a doctor renowned for his compassionate and holistic approach to the treatment of the whole patient, which, in her case, involved injections of vitamin supplements.

Clearly, Agnes was a case — but of what? George and the sons had a family-dynamic explanation. The changes and departures in the family had diminished her formerly central role as a mother, and she was filling in this loss with illness. They hoped that I would be able to redirect her energies, especially toward resolving conflicts in what remained the central part of the family, her relationship with George. He declared that he was available to work on this if I recommended it.

In Chapter 5, I referred to the problem of family-system formulations in situations in which the players are not equals. To accept that Agnes' symptoms had resulted from an attempt to restore her once-central family role would have meant treating her as equal to the other players. But giving a name to her inequality, a diagnosis, presented us all with a workable program of change.

Agnes met the requirements set down in DSM-IV for major unipolar depression. She had depressed mood, her thinking was hopeless and helpless, and she had enough sleep disturbance and weight loss to place her in that diagnostic box. I invited the family to unite against this external enemy — external in the sense that, although it was located within Agnes' nervous system, it had the status of an illness, rather than of a failing.

The appearance of depression, I explained, is naturally related to life events, especially losses; moreover, depression, anxiety and physical illness are sometimes difficult to differentiate. Many of Agnes' pains and weaknesses could be expressions of depression, called "somatization." In some parts of the world, depression is mostly experienced as fatigue and physical pain, such as headache. I acknowledged that we must proceed with extreme care because of Agnes' sensitivity to medications. I urged her to check out the advisability of taking an antidepressant with her other consultants, especially the nutritionist, who, Agnes said, would be able to tell if she was allergic to it.

I agreed with George that too many cooks were involved here, yet the time was not right to fire any of them. Instead, we hired another, one of whose specialty everyone approved. An occupational therapist came to the house a couple of times a week and accompanied Agnes on experiments in independence. Agnes would meet the woman at destinations and activities progressively further from the house. After a few months, Agnes was taking pride in her ability to get out on her own and drive her car again, and she eventually terminated the services of the companion. She was able to do this because the therapy had consisted of a progressive series of triumphs over the symptoms of depression that held her back. These symptoms — the headaches, leg weaknesses, and other physical ills — were legitimate medical handicaps that could be overcome by rehabilitation under professional supervision. Meanwhile, the drug expert sorted through a series of antidepressants until finding the one to which she objected the least, and inched up the dosage slowly enough for her to tolerate the many side effects.

Keeping our discussions well within the medical model of depression, we measured Agnes' progress with charts and careful record keeping. The progress notes she herself wrote in her journal were detailed, like her research files at work. Having dispensed with the occupational therapist, we retired the nutritionist as well. We reduced meetings with me from two to one a week and began to take up some of the issues of control between Agnes and George. Her husband was enthusiastic about her progress, and they experimented with other forms of talk besides their usual debates. Thus we arrived at family dynamics by a circuitous route, as a subtheme to the management of depression. Family conflict was another area where Agnes learned to be effective by standing up for her point of view as an increasingly healthy person.

Agnes' was a very slow and expensive treatment, lacking the panache of a systems master. I kept wondering what Minuchin or Bowen would have done: Would they have cleared all this up with a few brilliant interviews? I doubt if they would have encouraged Agnes, as I did, to join a group of ex-hospital patients in meetings guided by the Recovery, Inc., handbook. Attending their meetings gave her the experience of helping people much sicker than herself and deciding that whatever diagnoses she had, she didn't have *theirs*. She still had the aches, pains, weaknesses, and dizziness; she just learned to tolerate them better. Apart from these symptoms, there were long periods when she was, in her own terms, active in her life and free of depression. But if the physical symptoms were expressions of depression, and the depression had improved, why did they persist?

A friend of the family urged Agnes to try another psychopharmacologist (something I hesitated to do), and, by good fortune, the one recommended was a colleague of mine at Columbia. He immediately sent her for a physical examination by a better internist than the one she had been seeing (the holistic vitamin injector who kept telling her that her heart sounded fine). The new internist, a cardiologist, gave her a very upsetting new diagnosis: coronary artery disease requiring bypass heart surgery. Suddenly, all her aches and pains were part of a new story. Were the weakness and pains that kept her from walking angina? Were the leg pains arterial insufficiency?

Agnes underwent surgery too quickly to dwell on these now-academic questions. She had become a heart case, and was only incidentally a psychiatry case. I saw her through the long, slow, painful and (for a time) depressing recovery from the operation. Although she had some setbacks, her family's attitude was now different. The story line of recovery from heart surgery and return to a life that is good for the arteries — healthy diet, exercise, heart medicines — is a medical campaign. It is all struggle, with no traces of the stigma that had been associated, even in this very understanding family, with the treatment of depression. Agnes and the family no longer tried to distinguish physical from psychological causes. A new medical team was working on her rehabilitation, and she entered at length on one of her best periods of depression-free, but still physically limited, function. She went out into the world actively and, on her own, took a course on the history of costume design, a subject she had long wanted to revisit. She joined George in trips to visit their children and grandchildren and generally, from her point of view, came almost up to speed.

A few years later, like some people with serious arterial disease, Agnes needed a second bypass operation and she entered the hospital again, a game but understandably discouraged veteran. I went to visit her, and when I watched her walk toward me down the long hospital corridor, I was shocked. Suddenly I saw her in a completely different light: she obviously had Parkinson's disease. The fixed stoop, the short, shuffling steps, and the arms not swinging at her sides were unmistakable signs of the minute degeneration of brain centers in that disease. Determined not to miss a second diagnosis, I called her internist, who said, "Oh, that poor woman! Hasn't she had enough?" We agreed to get a neurological consultation, but not to discuss this development until after the surgery. The neurologist confirmed the Parkinson's disease, but pointed out that, in many ways, it was not advanced. Agnes' speech, facial expression, and voice modulation were all normal. The symptoms of Parkinson's can appear quite independently, he noted, and at different times over the years of slow development. They include dizziness, weakness, anxiety about falling, stiffness, pain in the extremities, and — depression!

So I had to look at the case again. The whole story, from beginning to end, could be the slow development of Parkinson's disease, a neurological condition with well-known causes and treatments, with a national foundation supporting research, and with no taint of moral failing, as in hypochondria. Depression in Parkinson's is either a side effect of an imbalance of neurohumors, whose primary effect is on the coordination of movement, or perhaps the result of feeling overtaken by mysterious aches and weaknesses for which there is no explanation or cure. This final, thoroughly medical-biological, view of depression as a chemical imbalance in response to vulnerability and provocation by another disease leaves the patient even more blameless.

Agnes had a harder time recovering from the second heart operation, and this time, she had a new enemy in Parkinson's. George and I, now seasoned consultants to one another as Agnes' caretakers, joined the cardiologist, the psychopharmacologist, the cardiac rehabilitation people, and the new member of the team, the neurologist. And even though all of us, very much including Agnes, now saw our work as a holding action against an illness that was even less forgiving than coronary artery disease, our morale was different from what it had been when we thought that depression alone was the problem. Everyone, including Agnes, was now more generous and tender, more forgiving. One of the keys to her new outlook, Agnes said to me recently, was not being angry at George anymore. That had changed around the time of the first heart operation and continued as an improving mutual understanding in the face of new challenges. He had really been wonderful about all this.

§

As I write, Agnes is still gallantly fighting Parkinson's and a series of strokes and other arterial defects. Most cases of depression are not so complicated by medical puzzles. But Agnes' case is of interest precisely because it illustrates the difference between doing epidemiological science and treating patients. She is not a typical case, and on that account would be eliminated from many studies of depression. But then many, perhaps most, cases are not typical, when you get to know them from inside. The way they become typical is by a construction of their story to match the type described in the epidemiology.

Patients as atypical as Agnes are the challenge (some would say the headache) of general practice because they do not fit neatly into diagnostic boxes. Their doctors, as well as their friends and families, wish they would follow directions, take their medicine, and get better. And the patients themselves would like nothing better than to follow that culturally approved path to recovery. But their bodies know it isn't working. They need more diagnostic investigation and more support, not less, since they may have more than one illness (Halberstam, 1967).

On the other hand, Agnes' case also illustrates the specific usefulness of entering into a diagnostic box, of being regarded as typical enough for the "depression" label. Apart from the "medical" effect of the treatment (antidepressant medication and behavior therapy), she gained from that label the ability to identify her own plight with that of a well-publicized and sometimes actually present group of other sufferers. She gained a "reference group," even a support group whose meetings she attended. She formed friendships with people who had had similar experiences. She read and clipped articles about depression in the newspapers. She kept a journal, and I gave her my notes from time to time, both records of ups and downs, but general progress. The medication she was taking was a "serotonin re-uptake inhibitor." I drew her diagrams of molecules of serotonin going across nerve synapses, with the medication blocking their return.

Through all of these actions, Agnes participated in a large and important cultural institution, a citizens' health campaign, whose main source of information is epidemiology. By choosing this audience for her story, Agnes entered a vast liminal congregation of cobelievers. And by visualizing her depression as an enemy, she was able to gain the same purchase on it that White and Epston and the *espiritistas* provide when they externalize the problems of their clients.

Placement in the depression box has the advantage of giving a name to despair, something felt to a degree by all patients, all candidates for diagnosis. In other boxes, however, the fit is a real problem, less because of the uncertainty of the diagnosis than because of the dilemma that a certain diagnosis presents to the person who is deciding whether or not to become a case. For me, these have been the most absorbing problems in my practice as a psychiatric consultant to families with mental illness.

§

The first difficult box is mania, the "up" phase of bipolar disease, also called manic-depressive disease. Occasionally, the candidate for this box accepts the diagnosis but finds taking pills to stop the mania a ridiculous proposal. He agrees only when his family forces him to look at the trail of consequences that his recklessness is leaving for others, and the ultimate danger to himself. Sometimes he must be brought forcibly to a hospital before he can begin this reflection. But the most interesting and difficult situations are those in which the patient has not yet met all the criteria for the mania box, but everyone except he himself can see it coming. Everyone except the patient knows that something is not right with him, but he is blaming everyone except himself.

I can recall many such stories, here collected into a fictional composite I will call Eddie. Eddie's father, a colleague of mine, is a clinical psychologist who runs drug trials for a university psychiatry department, and Eddie, age 30, is a member of the People's Labor Party, a group that holds rallies in our neighborhood at election time, and even enters candidates in local elections. Eddie is one of their best speakers. He also has been giving speeches at home, ever since he was about 10 years old. In fact, he lectures at home so often and so passionately that his younger sister is embarrassed to bring her friends there. Eddie's Marxist position is that his father's profession is part of a capitalist plan to tranquilize the proletariat into submission, to zap them with Prozac and make them more efficient and docile workers. This enterprise pays his father much more than his mother, a social worker in private practice, earns. Eddie tells me that she is always bugging him with absurd modernist-positivist pseudoscientific Freudian claptrap about how his problems result from infantile conflict with his father. Eddie consented to visit me because his father assured him that I wouldn't give him any of *that*.

On the other hand, Eddie knows that his father and I have discussed the possibility that Eddie's problems might be attributable to bipolar disease — an entity defined by the modernist-positivist science of epidemiology. Epidemiology is one of his father's main professional tools, and my own master's diploma in that science hangs on my office wall. As Eddie arrives, he inspects it with a little smile of greeting the enemy, and we sit down to talk about his options.

Eddie has read all his father's books and is sure that he does not have bipolar disease or any other disease, for that matter. He is willing to talk to me about only two problems. The first is that he has once more lost a girlfriend to whom he had a passionate attachment. It has happened to him in the past with agonizing regularity, and this time, as has also happened before, she said that she would come back to him if he got himself straightened out.

The second problem is a new one. His friends in the People's Labor Party have told him that he disrupts their discussions, can't stick to the point, won't yield the floor, and has been proposing wilder and wilder agendas. They don't want him to attend any more meetings. That got his attention and made him willing to discuss some medication possibilities.

Eddie doesn't like his father's hints and suggestions that he has bipolar disorder because it turns his protest against injustice into a disease, just as his mother's way of thinking turns it into a complex. To his surprise, I agree with him. I say I certainly want to keep his protest completely separate from whatever is getting on his nerves. But I do think that his nervous problem has pulled a sneak attack on him while he was looking the other way.

"Can we think about it for a moment?" I ask.

"Sure," he says, locking onto my gaze and sitting forward.[2]

"You've obviously thought about bipolar disorder and decided you don't have it. How did you work that out?"

"I know the checklist by heart. Increased activity or restlessness, racing thoughts, elevated mood, grandiosity or irritability, pressured speech, recklessness, decreased need for sleep. Sounds like most of the really interesting people I know, but if you have any three out of seven, bingo! You're manic-depressive! Step right up and get your booby prize, lithium carbonate. Rock salt. How did the drug companies figure out a way to charge so much for a hundred milligrams of rock salt? Kills your kidneys, never mind your spirit. Is that what you have in mind for me?"

"I certainly wouldn't suggest lithium unless we agreed that it would be the best for you, and there are other drugs for manic-depressive illness. But I don't know if that's what ails you. I don't know what you want help with. Can we talk about that?"

"Even if I believed that three-out-of-seven stuff was science rather than bingo, I wouldn't make the cut. Recklessness? I don't have the money for reckless spending; in fact, I'm a total tightwad. I never had to get much sleep; my restless activity has always been in the service of the party — a cause that buoys me up in a way you must find hard to understand. I've always talked too much and too fast to suit most people, but I get things done, I really do — ask anyone."

"Let's talk about what you want to change, what you want help with."

"I want to avoid being pigeonholed, electroshocked, lobotomized. Remember *One Flew over the Cuckoo's Nest*? My favorite movie. My parents are just like Nurse Ratched."

"It's one of my favorites, too. Actually, your father and I have talked about how important it is to help you stay out of the hospital, not that you're in any immediate danger. I think, if we work together carefully, we can succeed at least in that. I want, above all, to help you avoid a

---

[2] Although this dialogue, like the rest of Eddie's story, is fictional, it is based on vivid recollection of many such conversations.

psychiatric emergency by working with you and your family to get control over this while it's still easy to do. I understand you've had a couple of nights with no sleep. Does that bother you?"

"Ah, the famous prodromal sign! The sleep disturbance. You and Dad are getting ready to put me in one of his clinical trials. But I don't fit!"

"Actually, your dad is the one who told me about the best argument against pigeonholes. You might be interested. Can I tell you about it? Two very distinguished epidemiologists, Blacker and Tsuang (1992), wrote a paper about manic-depressive disease as the ideal psychiatric diagnosis. Compared with all the others, it really is quite distinct. It's got everything a diagnosis should have (and so few do): a unique symptom description, a unique pharmacology, and one of the clearest heredity patterns. A couple of people have even claimed to have found the gene for it."

"Yeah, that guy at Columbia. And then he turned out to be wrong – I read all about it. I know my dad has three relatives on his side of the family that he says were bipolar. The only one I've met is his father, who was certainly weird enough. My dad avoided going to restaurants with him because he would talk to the people at the other tables, trying to pick up the women. It was really embarrassing."

"You remember that? Maybe, like most of us, your dad became interested in psychopathology from early experience. Anyhow, Blacker and Tsuang said that if there is a diagnosis in psychiatry, manic-depressive is exhibit A. And then, they said, look what a mess it is. It shades off into everything that is like it on every side. The walls of the box are really full of holes. You can hardly find a typical case. So they suggested that we think about doing away with diagnosis by inclusion criteria and instead look at symptoms as traits, or even states, that you can put on a scale. Two points of sleep disturbance, five points of pressured speech, a little of this, some more of that. It would make psychiatry more like the rest of medicine, where you can have a little hypertension and some shortness of breath, without having to put it all into one illness. What do you think of this approach? Suppose we skip the manic-depressive diagnosis. Can we just talk about what symptoms you would like to change?"

For the first time, Eddie seems to take a breath. He closes his eyes. "Okay. The sleeplessness is bothering me. I know I need to get some sleep."

"Good. I can give you something to help you reset your sleep schedule. What about 'irritability'? Are you feeling touchier than usual?"

"My friends say I've become a total pain in the ass. I think that's why they threw me out of the meetings." As he says this, Eddie's eyes fill with tears and he begins to sob, recalling the shame of that confrontation. He goes rapidly from tears to anger to tears again. But eventually, as he calms down, we begin to work out a plan of medication and consultation with his family.

"I want to meet with you and your parents," I say, "maybe your sister too, if she will come, to talk about this problem as something that's everyone's concern. My experience with families that have lived with this problem — illness, illnesses, symptoms, whatever you want to call it — is that they eventually come to see it as a condition of life with which they all can help. Whatever it is may appear at the moment to be located in you, but if you look at your family's experience, the presence of this kind of tension over unpredictability and the need for control goes back further. Your father was concerned about it in his father, and, in many ways, your family has been occupied with controlling what they fear is uncontrollable.[3] For parents, it comes from despair over having bright children who appear to be deliberately throwing their lives away, a kind of outrage and righteous resentment of waste and disorder. And in time the children come to feel the same kind of resentment toward their parents."

"Dad and I have fights that my mom describes as moral shoot-outs. His weapon is scientific, mine is political, and then Mom comes in blazing with psychodynamics."

"Have you considered the possibility that shoot-outs are actually a destructive practice in your family? That they alienate and wound you rather than bringing you to a common solution?"

"Their common solution is for me to shut up. But I'm 30 years old, and I need some respect."

"Let's see how you could get that, and how they could give it. That would be an important thing to have a family meeting about."

As we make our appointment for the next meeting, I reflect on the familiarity of this scene. Families with a bipolar member, however well or badly the label fits, when assembled into multifamily groups recognize these patterns of scornful, wounding debates (Moltz & Newmark, in

---

[3] This idea that the families of patients with manic-depressive disease are especially moralistic and striving, occupied with control and achievement, was originally expressed by Mabel B. Cohen in 1954 (Cohen, Baker, Cohen, et al., 1954), and has been one of the elements of the family therapy of Stierlin's group in Heidelberg (Stierlin, Weber, Schmidt, & Simon, 1986).

press). They help each other to become more skillful at defusing conflict. They are able to substitute problem solving for these endless interruptions and standoffs, just as families with a schizophrenic member replace their peculiar communication difficulties with problem solving (see Chapter 3) (McFarlane, Lukens, Link, et al., 1995).

The essential move in this treatment is to free the patient from the moral implications of being in the diagnostic box, which his mood and his pride rebel against, while preserving the advantages of that medical experience: using medication and behavior monitoring to control symptoms. The family and the patient eventually learn to live with the fact that definitively distinguishing between some symptoms of mania — excessive irritability, uncontrolled enthusiasm — and the ups and downs of a passionate life is impossible. No medical expert can sit in the family and sort these behaviors out, except in the extremes of the highs and lows. At other times, the family members have to learn to consult constructively with each other, to build on their own experience (Moltz, 1993). Eventually they get the best of both kinds of thinking, the moral narrative and the medical-scientific. The multifamily groups add a community of concern that relieves the family members of the sense that they are the only people crazy enough to have these experiences. And they can read in Kay Jamison's (1993) remarkable book *Touched With Fire* about the great artists and thinkers who have been similarly afflicted.

§

The diagnostic box to which I want to return now is one that I introduced in Chapter 3: borderline personality disorder. I described there the group therapy that Marsha Linehan has devised for working beyond the protest of the traumatized child. Getting to the point where that kind of therapy can begin is, in my experience, partly a matter of accepting and dealing with the objections that the patient has to the assumptions of the diagnosis.[4] The epidemiology of BPD indicates that the condition

---

[4] See Berkowitz and Gunderson (in press) on the use of multifamily groups for borderline personality disorder. They say, without offering a solution to the problem, that the patients' resistance to the "deficit" characteristics of the diagnosis is a major obstacle to success, and indeed patients, for the most part, refuse to attend such meetings.

is caused partly by trauma and partly by a temperamental vulnerability to the effects of that trauma. On the other hand, the vulnerability may in turn be the result of the trauma (van der Kolk, 1997).

Suppose the patient, almost always a woman, cuts through this balanced discussion with an attack. She says, "Listen, if you call me a borderline, I know what that means — on the borderline of psychotic. Not completely crazy, but close enough to it at times that my judgment about people is not to be trusted. It says I'm paranoid, narcissistic, depressed, demanding. Demanding that you pay perfect attention to the injuries I have sustained in my life. Maybe you don't like that demand, but when I was a child, no one paid any attention: quite the opposite, my parents told me what a burden I was, how unreasonable, how troubled. They had no idea *they* were *making* me doubt my judgment, and I didn't either — I just thought I was mixed up or bad. Finally I discovered anger, and it has been my liberator. It has helped me to challenge the parents and therapists who blame me for this and make them yield the few concessions of respect I have received. Sometimes I look for the ideal, the perfect therapist who could 'really understand me.' But mostly I've learned to distrust helpers, especially therapists who claim to be better than parents, calmer and smarter. In the end, like parents, they want to straighten me out. They want to make me behave, 'grow up,' realize what my misunderstanding contributed to the problem, or contributes to situations like this now where I'm sitting here attacking you. You want me to learn how I misconstrue encounters in my life, and that means I'm supposed to believe the other person is not jerking me around. If I think so, I don't know what I'm talking about. Now you want me to think of all this as a medical diagnosis, a disorder of *my* personality that lets everyone else off the hook."

The psychiatrist listening to the attack is in a dilemma. Epidemiology has demonstrated that childhood maltreatment is a cause of some personality disorders (Johnson, Cohen, Brown, Smailes, & Bernstein, 1999), while outcome research has shown that behavioral treatment that does not focus on that causal factor is more effective than the psychodynamic treatments that do (Linehan, Tutek, Heard, & Armstrong, 1994). But my experience is that in order to secure the benefits of this science, from the patient's point of view, it may be necessary to exhaust the narrative of abuse. It may be necessary to hear to the end the story of the child's anger as she tracks down the culprits in her life and brings them before the bar of her own truth and forgiveness.

A further response, which I learned from David Epston, is to follow the patient as far as everyone, including the patient, can bear to be followed, down the road to the recognition or confrontation that the patient imagines. It may even be possible for the parents to apologize. Or, if this is not possible, the therapy can recreate the situation in childhood — reenact it much in the way that Michael White reenacts conversations in the form he calls, "Say hello again" (White, 1989). The therapist can accept and admit and apologize for the injury on behalf of the world of parents, therapists, and others who have tried to "bring her to her senses."

Once this protest is followed to the end, the patient may need to acquire some skills, in the manner of Linehan. When that point is reached, my gloss on the Linehan therapy is to say to the candidate for the BPD box, "When you find yourself in a futile debate about whether you were injured as a child or whether you brought it on yourself, give up the debate. Both may be true, but as a plan for recovery, neither is useful. And both are untrue, in the sense that the real problem is a vulnerability for which neither you nor your parents are responsible. Go on to making up for lost time by learning how to take care of yourself, learning how to do some of the things you didn't learn before, regardless of who's to blame for your not learning them."

§

The last story concerns a group of diagnoses that may, in fact, overlap. Epidemiologists are still working out their co-occurrence or "comorbidity." They have in common a responsiveness to antidepressive medication.[5] The last episode in the story of the Vargas family concerns a diagnosis that arrived just in time to save a family system when it seemed that nothing else could.

§

---

[5] Some of these diagnoses are attention-deficit disorder, obsessive-compulsive disorder, panic attacks, and social phobias. For a discussion of comorbidity and other adventures into this area of epidemiology, see Hornig (1998), Kessler and colleagues (1944), Pliszka (1998), and Murphy & Barkley (1996). Brown (2000) and Hollander (1997) are important resources for clinicians.

Fausto Vargas wanted to make an appointment with me. He had read a book, which he brought with him to my office: *Driven to Distraction* by Edward Hallowell and John Ratey. This is a book about attention-deficit disorder, written by two psychiatrists who have had it. It describes the disorganization, distractibility, and driven thoughts of people with this illness. Maria had given him this book, he said, and it was absolutely amazing. It was him. His whole life was there, including his trouble studying at school. His only good grades were in literature, because novels were the only books on which he could concentrate. The enormous effort he required to concentrate, to stay organized, the anger at his children when they were not putting in the same maximum effort at school that he had — it was all there. As I talked with Fausto about his new discovery of himself as a person with a deficit of attention, I was struck by two things. One, I would have missed the evidence for it because I had not asked, and two, the more he talked, the more I saw hints of other diagnoses in a slightly different direction: obsessive-compulsive disorder, for example. He described ruminating, returning thoughts, an inability to get things out of his mind — certainly an obsessive way of looking at experience. Well, no matter, the medical treatment of each of these sets of symptoms is the same. Fausto started to take an antidepressant.

Within a few weeks, he was a changed man. Calm, generous, approachable, his old self was an object of curiosity to him now as he kept stumbling over all his bad habits of a lifetime. He and Maria made a new beginning on their life together, with both children living out of the house. What a difference!

They were just beginning to cultivate some parts of this new Eden when a lightning bolt struck. Fausto discovered that during the years before this change, Maria had been having an affair. All those clicks on the answering machine of which he had been so suspicious! What amazed me was that Fausto spent only one maddened day thinking about divorce and revenge. As he recovered his balance, his attitude toward Maria's affair was this: all three participants were responsible, but he and Maria, in particular, were victims of his illness. He was enraged at the thought of the other man, the snake in the garden, the seducer. But he could see that Maria had good reason to feel alienated from him as he was before, and he was determined to go on changing with the help of the medication and by working with me, alone and with Maria.

That is what we did, painfully, revisiting his suspicions and obsessions over and over until they both recovered a working confidence in themselves and each other. Maria's recovery from this episode in her life, and her shame and depression about it, was particularly painful. I saw them both individually and together. The rest of these intertwining therapies is a different story. Fausto and I had to explore many alternative ways of accounting for his change in outlook. But what saved the family from exploding at the crucial moment was his ability to see an illness as having blighted his life, rather than himself as the author of his troubles, or Maria as a traitor from whom he needed to be cut off.

Fausto's case is not typical of anything in the psychiatric literature. But he is very specifically helped by his medication; he used to be able to tell within a day if he forgot to take it. At the beginning, that was an important badge of membership, as well as a therapeutic effect. And now something interesting is happening: he goes for periods without it because he has learned how. His nervous system can step up from the footstool that the medication provides to use this, its highest function: learning how to learn from experience. And his changed point of view permits the first serious work on his marriage.

By finding his story in the book about attention-deficit disorder, he made a crucial shift of membership. This is happening more and more as people read and investigate for themselves the benefits and hazards of identifying their problems in psychiatric terms. Psychiatry is a medical practice that requires skill in both science and narrative. It gets its stories from books that the patients and families are reading, as well. Political movements, such as the National Alliance for the Mentally Ill, have completely changed the philosophy of the management of schizophrenia toward that of a social campaign (the beginnings of which I described in Chapter 5). That diagnosis, the part of psychiatry where I started out, was the earliest prototype of this kind of transformation: from a secret story of mystery, despair, and moral failing to one of membership in affliction, a public campaign, and partnership with the medical profession.

And thinking again about psychiatric diagnosis, as I said to Eddie, we may be heading for a new epidemiology, getting rid of the bingo boxes and instead using symptom scales that measure how symptoms change over time, how they occur together, and what they predict about both illness and the strength to combat it. That would be a new and very interesting science, much closer to the narrative of life as it is actually lived.

CHAPTER FOURTEEN
A Seder in Princeton

THE NARRATIVE APPROACH BRINGS the power of authorship to the real authorities, the storytellers themselves. In writing this book, I began to think about the effect of authorship on my own life — the public witness, the chance to rewrite, reclaim. Performing life as a book is something like marriage-as-therapy that I mentioned at the end of Chapter 7. The public performance, of either memoirs or marriages, requires a special kind of discovery, in the sense of revealing oneself. It is the truth of outward commitment and intention, the discovery before an audience. As I thought about this similarity of writing and marriage as public forms of narrative, I wondered how to end a book that was also about rewriting history and inventing ritual. The answer dropped into my life last April. Margaret's sister Nancy invited us to her home in Princeton for Passover.

§

This would be an unusual event, partly because of the absence of children or grandchildren: it would be just the four of us, Margaret and me, Nancy and her husband, Immanuel — the grandparents, ages 64 to 75. Passover means children to me. The Passover suppers Margaret and I have attended have reminded me of Christmas, in the sense that both Passover and Christmas are feasts for telling stories to children. The youngest child at Passover asks four questions about how the meal on this night repeats the story of the delivery of the Jews from slavery in Egypt. Children at Christmas visit the Christ child born in a manger and receive the gifts of the Magi. Actually, Christmas Eve is Margaret's favorite festival, to which she invites friends to trim the tree, especially those she knows are not having their own celebration. Margaret's family never celebrated any Jewish holidays. I suppose friends invite us to Passover, knowing we lack it — the way we invite friends to Christmas Eve.

And I remember that this Passover is also unusual because it has been many years since we last celebrated together. Once, in the 1970s, Nancy invited us and our children to a feminist Seder that a friend of hers was preparing, and something prevented us from going. That was the first I had heard of rewriting the Passover ceremony, bringing it up to date. (Of course, Margaret and I rewrote our marriage ceremony: we started with the Episcopal Book of Common Prayer, took out the Trinity and put in the wine cup and a Hebrew blessing.) Generally, there have been Thanksgivings and birthdays at our house, and dinners and birthdays, and a wedding, at Nancy's house, and I have always accepted that we did Christmas and they did Passover with different circles of people.

Margaret and I find our seats on the train to Princeton. I wonder what just four of us will do with a responsive reading of the Haggadah. You have to have enough people to take turns, and Margaret and I don't know the songs. As we settle down for the ride, we agree that, however odd it will be to have only grandparents at a feast for the instruction of children, this is just the right moment for the four of us to get together.

We are the core of the Rabi family in which Immanuel and I are the sons-in-law. Immanuel has a younger brother, but basically this is the family as Margaret and I think of it. It is partly kept together by the responsibility the four of us have for the care of three old women, Margaret and Nancy's mother, Helen; Helen's sister, Agnes; and their father's sister, Gertrude. Their father died 12 years ago, leaving the means and the instructions for the care of Helen and Gertrude. Each of these women is verging on 100 (Agnes has passed it) and they reside — mostly in bed, but in good health, considering — each in a separate Manhattan apartment, attended by the female members of a large Jamaican kinship. None of them is what you would call dying, just very slowly fading. The maintenance of this spectral oldest generation — medical, technical and financial, but above all, interpersonal Jamaican — has occupied the attention of the four of us for at least a decade. And since Margaret is the sister who lives closest, it has occupied her most of all.

Margaret starts to do the *Times* crossword puzzle, but soon falls asleep. She is exhausted these days, coping with too many things, her work, the old women, me writing this book. I have brought a chapter of it along to work on on the train, but instead I look out of the window at the passing New Jersey countryside.

I think that living in Manhattan is the obvious reason for Margaret's life being consumed with these women, but there is also something about her place in the family. Ever since I have known her, she has been the person who somehow stands up for the idea of what the family should be. She brought together her mother and her mother's brother Eddie after many years of estrangement. Soon after we were married, Margaret took me with her to the Bronx to visit her mother's mother. Few in the family made that trip to see Rose Newmark in the old age home run by the Workman's Circle, the socialist union her husband had helped to found. *De Arbiter's Ring,* as she called it in Yiddish, was a great disappointment to Rose Newmark. She confided to us over a glass of tea in the dining room, "You know who is here? A bunch of has-beens!"

As the newly green fields and brown warehouses of New Jersey slide by, I pick out an occasional flowering tree. One is a dark pink crabapple like the one we planted in our back yard in Washington. It is a little early this year for the white cherry trees in Manhattan's Riverside Park, under which Margaret and I sometimes drink a furtive martini to welcome the spring. That and a supper of shad, asparagus, new potatoes, and strawberries is our spring festival and special meal.

Of course, Easter, not Christmas, is the real Christian parallel to Passover. I think about the coincidence of this Passover, a Thursday, with the Thursday night of Holy Week, when Christ celebrated His last Passover, the Last Supper with His disciples. Both Easter and Passover are feasts of commemoration, special spring meals, the very eating of which is a repetition of a story and a ritual. The older ritual was to remember the Jews' liberation from slavery, when the avenging angel passed over their houses, sparing their sons, but smiting the first born of the Egyptians, not only their children, but their cattle as well. And the other was when Christ celebrated the Passover, and in the same ritual prepared for His own sacrifice, saying as He broke the bread and drank the wine, "Do this in remembrance of me." I never liked thinking of all this in school when it was a weekly obligation to sit through communion, but that obligation prepared my mind for falling into the deeps of the music when in college I listened over and over to Bach's "St. Matthew's Passion."

Nancy and Immanuel's house in Princeton is a short walk from the station, and we make our way through the last of the afternoon sun, past the lawns and stone walls of the houses around the university. This kind of neighborhood with sidewalks does not seem to me so alien as the "real country" suburbs in which my parents lived. Living in real country meant that it was hard to get there and once you got there, there was nothing to do. Having come home to New York City, those country places — Bedford, New York, and Fairfield, Connecticut — always felt like enemy territory.

But I liked visiting Princeton for Christmas shopping when the children were small. That was how I got to know these streets. As we arrive at the white house with the big front porch, we are carrying a basket with our contribution to the feast. Margaret bought one jar of gefilte fish from each of the five principal delicatessens of Manhattan's Upper West Side.

Nancy and Immanuel are putting the finishing touches on the meal — soup, roast chicken, green beans, and potatoes — but first, of course, there will be the ritual eating and reading, the matzos and wine and the plate of five foods prescribed in the Haggadah. The table is set, silver and crystal on the white tablecloth, the stack of unleavened matzos under a white napkin. Immanuel hands around the Haggadah books. This version was edited and translated by his Aunt Tamar, sister of his mother, Tehilla.

I am impatient with the ceremony of waiting and not eating or drinking until the prayers have all been offered, raising the cups of wine but not drinking until the right time. As we read along, however, I become interested in the way the ceremony is written. This Haggadah is about food and celebrating the liberation from oppression, not about revenge. All the curses and invidious comparisons seem to have been omitted, and when we come to the recitation of the plagues upon the Egyptians, for the first time, I do not feel as though I am an Egyptian in disguise at the table.

The reading is also shorter than I remember, and it is not long before we are at the end, putting aside the ritual sweet wine for the good Bordeaux to go with the chicken. "That was wonderful," Margaret says, "Tamar took out all the embarrassing parts. Wasn't there a wicked son in the old version?"

"Yes," Immanuel says, "she kept the wise, the simple, and the young sons, but she re-named the wicked son 'skeptical.'"

"Bowdlerizing the Haggadah! Maybe taking out the bad parts is something both sisters did. Remember how your mother used to change all the fairy tales she read so that nothing bad happened in any of them? The children were mystified, because the stories didn't have any point. But somehow Tamar's rewriting works for this ceremony. Why did she leave in all those details of how each rabbi calculated a different number of plagues for the Egyptians?"

"I'm not sure. It's like a child's game — maybe an encouragement to children to come up with their own theories. But in a way, rewriting the Haggadah is nothing new. It's been rewritten for centuries."

"Actually, calling the wicked son skeptical is quite a modern touch, in a way. It gives him an interesting motive, rather than just labeling him bad."

Dinner begins with a sampling of the gefilte fish. During the main course, the talk turns to slavery, ancient and modern. We have been watching a Public Television series about the history of slavery in America that showed its effect not only on the African slaves, but also on the owners, brutalizing the whole society. And thinking about the release of the Jews from bondage, Nancy says, in Israel, the campaign to constrict and subdue the Palestinians is having the same effect on the Israelis.

I like talking with my sister- and brother-in-law. My memory goes back to the first conversations among the four of us. Our first child, Jessica, was just a baby in the airplane seat between us when we flew out from Washington to San Francisco to spend a spring vacation with Nancy and Immanuel and their children. Our son Alexander, who reckons his age in the Chinese fashion, from the date of conception, likes to say that he was conceived in San Francisco, and so he was. I remember the room in which we stayed, with its high gables and rafters at the top of their house on a hillside in Berkeley. The University of California campus was still recovering from the shock of the student revolts that year, 1964, and the four of us talked about what a different growing up our children would have, not like the conformist experience we had all gone through.

The four of us took a trip up the coast to Big Sur and stayed at a little hot springs resort that had not yet been renamed Esalen, but I could see on its bulletin board that Fritz Perls and Virginia Satir were giving seminars there on the gestalt and family approaches to psychotherapy. Margaret and I tried to explain to Nancy and Immanuel what this new way of doing therapy was all about.

As he divides the last of the Bordeaux among our glasses, Immanuel says, "Speaking of Israel and the Palestinians, you know Tamar was the last of our family to live in Jerusalem. My grandparents bought property in the Arab part, and established a yeshiva, in complete peace with their Arab neighbors. When the land was condemned to build a bus station, there was no member of the family still living in Israel, but the relatives in the United States received compensation."

Margaret says. "I wonder if Arabs whose land is taken ever receive that kind of consideration."

Dessert is sherbet and berries, delicious. None of us can drink coffee any more, so we clear the table and move to the kitchen, where we return our attention to the five jars of gefilte fish, with much discussion. After a blind tasting, the winner is Williams' Barbecue. Immanuel and I load the dishwasher and start cleaning the pots while Nancy and Margaret go to the sofa and chair at the porch end of the kitchen.

Margaret begins to tell Nancy about our trip to Australia to attend "Adelaide '99," a conference on "narrative therapy and community work" organized by the Dulwich Centre. Margaret becomes involved in describing the elaborate opening rituals of the conference. "Before they started one of the preconference workshops, they had to search to find a person from the Aboriginal group that lived in that part of the country, to invite us to make use of the conference building. The New Zealand workshop leaders had forgotten about it until that morning, and it took a while to locate a woman who worked in one of the offices, and who was a descendant of the right group."

"It took quite a while to get down to business," I break in.

"But that was the interesting part," Margaret says. "I realized after a few days that the conference was not about getting down to business in the usual sense of a scientific and technical agenda. There were all those people from around the world. The design of the conference was to give them room to tell their stories. It wasn't about coming to conclusions or settling controversies."

I see her point, and as I go on wiping dishes, I think back to other experiences at the Adelaide conference. It was not a scientific conference, where data are presented, and possibly challenged. It was a narrative ritual. That explains the experience we had in attending it with Alan Rosen, a psychiatrist and epidemiologist, and, like us, a creature of the scientific world. Between meetings, he talked to David Epston about publishing a statistical paper on David's work with asthma. Alan directs a community mental health service in Sydney, and at this conference his was the scientific voice, taking exception, arguing. He was frequently silenced for raising these arguments, and I hadn't understood this until now. Margaret's point also made sense of another detail: On the second day of the preconference workshop, the New Zealand group included Alan in the morning welcoming ceremony, and he told some wonderful stories about his family. They were saying to him, "This is the way we want you to participate."

"The people there, from different countries and with different ways of working, would have been upset by 'scientific' controversy, and to no purpose," Margaret says. "The miracle was that we all watched and heard about each other's ways of going about our work, and came to understand each other. It's one of the few meetings we've attended where there was no backbiting during the coffee breaks. Maybe scientific argument is for journals, not therapy conferences."

And in a similar way, maybe family business is not for feast days, I think, as we put away the last of the dishes. We'll take up the things we have to settle at breakfast. Margaret and I start to tell Nancy and Immanuel about the rest of our Pacific trip, the tour in Japan and Taiwan, with Alexander. Studying for his oral exams in Chinese history has made Alex the perfect Asian tour guide and translator. As we all go slowly upstairs to bed, talking about our travels, I look at the paintings by their daughter Lizzie and her husband, Tom, that cover the walls of the house and march up the staircase wall. What a pleasure it is at this time of life, the way things come back from the children!

In the upstairs hall, we say goodnight, and Margaret and I turn in to the bedroom where Nancy has put her Tibetan Buddhist altar in the corner. Buddhism, I realize, was a gift Nancy got from her children. I think about the evening as we get ready for bed, and wonder if Buddhism has anything to do with Nancy's quiet receptivity to the way Margaret and I talk about our hobbyhorses.

The next morning at breakfast we set a date to meet and talk about Helen's finances. Immanuel will look at nursing homes in New Jersey. In thinking about nursing homes, we have our doubts about whether the old women will get there before we do. "One of the things I learned in Taiwan was Mah-Jongg!" I say. "I'm ready to go."

We all get into their car for the drive to the train station. "This was such a wonderful visit," Margaret says. "I was awake at night thinking about a Seder ritual that would work for our family. Our Easter is centered in Washington and Holy Week because our son-in-law is a member of his church choir. He spends that week in rehearsal, and the children go to church. But maybe Jessica would just bring the grandchildren to our house some other time. At least Anika is old enough, she's 4."

Nancy says, "It seems as though it is important to do the ritual at the same time as it is being done by everyone else — there is a certain energy that comes from that."

"I don't know," Margaret says, "We could do it anytime in the spring. Our family seems to be pretty flexible about these things. Anika goes to an Orthodox preschool and she can say the Hebrew blessings."

As we wait for the train, Nancy talks about a book she has been reading, *The Jew and the Lotus*. It's by a member of a group of Jews who were invited by the Dalai Lama to tell him how they dealt with the Diaspora, the problem of persecution both at home and abroad. The author's point is that the Jews learn more from the consultation than the Dalai Lama does. "I think," Nancy says, "that there is a rising interest in spirituality everywhere, maybe just as a result of people comparing experiences. You can see it in the return of interest in the Jewish kabbalah and in mysticism."

The arrival of the train to New York interrupts this discussion, and with more thanks and farewells, we climb aboard. As we settle into our seats and wave, Margaret says, "I never know what people mean by 'spiritual.'" The train starts moving and she continues to look out of the window, as if this were something she has been thinking about for a long time. "Mark Twain wrote a story about people on a raft in the ocean, and they soon discovered that they had to get along together. The idea of being on a raft dictates a moral order, a shrinking world. Some one said to me, 'Margaret, you really fan the little sparks of friendship.' Perhaps that's my spiritual practice, because I really believe that we are on a raft. We'd all be happier if everybody did that, and it's what I need to do. It's valuable in and of itself as a practice. Maybe for me it comes from moving so often and going to so many schools."

How different from my response, I think, is her reaction to many moves and many schools. "Can I write down what you are saying?" I ask, getting out a pad of paper.

"Sure," Margaret goes on, hardly noticing: "I'm so glad Nancy did this. We could put a Seder into our family's Holy Week. The kids would like it, and it wouldn't take long. Do we have to do it on the same night as everybody else? I don't think so. It's the story and what we make of it that are essential after all — the story of liberation, and having a meal together — organizing something over the generations.

"I thought that in Tamar's Haggaddah, the eating and enjoying yourself had such salience. The herb, the fruit of the vine, the bitter herb, the bread, the focus on food. It would just be fun for the children. Manischevitz wine is a child's drink. We could take turns being the youngest. Talking about it, passing down the knowledge. That's our job, to pass down knowledge. To counter the wars these days that destroy knowledge and tradition, killing intellectuals, wiping out villages, burning books, destroying records, capturing the children. Like what we did to the Indians and the Australians did to the Aboriginals — 'boarding schools!' Trying to make the children into well-meaning slaves."

She turns to me. "Wouldn't that be fun, to have a meal like that?"

"It would be lovely," I say.

"Particularly if you didn't have to do it every year. Some years, we could just have the gefilte fish or our traditional spring dinner with the shad and the martinis. Or the paschal lamb. I would want the children to have a Jewish presence strongly there in a weak way."

"So would I," I say, remembering the pleasure I took in just the touch of an Episcopal education our children got from attending Cathedral School in our neighborhood. Jessica sang in the Cathedral choir. It suddenly occurs to me that Christ was rewriting the Passover service when He instituted the communion with bread and wine. "Rewriting the Haggadah," I write in my notes. "Rewriting history, inventing ritual." Then, remembering a quotation I heard from a friend who is a historian, I write, "Every generation rewrites history to deal with the issues that it has to face — passing down knowledge is part invention, part transmission."

"Why ritual?" Margaret says. "And why all that repetition, every time and over again? Repetition allows for new meaning. The Seder is for multiplying stories; the good part of Judaism is the multiplication of interpretations, the rabbis talking about the number of the plagues, each telling a different story. We could also tell your story of fighting for the mentally ill in the Bronx. Like all these stories, it's oppression followed by liberation and prospering. That's what those stories of Michael and David are about. This is what family therapy is about."

I put down my pen. "I was thinking," I say, "about the difference between two kinds of ritual — between reciting a creed about what you believe, and having many different stories to choose among. It's the difference between the Nicene Creed defining the attributes of God and the hall of the thousand Buddhas that we saw in Nara."

"The creed is a formula. Every time you fall for a formula, you risk harming someone. Wars were fought over one phrase of that creed," Margaret says. "On the other hand, as a therapist, you owe people the skill of what you know how to do — that kind of leadership. The Seder needs a leader. Helping people to tell a good story. There is no way out of complexity; however, that's your job, to help people out of complexity. We were lucky to have World War II to grow up with. It gave us a model of leadership. We learned a different meaning for such words as 'resistance' and 'defense.' The Resistance was the French Underground. The Defense Effort was a good thing. In our neighborhood. in Cambridge during the war, we had a fort that was being defended — boys against girls — the girls were *defending* something."

As we enter the tunnel to Pennsylvania Station, the windows are dark and the lights in the car come on. "I've written it all down," I say, putting my pad away.

Margaret looks at me. "Good," she says, "It will take some doing on both our parts. One of the things I got out of the trip to Australia and Japan was a realization that I am going to stop running the family for everybody else."

I have heard Margaret say this before, but she sounds like something about the trip confirmed it for her. If she doesn't run it, who will? I remember her worry about losing touch with her family after the old women — especially her mother — die. It is a worry that would not have occurred to me. There have always been more than enough people in my life. She has always been enough family for me, she and the children. But I would not be enough family for her.

Now, as we collect our bags and the train comes into the station, I try to put myself into this story of travel and change. What do I want? No. What are my intentions? My pilgrimages up until now have been solitary, trips to an arts camp in the summer, for example, where I painted landscapes all day and wrote the first chapters of this book at night. One summer, Margaret came as well, and, in addition to playing Scrabble with all comers, she wrote — the stories she told our children. Passing down knowledge.

As we head off through the crowd at Pennsylvania Station, I realize that I would welcome more company on the raft now than I did in those days, five years ago. Maybe this pilgrimage to Princeton has taken us across a border in time. Here we are, heading for retirement, the book written, the work done, ready to begin again.

EPILOGUE:
An Open Letter to
Family Therapists

I WROTE THIS BOOK FOR THE GENERAL READER, hoping that family therapists and others in the mental health business would enjoy it as a story to compare with their own, and perhaps recommend it to nontherapist friends who are curious about our work. With that nonprofessional audience in mind, I have avoided, where possible, the kinds of discussions that enliven our journals and warm the exchanges in the bar during meetings of the American Family Therapy Academy. It is time, here at the end, to address some of the problems that we face as a profession. First, I want to review the problems created by our hunger for the assurance of a general theory. And then I want to address the more serious question of our survival as an effective force in the psychotherapy business.

Our habit of becoming overinvolved with the general ideas of our heroes, taking them literally as the heralds of revolution, has led us astray in two ways: we have wasted time and energy arguing about doctrine, and in some cases we have ended with the pointless conclusion that we are divided from one another into philosophical schools (Chapter 8).

Doctrinal argument was the way classical psychoanalysis alienated itself from everything else, as I said in the earlier chapters, and we should take care not to repeat that history. Psychoanalysis had many other ways to go other than this scientistic isolation, as can be seen from this quotation from 30 years ago[1]:

---

[1] Novey, Samuel (1968). *The second look: The reconstruction of personal history in psychiatry and psychoanalysis.* Baltimore: John's Hopkins Press (quoted by J. Philip Stanberry, *Readings*, 14:3, 1999, p. 10).

This is my behavioral sense of it, that each of us goes around with a curriculum vitae, with a sense of who we are, where we've been, and where we're going. This is in people who are having difficulties, an unfortunate one. Suppose they get together with someone and gain what I call perspective, get a second look. Get the view of prior events to be looked at again — not prior events as they happened but today's view of those events. If this is modified, I think there is an accompanying modification of the people themselves.

That sounds to me like the very essence of narrative, and if we had heard more of such straight talk (this was from an analyst in 1968), and less elegant theory, we would be further along toward the kind of synthesis of approaches I have been talking about.

Family therapy also ran the risk of isolation — seeing ourselves as part of a distinctive school — thinking that in the Batesonian concept of "systems" we had something new and unique. I remember how taken we were by these ideas; Margaret and I used to take turns reading Bateson's *Mind and Nature* to each other. Lynn Hoffman and I would puzzle over the detection of "positive feedback" versus "negative feedback" phenomena in our clinical cases. In seminars, many of us tried to figure out how to tell whether we were achieving "second-order change," or merely plain old first-order change, the kind that didn't really reset the system.

In fact, I think we were enthralled with Batesonian systemic thinking because it seemed like such a change from Freudian positivism, and because it provided an intellectual thread to follow through the jungle of novel practices that family therapy presented. People were trying everything, and nothing had been tested. We had to have an image in mind. If we had taken systems thinking as a biological metaphor rather than as a religious text, or as a scientific handbook, we could have avoided excesses of fidelity such as the Milan method, whose literal approach managed to combine the worst of both psychoanalysis and system cybernetics (Chapter 11). Bateson was appalled at some of the things that family therapists did in his name (Bateson & Bateson, 1987, p. 204).

A third instance of this literal approach to theory is a strangely intense debate that took place inside the circle of narrative "schools." Some postmodern thinkers were so taken with the idea of the narrator as the ultimate authority that they began to believe that no other perspective was valid, or even knowable, and they found scientific support for this in the biology of Umberto Maturana (Dell, 1985). Perhaps they were seduced into this literal belief because it seemed to settle the problem of alliance with the patient under difficult circumstances.

Barbara Held took this subject on in an interesting analysis, *Back to Reality, A Critique of Postmodern Theory in Psychotherapy*.[2] She pointed out that the extreme position of the social constructionists is a way of skirting the clinician's dilemma, which is to try to know the powers and limitations of both the narrative and scientific diagnostic point of view. I argued in favor of this in Chapter 13. Every clinician has the dual and inescapable responsibility to comprehend both the knowledge of the outside world and the knowledge that is in the patient's head. If they conflict, whatever is useful of each has to be somehow brought together, and that is no more a matter of simply joining the patient's experience than it is of simply appealing to medical authority. The combination of the art and the science is more difficult than that, and the path to doing no harm lies through the middle of the conflict, a path one must follow with one's eyes open.[3]

§

Grand theoretical ideas are useful as inspiring metaphors. Now, two academic generations after Bateson, it is possible to look back and see that systems thinking was a metaphor for organic interrelatedness, for an interest in how life at all its levels of complexity actually went on. As Bateson knew, it was a concept that had been there since the great French physiologist Claude Bernard described homeostasis — the regulation of blood pressure, blood sugar, temperature, and countless other biological mechanisms — in the middle of the nineteenth century. This was the physiology that inspired the young John Dewey as a college student

---

[2] As I read Held's book (Held, 1995), I was struck by the fact that she did not refer to herself as a family therapist, or to the 11 out of 15 people she was talking about who were primarily trained or known as family therapists.

[3] I have watched narrative therapists — myself included — do damage by sticking exclusively to the client's own story when a darker possibility needed to be investigated. Childhood autism, affective disorders, and addictions are easy to miss if the therapist is paying attention only to the hopeful side of the family's narrative.

in the 1880s. Follow me for a moment into Dewey's reflections on the source of his inspiration. I think reading them in detail provides a positive example of how to look at grand ideas like general systems theory.

Toward the end of his career, in 1929 at the age of 70, Dewey looked back on his senior year in college at the University of Vermont, where he had been able to take an elective course.[4]

> That was a rather short course, without laboratory work, in physiology, a book of Huxley's being the text. It is difficult to speak with exactitude about what happened to me intellectually so many years ago, but I have an impression that there was derived from that study a sense of interdependence and interrelated unity that gave form to intellectual stirrings that had previously been inchoate, and created a kind of type or model of a view of things to which material in any field ought to conform.

The scientific representations of the course provided a metaphor:

> Subconsciously, at least, I was led to desire a world and a life that would have the same properties as had the human organism ... I date from this time the awakening of a distinctly philosophic interest. (p. 4)

Dewey makes it clear that it was not Huxley or Bernard, but another physician, William James, who showed him how to turn this vision into a working approach to philosophy.

> I doubt if we have as yet begun to realize all that is due to William James for the introduction and use of this idea. ... anyway, it worked its way more and more into all my ideas and acted as a ferment to transform old beliefs.

And the fermenting idea was specifically not to be taken literally; it was not a mechanism, a "schematism":

---

[4] Dewey, 1930. I am indebted to Laura Chasin for showing me this.

If this biological conception and mode of approach had been prematurely hardened by James, its effect might have been simply to substitute one schematism for another. But it is not tautology to say that James's sense of life was itself vital. He had a profound sense, in origin artistic and moral, perhaps, rather than "scientific," of the difference between the categories of the living and the mechanical; some time, I think, someone may write an essay that will show how the most distinctive factors in his general philosophic view, pluralism, novelty, freedom, individuality, are all connected with his feeling for the qualities and traits of that which lives. Many philosophers have had much to say about the idea of organism; but they have taken it structurally and hence statically. It was reserved for James to think of life in terms of life in action ... (p. 15)[5]

This was prophetic. Bateson, in fact, wrote that essay in *Steps to an Ecology of Mind*. Here is the distinction between the rules that apply to the inanimate world of mechanics, the *pleroma*, and the world of life in action, the *creatura* (Bateson, 1972). This physiology also provided, as Bateson later pointed out in the psychiatric textbook he coauthored (Ruesch & Bateson, 1968), a model for the social nature of mind.[6] As Dewey put it:

The objective biological approach of the Jamesian psychology led straight to the perception of the importance of distinctive social categories, especially communication and participation. It is my conviction that a great deal of our philosophizing needs to be done over again from this point of view, and that there will ultimately result an integrated synthesis in a philosophy congruous with modern science and related to actual needs in education, morals and religion. The characteristic traits of the

---

[5] How different this vision of biology was from that of Freud, who was also a neuroanatomist and neurophysiologist, can be appreciated by reading Sulloway (1992) on Freud's brief career as a medical researcher.

[6] George Herbert Mead (Chapter 4), the principal originator of this Batesonian idea, was a graduate student with James at Harvard. He, James, and Dewey developed this aspect of psychology in different ways — Mead most explicitly.

science of today are connected with the development of social subjects – anthropology, history, politics, literature, social and abnormal psychology and so on. The movement is both so new, in an intellectual sense, and we are so much of it and it is so much of us, that it escapes definite notice. (p. 17)

Bateson was working out the "social categories of communication and participation" and produced a synthesis "congruous with modern science, education, morals and religion." If we had been able to take his apparently mechanistic cybernetics with a grain of salt, we might have been more inspired and less possessed by him.

§

If we are not to expect certainty from theory, where will it come from? The really important differences among us are those that stem from practice and its consequences, and we need to inquire deeply into those. That inquiry involves outcome research — and process research in which instead of reading each other's theoretical papers we look at each other's videotapes.[7]

For me, being in new places, presented with new problems to solve with new clinical populations, and having to demonstrate some new measure of effectiveness, if only to oneself, these were the circumstance that led to invention. I think the same must have been true of Minuchin at Wyltwick and Bowen at NIMH, to mention two famous instances. I know firsthand the people at the Ackerman Institute who have taken on specific projects such as Peggy Papp's work with depression in married couples, Virginia Goldner and Gillian Walker's work with spouse violence, Marcia Sheinberg's project for sexually abused children and their families, the large group working on the effects of fertility treatment on marriage, and so on (Diamond, Kezur, Meyers, et al, 1999). Sharply defined clinical practice produces the grain and grit of progress in our work.

---

[7] A respondent at a recent conference on narrative approaches asked rhetorically if anyone had ever changed his or her therapeutic practice as a result of outcome studies. The answer is "Yes." See the treatment of schizophrenia and borderline personality disorder in Chapter 13.

Is a larger synthesis possible? If I cast about for it in my experience, the closest I come is a kind of carefully described eclecticism. James and Melissa Griffith's *The Body Speaks* (1994) is my most recent reading of this kind. They combine hypnosis, medical psychiatry, family therapy, spiritual dialogue and narrative work in a general medical hospital that I think must be a very fortunate place. Reading their stories gives a picture of what the general practice of psychotherapy could be like if we were all trained to do our best.

§

Now to turn to the most serious threat we face. The history of public psychiatry (Chapters 2, 3, and 5) must have seemed to many readers like a trip to the lost, drowned city of Atlantis. The waters have closed over it. The agents of state budgetcutting and the cynical debauch of "managed care" have not only destroyed the system of service delivery we were beginning to construct so painstakingly in the 1970s. They have also taken with it the structure and the motivation for training. Insurance companies are not interested in training. It is an expense they want someone else to bear.

The charge the insurance lobby has made, that publicly supported medical care will not work in America, is not true even to our own experience.[8] When I was a resident at Bronx Municipal Hospital in 1961–1963, I was part of the New York city hospital system, one of several publicly funded health systems in the country. Patients who could afford to pay, paid, and those who could not pay were treated free of charge. It was a two-tier system of social medicine like those of many European countries. Later, when I worked for the New York state hospital system, I came even closer to socialized medicine, a system supported completely by taxes in recognition of an obvious and historical public need. Both of those city and state hospitals, with help from the federal government, included training as an expense in their budgets, and as a major concern in the way they allocated staff time and responsibilities. Even the most private hospitals sought, and still seek, university affiliation and teaching

---

[8] The Congress and the executive branch in Washington depend on Walter Reed Army Hospital for their medical care, and endorse it with the taxpayers' money. The quality of public medicine depends on the intentions of its designers.

programs as a way of maintaining quality. It was obvious that all of us needed to go on learning from each other, that teaching and learning were needed not only for the credentials the risk managers worry about, but were the life and conscience of the profession. In psychiatry, learning is a metaphor for healing itself (Chapter 6).

The mess of pottage for which we exchanged this great public trust seemed like a minor side dish at first. Some of the patients, mostly working class, had a hard time paying the increasing costs of care. Health insurance payments for some or all of their treatment had been available since the 1940s, and increased noticeably in the 1960s. It seemed like a small matter, even a humane policy, but it introduced two considerations that have now overwhelmed and destroyed the system. One is that illness is something one can be insured against, like a flood or a bent fender, rather than something that is our common lot, like the need for water or for rescue from fire. And following that is the second heresy, that insurance companies should have something to say about treatment. Instead of facing the social problem of the rising cost and fair public distribution of medical care, we thought of it as something the insurance industry in its wisdom would somehow take care of, the way they miraculously pay for major surgery.

That is how it happened. I am amazed and touched at the hardiness with which family therapy survives in this environment. The Ackerman Family Institute continues to get students. People still want to learn it, in spite of having no family diagnoses to put down for their insurance forms, and often no payment for the treatment that they do. What we have to do is hold on to training programs, against the tide, until the tide turns, as it must eventually. People will eventually recognize that the insurance companies, by swallowing health care whole, have created a public entity that will have to be regulated and reorganized after they are through digesting what they can. They have already begun to spit out the Medicaid part. It is our bizarre American way of making social change, and we will eventually figure it out after much destruction, with hospitals and even medical schools killing each other off, trying to merge, like banks, for economies of scale.[9]

---

[9] Turning medicine into a "free market" not only has been bad medicine, it has been an economic failure for everyone except the biggest profit-takers. See Kuttner (1997), especially Chapter 4, "Markets and Medicine."

The political challenge that faces us, and everybody else, in the years ahead is to find some way to put the public system back together again after its savage dismemberment. Meanwhile, we have to keep training alive. In 1980 a group of us at the Psychiatric Institute put together a Public Psychiatry Fellowship for beginning psychiatrists in the public sector, a postgraduate year of study and experience to help them find a good place to work in what is left of that system. And we offer training in family therapy.[10] I go back once a year to give a seminar for that group, and I am amazed at the ingenuity with which people who are really determined to take care of the poor, the addicted, and the seriously ill continue to do so in the trenches of this bombed-out terrain. That is what we need to keep learning how to do, until the public is disgusted enough to face its responsibility — and its interest in its own health — and vote the jackals out.

---

[10] The Public Psychiatry Fellowship thus allows the state to pay the salaries of a faculty who both teach the fellows and provide family therapy training to the rest of the Psychiatric Institute.

REFERENCES

Ackerman, N. W. (1966). *Treating the troubled family*. New York: Basic Books.

Anderson, C., Hogarty, G., & Reiss, D. (1980). Family treatment of adult schizophrenic patients: A psychoeducational approach. *Schizophrenia Bulletin, 6,* 490–505.

Anderson, C., Hogarty, G., & Reiss, D. (1981). The psychoeducational family treatment of schizophrenia. In M. Goldstein (Ed.), *New developments in interventions with families of schizophrenics*. San Francisco: Jossey-Bass.

Anderson, H., & Goolishian, H. A. (1988). Human systems as linguistic systems: Preliminary and evolving ideas about the implications for clinical theory. *Family Process, 27,* 371–393.

Asch, S. E. (1951). Effects of group pressure upon the modification and distortion of judgements. In H. Guetzkow (Ed.), *Groups, leadership and men*. New York: Russell & Russell.

Auerswald, E. (1968). Interdisciplinary vs. ecological approach. *Family Process, 7,* 202–215.

Bachofen, J. J. (1967). Myth, religion and mother-right. R. Manheim (trans.). Princeton, NJ: Princeton University Press.

Bamberger, J. (1974). The myth of matriarchy: Why men rule in primitive society. In M. Z. Rosaldo & L. Lamphere (Eds.), *Woman, culture and society* (pp. 263–280). Stanford, CA: Stanford University Press.

Bass, E., & Davis, L. (1988). *The courage to heal*. New York: Harper & Rowe.

Bateson, G. (1958). *Naven*. Stanford, CA: Stanford University Press.

Bateson, G. (1972a). The cybernetics of "self": A theory of alcoholism. In G. Bateson, *Steps to an ecology of mind*. New York: Ballantine Books.

Bateson, G. (1972b). Form, substance and difference. In G. Bateson, *Steps to an ecology of mind*. New York: Ballantine Books.

Bateson, G. (1979). *Mind and nature, a necessary unity*. New York: Dutton.

Bateson, G., & Bateson, M. C. (1987). *Angels fear: Towards an epistomology of the sacred*. New York: Macmillan.

Bateson, G., Jackson, D. D., Haley, J., & Weakland, J. (1956). Towards a theory of schizophrenia. *Behavioral Science, 1,* 251–264.

Beels, C. C. (1981). Social support and schizophrenia. *Schizophrenia Bulletin,* 7(1), 58–72.

Beels, C. C. (1989). The invisible village. *New Directions for Mental Health Services, 42.*

Beels, C. C., & Ferber, A. S. (1969). Family therapy: A view. *Family Process, 8,* 280–318.

Beels, C. C., Gutwirth, L., Berkeley, J., & Struening, E. (1984). Measurements of social support in schizophrenia. *Schizophrenia Bulletin, 10*(3), 399–411.

Bell, J. E. (1967). Family group therapy — A new treatment method for children. *Family Process,* 254–263.

Berkowitz, C. B., & Gunderson, J. G. (in press). Multifamily psychoeducational treatment of borderline personality disorder. In W. R. McFarlane (Ed.), *The multifamily group.* New York: Guilford.

Berne, E. (1986). *Transactional analysis in psychotherapy.* New York: Ballantine Books.

Blacker, D., & Tsuang, M. T. (1992). Contested boundaries of bipolar disorder and the limits of categorical diagnosis in psychiatry. *Amercian Journal of Psychiatry, 49,* 1473–1483.

Bowen, M. (1978). *Family therapy in clinical practice.* New York: Jason Aronson.

Bremner, J. D., & Marmar, C. R. (1997). *Trauma, memory and dissociation.* Washington, DC: American Psychiatric Press.

Brown, G. W., & Harris, T. (1978). *Social origins of depression: A study of psychiatric disorders in women.* London: Tavistock.

Brown, T. E. (2000). *Attention-deficit disorders and comorbidities in children, adolescents, and adults.* Washington, DC: American Psychiatric Press.

Brumberg, J. J. (1988). *Fasting girls.* Cambridge, MA: Harvard University Press.

Bruner, J. (1990). *Acts of meaning.* Cambridge, MA: Harvard University Press.

Burgess, E. (1926). The family as a unit of interacting personalities. *The Family,* 7(1), 3–9.

Burns, D. D. (1998). *Feeling good: The new mood therapy.* New York: Avon.

Carr, A. (2000). Evidence-based practice in family therapy and systemic consultation II. *The Journal of Family Therapy, 22*(3), 273–296.

Chamberlain, S. (1990). The new ethnography: "Windmills and giants." *Dulwich Centre Newsletter 2,* 39–46.

Chapman, A. H. (1976). *Harry Stack Sullivan: The man and his work.* New York: G. P. Putnam's Sons.

Chess, S., Thomas, A., & Birch, H. (1963). *Temperament and behavior disorders in children.* New York: New York University Press.

Cohen, M. B., Baker, G., Cohen, R. D., Fromm-Reichmann, F., & Weigert, E. (1954). An intensive study of twelve cases of manic–depressive psychosis. *Psychiatry, 17,* 103–137.

Crews, F. (1994). The unknown Freud. *New York Review of Books,* February 3.

Cushman, P. (1995). *Constructing the self, constructing America: A cultural history of psychotherapy*. Reading, MA: Addison-Wesley.

Darnton, R. (1968). *Mesmerism and the end of the enlightenment in France*. Cambridge, MA: Harvard University Press.

Decker, H. S. (1991). *Freud, Dora and Vienna 1900*. New York: Free Press.

Dell, P. F. (1985). Understanding Bateson and Maturana: Toward a biological foundation for the social sciences. *Journal of Marital and Family Therapy, 11*, 1–20.

DeSisto, M., Harding, C. M., McCormack, R. V., Ashikaga, T., & Brooks, G. W. (1995). The Maine and Vermont three-decade studies of serious mental illness. *British Journal of Psychiatry, 167*, 331–342.

Dewey, J. (1930). On experience, nature and freedom. In R. J. Bernstein (Ed.), *The library of the liberal arts* (Chap. 41). Liberal Arts Press.

Diamond, R., Kezur, D., Meyers, M., Scharf, C. N., & Weinshel, M. (1999). *Couple therapy for infertility*. New York: Guilford.

Dinsmore, C. (1991). *From surviving to thriving: Incest, feminism and recovery*. Albany: State University of New York Press.

Eisler, R. (1987). *The chalice and the blade: Our history, our future*. New York: Harper & Rowe.

Ellenberger, H. (1981). *The discovery of the unconscious: The history and evolution of dynamic psychiatry*. New York: Basic Books.

Falloon, I. R. H., Boyd, J. L., & McGill, C. W. (1984). *Family care of schizophrenia*. New York: Guilford.

Falloon, I. R. H., Boyd, J. L., McGill, C. W., Razani, J., Moss, H. B., & Gilderman, A. M. (1982). Family management in the prevention of exacerbations of schizophrenia: A controlled study. *New England Journal of Medicine, 306*(24), 1437–1439.

Faris, R. E. L. (1967). *Chicago sociology 1920–1932*. Chicago: University of Chicago Press.

Ferber, A. S., Mendelsohn, M., & Napier, G. (1972). *The book of family therapy*. New York: Science House.

Forrester, J. (1997). *Dispatches from the Freud wars: Psychoanalysis and its passions*. Cambridge, MA: Harvard University Press.

Foucault, M. (1965). *Madness and civilization*. New York: Pantheon.

Frank, J. (1991). *Persuasion and healing: A comparative study of psychotherapy*. Baltimore: Johns Hopkins University Press.

Fraser, C. (2000). "Mary Baker Eddy" by Gillian Gill. *New York Review of Books, 47*(7), pp. 49–52.

Freeman, D. (1998). *The fateful hoaxing of Margaret Mead: A historical analysis of her Samoan research*. Denver: Westview Press.

Freud, S. (1896). The etiology of hysteria. *Standard Edition* (Vol. 3, pp. 189–221). London: Hogarth.

Freud, S. (1909). Five lectures on psychoanalysis. *Standard Edition* (Vol. 11, pp. 3–55). London: Hogarth.

Freud, S. (1911). Psychoanalytic notes on an autobiographical account of a case of paranoia (Dementia Paranoides). *Standard Edition* (Vol. 12, pp. 3–79). London: Hogarth.

Freud, S. (1927). The future of an illusion. *Standard Edition* (Vol. 21, pp. 3–56). London: Hogarth.

Freud, S. (1930). Civilization and its discontents. *Standard Edition* (Vol. 21, pp. 59–145). London: Hogarth.

Freud, S., & Breuer, J. (1895). Studies in hysteria. *Standard Edition* (Vol. 2). London: Hogarth.

Fuller, R. C. (1982). *Mesmerism and the American cure of souls.* Philadelphia: University of Pennsylvania Press.

Garfinkel, H. (1984). *Studies in ethnomethodology.* London: Polity Press.

Garrison, V. (1982). Folk healing systems as elements in the community: support systems of psychiatric patients. In U. Rueveni, R. V. Speck, & J. L. Speck (Eds.), *Therapeutic intervention: Healing strategies for human systems* (pp. 58–85). New York: Human Sciences Press.

Gauld, A. (1992). *A history of hypnotism.* London: Cambridge.

Geertz, C. (1973). Thick description: Toward an interpretive theory of culture. (Chapter 1), In C. Geertz, *The interpretation of cultures.* New York: Basic Books.

Gilligan, S., & Price, R. (1993). Therapeutic conversations. New York: Norton.

Goldner, V. (1985). Feminism and family therapy. *Family Process, 24,* 31–47.

Goldner, V., Penn, P., Sheinberg, M., & Walker, G. (1990). Love and violence: Gender paradoxes in volatile attachments. *Family Process, 29,* 343–364.

Goode, E. (1999, November 2). New clues to why we dream. *New York Times,* pp. 1 & 4.

Goodheart, E. (1995). Freud on trial. *Dissent,* Spring, 236–243.

Gray, J. (1994). *Men are from Mars, women are from Venus.* New York: Harper Collins.

Gremillion, H. (1992). Psychiatry as social ordering: Anorexia nervosa, a paradigm. *Social Science and Medicine, 35*(1), 57–71.

Griffith, J. L., & Griffith, M. E. (1994). *The body speaks: Therapeutic dialogues for mind–body problems.* New York: Basic Books.

Gudeman, J. E., & Shore, M. F. (1984). Beyond deinstitutionalization: A new class of facilities for the mentally ill. *New England Journal of Medicine, 311,* 832–836.

Gunderson, J. (1990). New perspectives on becoming borderline. In P. S. Links (Ed.), *Family environment and borderline personality disorder* (pp. 151–159). Washington, DC: American Psychiatric Press.

Gurman, A. S., & Kniskern, D. P. (Eds.). (1991). *Handbook of family therapy, Vol. II.* New York: Brunner/Mazel.

Halberstam, M. (1967). Patients who make the doctor feverish. *New York Times Magazine, February 5*, pp. 18–19.

Hale, N. G. (1971). *Freud and the Americans.* New York: Oxford.

Hale, N. G. (1995). *The rise and crisis of psychoanalysis in the United States.* New York: Oxford.

Haley, J. (1968). An interactional explanation of hypnosis. In D. D. Jackson (Ed.), *Therapy, communication and change.* Palo Alto, CA: Science & Behavior Books.

Hallowell, E., & Ratey, J. (1994). *Driven to distraction.* New York: Pantheon.

Harding, C. M., Brooks, G. W., Ashikaga, T., Strauss, J. S., & Breier, A. (1987). The Vermont longitudinal study of persons with severe mental illness. II: Long-term outcome of subjects who retrospectively met DSM-III criteria for schizophrenia. *American Journal of Psychiatry, 144*(6), 727–735.

Hare-Mustin, R. (1994). Discourses in the mirrored room. *Family Process, 33*, 19–35.

Hartwell, C. E. (1997). The schizophrenogenic mother concept in American psychiatry. *Psychiatry, 59*(3), 274–297.

Havens, L. (1976). *Participant observation.* New York: Jason Aronson.

Held, B. S. (1995). *Back to reality: A critique of postmodern theory in psychotherapy.* New York: Norton.

Henry, J. (1971). *Pathways to madness.* New York: Random House.

Herman, J. L. (1992). *Trauma and recovery.* New York: Basic Books.

Herskovitz, M. (1940). *Economic anthropology: The economic life of primitive peoples.* New York: Norton.

Hollander, E. (1997). Obsessive-compulsive disorder: The hidden epidemic. *Journal of Clinical Psychiatry, 58 Supplements*(12), 3–6.

Hornig, M. (1998). Addressing comorbidity in adults with attention-deficit/hyperactivity disorder. *Journal of Clinical Psychiatry, 59* (Supplement 7), 69–75.

Hyde, L. (1979). *The gift: Imagination and the erotic life of property.* New York: Vintage Books.

Imber-Black, E., & Roberts, J. (1992). *Rituals for our times.* New York: Harper Collins.

Imber-Black, E., Roberts, J., & Whiting, R. (1988). *Rituals in families and family therapy.* New York: Norton.

Jackson, D. D. (1960). *The etiology of schizophrenia.* New York: Basic Books.

Jamison, K. R. (1993). *Touched with fire: Manic-depressive illness and the artistic temperament.* New York: Free Press.

Jaynes, J. (1990). *The origin of consciousness in the breakdown of the bicameral mind.* Boston: Houghton Mifflin.

Johnson, J. G., Cohen, P., Brown, J., Smailes, E. M., & Bernstein, D. P. (1999). Childhood maltreatment increases risk for personality disorders during early adulthood. *Archives of General Psychiatry, 56* (July), 600–606.

Kardec, A. (1953). *El evangelio segun el espiritismo.* (1st ed.). Tlacoquemecatl, Mexico: Editorial Diana.

Kemp, W. (1990). *The desire of my eyes: The life and work of John Ruskin.* New York: NoonDay Press, Farrar, Strauss & Geroux.

Kessler, R. C., McGonagle, K. A., Zhao, S., Nelson, C. B., Hughes, M., Eshleman, S., Wittchen, H.uU., & Kendler, K. S. (1944). Lifetime and 12-month prevalence of DSM-III-R psychiatric disorders in the United States: Results from the National Comorbidity Study. *Archives of General Psychiatry,* 51, 8–19.

Kiesler, C. A. (1982). Mental hospitals and alternative care: Noninstitutionalization as potential public policy for mental patients. *American Psychologist, 37,* 349–360.

Kleinman, A. (1988). *The illness narratives: Suffering and the human condiiton.* New York: Basic Books.

Kuttner, R. (1997). *Everything for sale: The virtues and limitations of markets.* New York: Knopf.

Laing, R. D. (1960). *The divided self.* New York: Pantheon.

Laing, R. D. (1965). Mystification, confusion and conflict. In I. Boszormenyi-Nagy & J. L. Framo (Eds.), *Intensive family therapy: Theoretical and practical aspects.* New York: Harper & Rowe.

Laing, R. L., & Esterson, A. (1964). *Sanity, madness and the family, Vol. 1. Families of schizophrenics.* London: Tavistock.

Lankton, S. R., & Lankton, C. S. (1983). *The answer within: A clinical framework for Ericksonian hypnotherapy.* New York: Brunner/Mazel.

Lasch, C. (1977). *Haven in a heartless world.* New York: Basic Books.

Lears, J. (1981). *No place of grace, antimodernism and the transformation of American culture, 1880–1920.* New York: Pantheon.

Lerner, H. G. (1985). *The dance of anger.* New York: Harper & Rowe.

Levi-Strauss, C. (1963). The sorcerer and his magic. In C. Levi-Strauss, *Structural anthropology* (pp. 167–185). New York: Basic Books.

Lewis, J. (2000). *Disarming the past: How an intimate relationship can heal old wounds.* Phoenix, AZ: Zeig, Tucker & Theisen.

Lewis, J. (1997). *Marriage as a search for healing.* New York: Brunner/Mazel.

Lidz, T., Cornelison, A. R., Fleck, S., & Terry, D. (1957). The intrafamilial environment of schizophrenic patients: II. Marital schism and marital skew. *American Journal of Psychiatry, 114,* 241–248.

Liebow, E. (1968). *Tally's corner.* Boston: Little, Brown.

Linehan, M. M., Tutek, D. A., Heard, H. L., & Armstrong, H. E. (1994). Interpersonal outcome of cognitive behavioral treatment for chronically suicidal borderline patients. *American Journal of Psychiatry, 151,* 1771–1776.

Lopez, C.-A. (2000). Franklin and Mesmer: A confrontation. In C.-A. Lopez, *My life with Benjamin Franklin*. New Haven, CT: Yale University Press.

Lubove, R. (1965). *The professional altruist*. Cambridge, MA: Harvard University Press.

Luepnitz, D. (1988). *The family interpreted*. New York: Basic Books.

Lusterman, D.-D. (1998). *Infidelity*. New York: New Harbinger.

MacGregor, R., Ritchie, K., Serrano, A. M., Schuster, F. P., McDanald, E. C., & Goolishian, H. A. (Eds.). (1961). *Multiple impact therapy with families*. New York: McGraw-Hill.

Malcolm, J. (1983). Books: Six roses ou cirrhose? *New Yorker* (January 24), pp. 96–106.

Malcolm, J. (1984). *In the Freud archives*. New York: Knopf.

Masson, J. M. (1992). *The assault on truth*. New York: Harper Collins.

McFarlane, W. R., Lukens, E., Link, B., Dushay, R., Deakins, S. A., Newmark, M., Dunne, E. J., Horen, B., & Toran, J. (1995). Multiple-family groups and psychoeducation in the treatment of schizophrenia. *Archives of General Psychiatry, 52*(8), 679–687.

McGinn, C. (1999). Freud under analysis. *New York Review of Books, 46*(17), pp. 20–25.

McGlashan, T. H. (1986). Schizophrenia: Psychosocial treatments and the role of psychosocial factors in its etiology and pathogenesis. In A. J. Frances & R. E. Hales (Eds.), *Psychiatry update: American Psychiatric Association annual review* (Vol. 5). Washington, DC: American Psychiatric Press.

Mead, G. H. (1962). Mind, self and society. C. W. Morris (Ed.), Chicago: University of Chicago Press.

Mechanic, D., & Rochefort, D. A. (1992). A policy of inclusion for the mentally ill. *Health Affairs*, Spring, 128–150.

Meyer, D. (1980). *The positive thinkers*. New York: Pantheon.

Miller, J. (1995). Going unconscious. *New York Review of Books,* April 20, pp. 59–65.

Miller, S. L. (1969). The origin of life. In S. Devons (Ed.), *Biology and the physical sciences*. New York: Columbia University Press.

Minuchin, S. (1974). *Families and family therapy*. Cambridge, MA: Harvard University Press.

Minuchin, S., Montalvo, B., Guerney, B. G., Rosman, B. L., & Schumer, F. (1967). *Families of the slums*. New York: Basic Books.

Mitchell, S. A. (1993). *Hope and dread in psychoanalysis*. New York: Basic Books.

Mitchell, S. A. (1999). Attachment theory and the psychoanalytic tradition; Reflections on human relationality. *Psychoanalytic Dialogues, 9* (1), 85–107.

Moltz, D. A. (1993). Bipolar disorder and the family: An integrative model. *Family Process, 32*, 409–423.

Moltz, D. M., & Newmark, M. (in press). Family groups for bipolar illness. In

W. R. McFarlane (Ed.), *The multifamily group*. New York: Guilford.

Murphy, K., & Barkley, R. A. (1996). Attention deficit hyperactivity disorder adults: Comorbidities and adaptive impairments. *Comprehensive Psychiatry*, *59*(Supplement 7), 393–401.

Myerhoff, B. (1992). *Remembered lives: The work of ritual, story-telling and growing older*. Ann Arbor: University of Michigan Press.

Newmark, M., & Beels, C. (1994). The misuse and use of science in family therapy. *Family Process*, *33*(1), 3–18.

Niederland, W. G. (1959). The "miracled-up" world of Schreber's childhood. *Psychoanalytic Study of the Child*, *14*, 383–413.

Nock, S. (2000). The divorce of marriage and parenthood. *The Journal of Family Therapy 22*(3), 245–264.

Novey, S. (1968). *The second look: The reconstruction of personal history in psychiatry and psychoanalysis*. Baltimore: Johns Hopkins Press.

Okin, R. L. (1985). Expand the community care system: Deinstitutionalization can work. *Hospital and Community Psychiatry*, *36*, 742–745.

Papp, P. (1980). The Greek chorus and other techniques of paradoxical therapy. *Family Process*, *19*, 45–57.

Perry, H. S. (1982). *Psychiatrist of America: The life of Harry Stack Sullivan*. Cambridge, MA: Belknap Press of Harvard University Press.

Pirsig, R. M. (1974). Zen and the art of motorcycle maintenance: An inquiry into values. New York: Morrow.

Pliszka, S. R. (1998). Comorbidity of attention deficit/hyperactivity disorder with psychiatric disorder: An overview. *Journal of Clinical Psychiatry*, *59* (Supplement 7), 50–58.

Putnam, F. W., & Carlson, E. B. Hypnosis, dissociation and trauma: Myths, metaphors and mechanisms. In D. J. Bremner & C. R. Marmar (Eds.), *Trauma, memory and dissociation* (pp. 27–55). Washington, DC: American Psychiatric Press.

Reik, T. (1946). *Ritual: Psychoanalytic studies*. New York: International Universities Press.

Rieff, P. (1959). *Freud: The mind of the moralist*. Garden City, NY: Viking.

Risen, J. (2000). How a plot convulsed Iran in '53 (and in '79). *New York Times*, April 16, Sec. A, pp. 1 & 14.

Ritterman, M. (1983). *Using hypnosis in family therapy*. San Francisco: Jossey-Bass.

Ritterman, M. (1987). Torture: The counter-therapy of the state. *Family Therapy Networker, January–February*, 43–47.

Rogers, C. R. (1995). *Client-centered therapy*. Trans-Atlantic Publications.

Rorty, R. (1991). *Objectivity, relativism and truth: Philosophical papers, Vol 1*. Cambridge, England: Cambridge University Press.

Rosen, A. (1994). 100% MABO: Decolonizing people with mental illness and their families. *Australian and New Zealand Journal of Family Therapy*, *15*, 128–142.

Rosen, A., Miller, V., & Parker, G. (1989). Standards of care for area mental health services. *Australian and New Zealand Journal of Psychiatry, 23,* 379–395.

Rosenblatt, A. (1974). Providing custodial care for mental patients: An affirmative view. *Psychiatric Quarterly, 48*(1), 14–25.

Rosenthal, D. (Ed.) (1963). *The Genain quadruplets: A case study and theoretical analysis of heredity and environment in schizophrenia.* New York: Basic Books.

Rothman, D. (1984). *The Willowbrook wars.* New York: Harper & Rowe.

Ruesch, J., & Bateson, G. B. (1968). *Communication, the social matrix of psychiatry.* New York: Norton.

Ryan, A. (1995). *John Dewey and the high tide of American liberalism.* New York: Norton.

Sander, F., & Beels, C. C. (1970). A didactic course for family therapy trainees. *Family Process, 9,* 411–423.

Sapir, E. (1968). Selected writings of Edward Sapir. D. G. Mandelbaum (Ed.). Berkeley: University of California Press.

Satir, V. (1964). *Conjoint family therapy: A guide to therapy and technique.* Palo Alto, CA: Science & Behavior Books.

Schafer, R. (1994). *Retelling a life.* New York: Basic Books.

Schatzman, M. (1971). Paranoia or persecution: The case of Schreber. *Family Process, 10,* 177–201.

Schreber, D. P. (1955). *Memoirs of my mental illness.* London: Dawson.

Searles, H. F. (1959). The effort to drive the other person crazy. *British Journal of Medical Psychiatry, 32,* 1–18.

Selvini-Palazzoli, M., Boscolo, L., Cecchin, G., & Prata, G. (1978). *Paradox and counter-paradox: A new model in the therapy of the family in schizophrenic transaction.* New York: Jason Aronson.

Serra, P. (1993). Physical violence in the couple relationship: A contribution towards the analysis of context. *Family Process* (32), 21–33.

Shalev, A. Y. (1999). Commentary: Beyond preclassified reality. *Psychiatry, 62*(4), 289–292.

Shephard, B. (1999). Still in shock: Treating the aftermath of trauma. *Times Literary Supplement,* July, pp. 4–5.

Sicherman, B. (1970). Adolf Meyer (1866–1950): Profile of a Swiss-American psychiatrist. Unpublished.

Simon, L. (1998). *Genuine reality, A life of Henry James.* New York: Harcourt Brace.

Sluzki, C. (1993). Toward a model of family and political victimization: Implications for treatment and recovery. *Psychiatry, 56,* 178–187.

Sluzki, C., & Veron, E. (1976). The double bind as a universal pathogenic situation. In Sluzki & Ransome (Eds.), *Double bind: The foundation of the communicational approach to the family.* New York: Grune & Stratton.

Sontag, S. (1977). *Illness as metaphor*. New York: Farrar, Strauss & Geroux.

Speck, R., & Attneave, C. (1973). *Family networks*. New York: Pantheon.

Spence, D. P. (1982). *Narrative truth and historical truth*. New York: Norton.

Spiegel, D. (1994). *Dissociation: Culture, mind and body*. Washington, DC: American Psychiatric Press.

Stack, C. B. (1983). *All our kin*. New York: Basic Books.

Stagoll, B. (1995). Coming across: Family therapy in Australia and New Zealand. *"Te putanga tai raro, out from down under."* Address to Australia–New Zealand Family Therapy Association, August 31, Wellington, NZ.

Steinem, G. (1994). What if Freud were Phyllis? New York: Simon & Schuster Audioworks.

Stierlin, H., (1976). The dynamics of owning and disowning: Psychoanalytic and family perspectives. *Family Process, 15*, 277–287.

Stierlin, H., Weber, G., Schmidt, G., & Simon, F. B. (1986). Features of families with major affective disorders. *Family Process, 25*, 325–336.

Stone, M. (1993). Etiology of borderline personality disorder: Psychobiological factors contributing to an underlying irritability. In J. Paris (Ed.) *Borderline personality disorder: Etiology and treatment*. Washington, DC: American Psychiatric Press.

Strauss, J. S., & Carpenter, W. T. (1974). The prediction of outcome in schizophrenia. I. *Archives of General Psychiatry, 31*, 37–42.

Sulloway, F. (1992). *Freud, biologist of the mind: Beyond the psychoanalytic legend*. Cambridge, MA: Harvard University Press.

Sulloway, F. J. (1996). *Born to rebel: Birth order, family dynamics and creative lives*. New York: McKay.

Tienari, P. (1991). Interaction between genetic vulnerability and family environment: The Finnish adoptive family study of schizophrenia. *Acta Scandinavica Psychiatrica, 84*, 460–465.

Tonigan, J. S., Toscova, R., & Miller, W. R. (1996). Meta-analysis of the literature on Alcoholics Anonymous: Sample and study characteristics moderate findings. *Journal of Studies on Alcohol, 57*, 65–72.

Turner, V. (1969). *The ritual process*. Chicago: Aldine.

Turner, V. W. (1982). *From ritual to theatre: The human seriousness of play*. New York: PAJ Publications.

Turner, V., & Turner, E. L. (1995). *Image and pilgrimage in Christian culture*. New York: Columbia University Press.

van der Kolk, B. A. (1997). The psychobiology of traumatic memory. *Annals of New York Academy of Science, 10*, 99–113.

Wade, N. (1998). Was Freud wrong? Are dreams the brain's start-up test? *New York Times*, January 4, p. 6.

Walters, M., Carter, E., Papp, P., & Silverstein, O. (1988). *The invisible web*. New York: Guilford.

White, M. (1989a). Pseudo-encopresis: From avalanche to victory, from vicious to virtuous cycles. In M. White, *Michael White: Selected papers*. South Australia: Dulwich Centre Publications.

White, M. (1989b). Say hullo again: The incorporation of the lost relationship in the resolution of grief. In M. White, *Selected papers* (pp. 29–37). South Australia: Dulwich Centre Publications.

White, M. (1990). Deconstruction and therapy. *Dulwich Centre Newsletter, 2*.

White, M. (1992). Men's culture, the men's movement, and the constitution of men's lives. *Dulwich Centre Newsletter, 3 & 4*, 33–54.

White, M. (1995). *Re-authoring lives*. South Australia: Dulwich Centre Publications.

White, M., & Epston, D. (1990). *Literate means to therapeutic ends*. New York: Norton.

White, M., & Epston, D. (1992). *Experience, contradiction, narrative, imagination*. South Australia: Dulwich Centre Publications.

Whyte, L. L. (1948). *The next development in man*. New York: Holt.

Winn, J. A., & Lesser, W. (1966). The day care center: A new dimension of treatment in a mental hygiene clinic. *Community Mental Health Journal, 2*(1), 79–81.

Winter, A. (1998). *Mesmerized: Powers of the mind in Victorian Britain*. Chicago: University of Chicago Press.

Wynne, L. C., McDaniel, S. H., & Weber, T. T. (1986). *Systems consultation: A new perspective for family therapy*. New York: Guilford.

Zwerling, I. (1965). *The second Strecker Award lecture*. Philadelphia: Institute of the Pennsylvania Hospital.

Zwerling, I., & Mendelsohn, M. (1965). Initial family reactions to day hospitalization. *Family Process, 4*, 50–63.

INDEX

n = note; r = reference only